ZOMBIES

A RECORD OF THE YEAR OF INFECTION

Field Notes by Dr. Robert Twombly

CHRONICLE BOOKS
SAN FRANCISCO

Library of Congress Cataloging-in-Publication data on file.

ISBN 978-0-8118-7100-6
ZOMBIES is produced by becker&mayer!, Bellevue, WA.
www.beckermayer.com

Design: Paul Barrett
Editorial: Amy Wideman
Production Coordination: Shirley Woo

ZOMBIES was illustrated by Chris Lane
and written by Don Roff.

The producer would also like to thank Steve Mockus
for his assistance in preparing this publication.

10 9 8 7 6 5 4 3 2 1

Printed in China
Chronicle Books LLC
680 Second Street
San Francisco, CA 94107
www.chroniclebooks.com

PUBLISHER'S NOTE

What follows is a found manuscript. The author/illustrator of this book, Robert Twombly, was a blood specialist native to Seattle, Washington. Dr. Twombly witnessed the worldwide necrotic infection that, as we now know, began suddenly on or around January 7, 2012. The infection lasted approximately one year, and during that time all known zombies either decayed enough to succumb to their physical limitations or were destroyed by pockets of human survivors.

Dr. Twombly's journal is a unique record of the time of infection in that it seeks to understand the undead by living among them. It is also the record of the author's day-to-day experiences at a time when such records were not commonly kept.

The manuscript was found inside an empty cottage in the town of Churchill, at the edge of Hudson Bay in northern Manitoba, Canada. The whereabouts and the fate of the author are unknown. His notations have been reproduced here in their entirety.

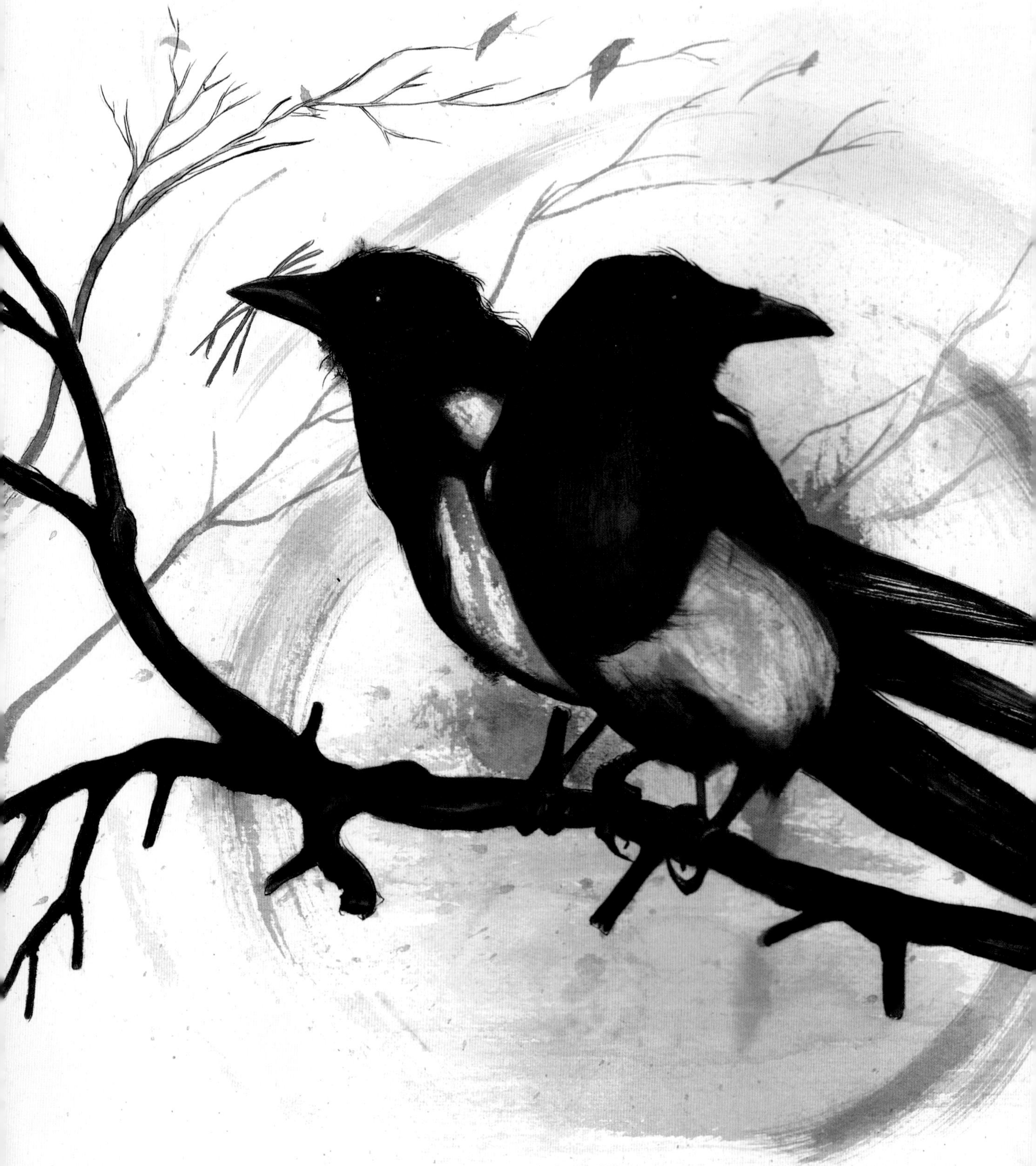

January 5, 2012

Saw a flock of Black-billed Magpies, 6 or 7 adults in the trees by the lake today.

Very strange to see them this far west!

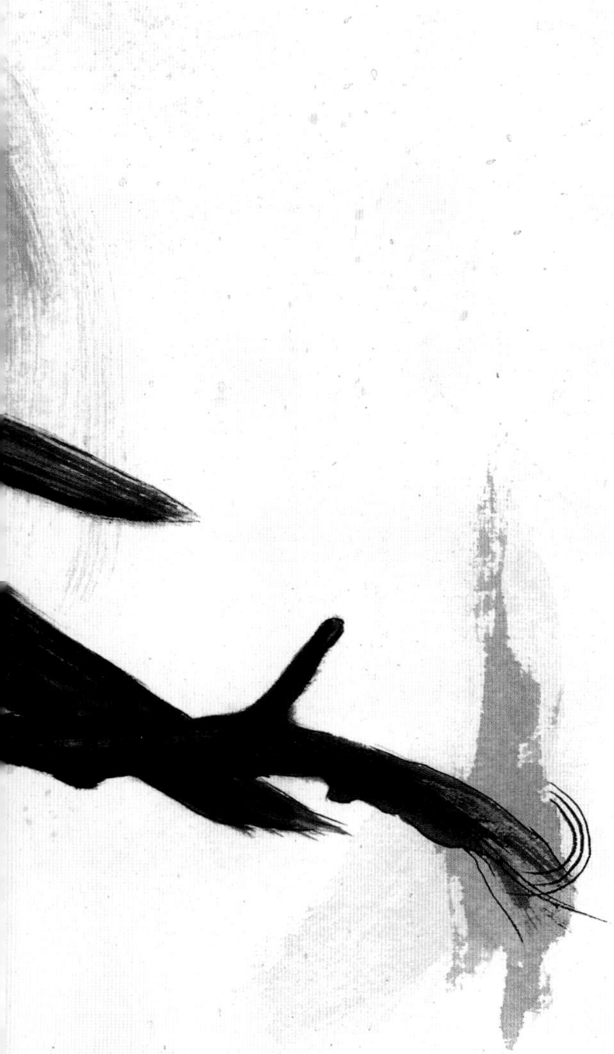

January 12, 2012

For the record, my name is Dr. Robert Twombly, age 32, Specialist in hematology-oncology at the Northwest Blood Treatment Center in Seattle, Washington. The NBTC lab occupies the top floor of a seven-story building adjacent to Lake Union. These are facts, and I record them because everything else right now is ~~hard~~ impossible to believe, and we need to start with the facts. I have my birding journal here, ink, etc. "Here" is I've barricaded myself in one of the lab rooms. Outside there's some sort of infection. It happened fast. I'm hoping that if I record as much as I can, and others are doing the same, we can ~~_____~~ I don't know, cure it? I don't know what IT is. No one seems to know what's happening. It feels like the end of the world.

Some of the headlines from the news, before the internet went down

Sudden Illness Fells Thousands

Global Pandemic Freezes Commerce
Airport, Shipping, Border Lockdown

Terrorists Lay Claim to Bio Weapon
Experts Deny Capability

CDC Emergency Summit
Conflicting Theories, Few Answers

Is It In the Air?
Contamination of Water, Food also Questioned

Attacks Reported Among Infected
Guard Mobilized to Secure Hospitals

On January 7, the first signs were the "breaking news reports" that people all over the world were getting sick. According to news reports, major cities have been hit hardest. Military units were mobilized to help, but of course there's no reason why soldiers would be any more immune to illness than civilians. Breathing filtration systems have not been helping. There is no help. When casualties vastly outweigh medical personnel—when treatments are, so far, ineffective—fear spreads even faster than disease. At first the reports of "attacks" weren't clearly [redacted] it wasn't clear that people weren't just killing each other in a panic of some sort, and the details were, I mean they had to have been censored or restricted, at least at first when that was still possible.

Estimates of the infection rate kept going higher before the news shut down, and it's difficult to figure by our remaining staff—though here where we might be able to help, more than anywhere else, people kept coming in rather than bunkering down at home—but it looks like downtown Seattle has a 90% infection rate. If the rest of the world is affected at anywhere near that. . . I don't know that a 90% infection rate is survivable, in terms of overall population. For the other 10%, is it just a matter of time until symptoms manifest?

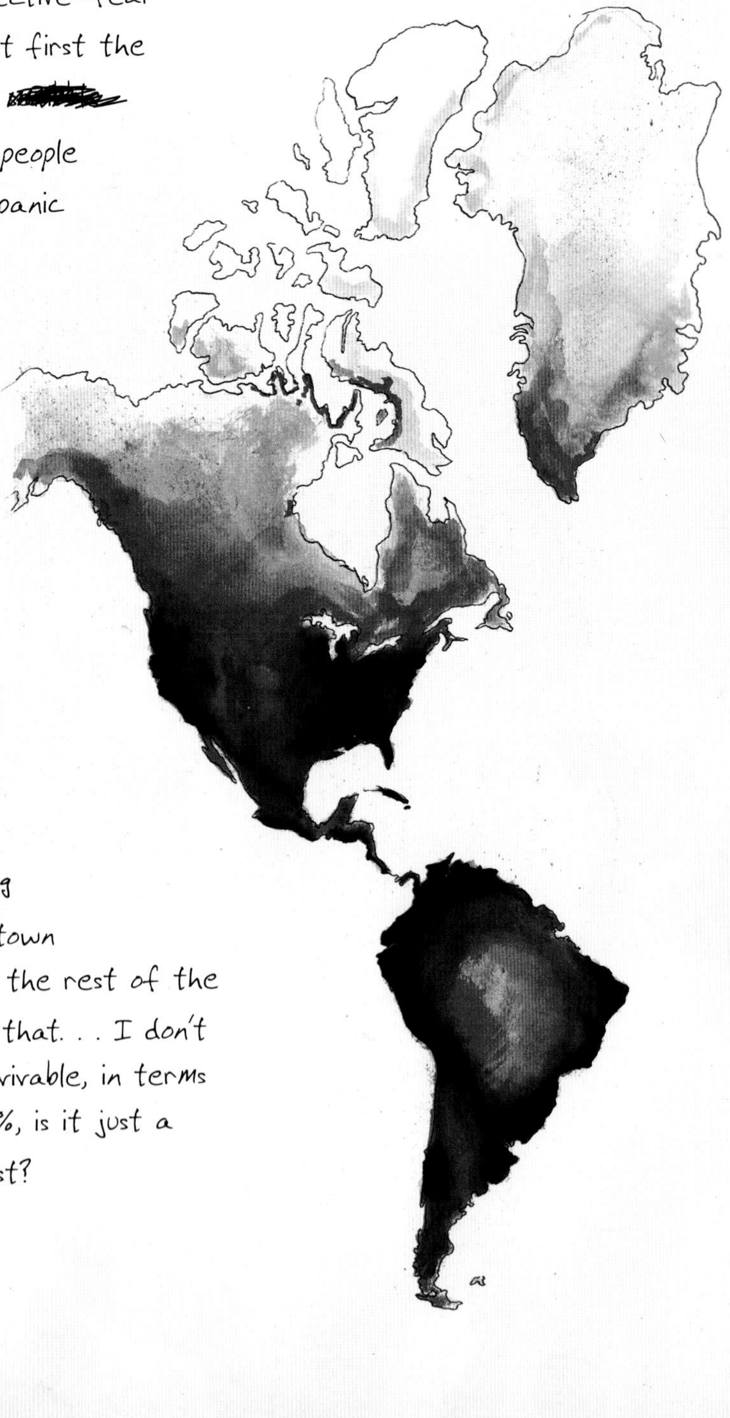

I have no idea why I've been one of the fortunate ones, or if I'll remain that way.

Here's where the infection stood on January 10.

I have to assume it's worse now.

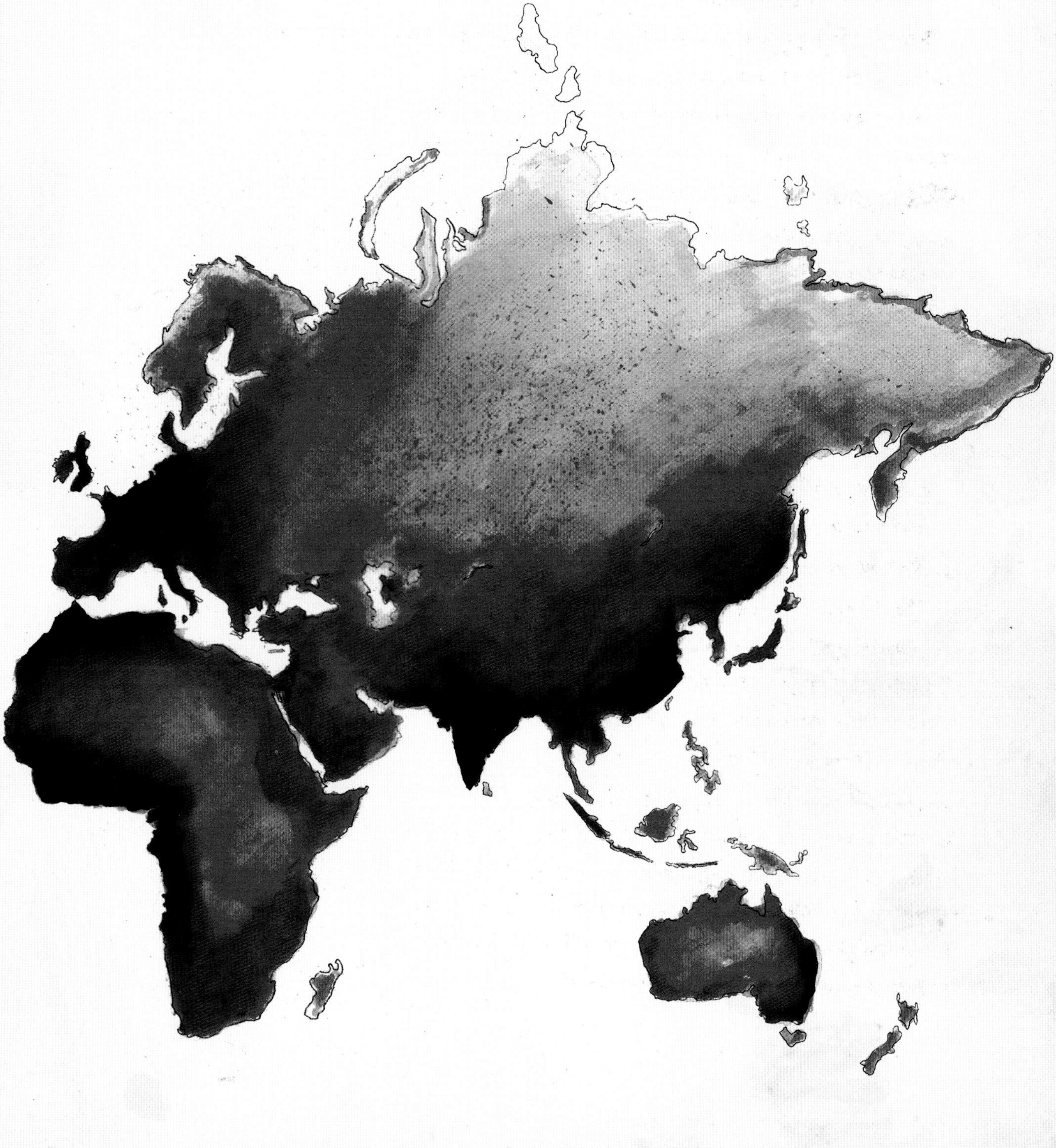

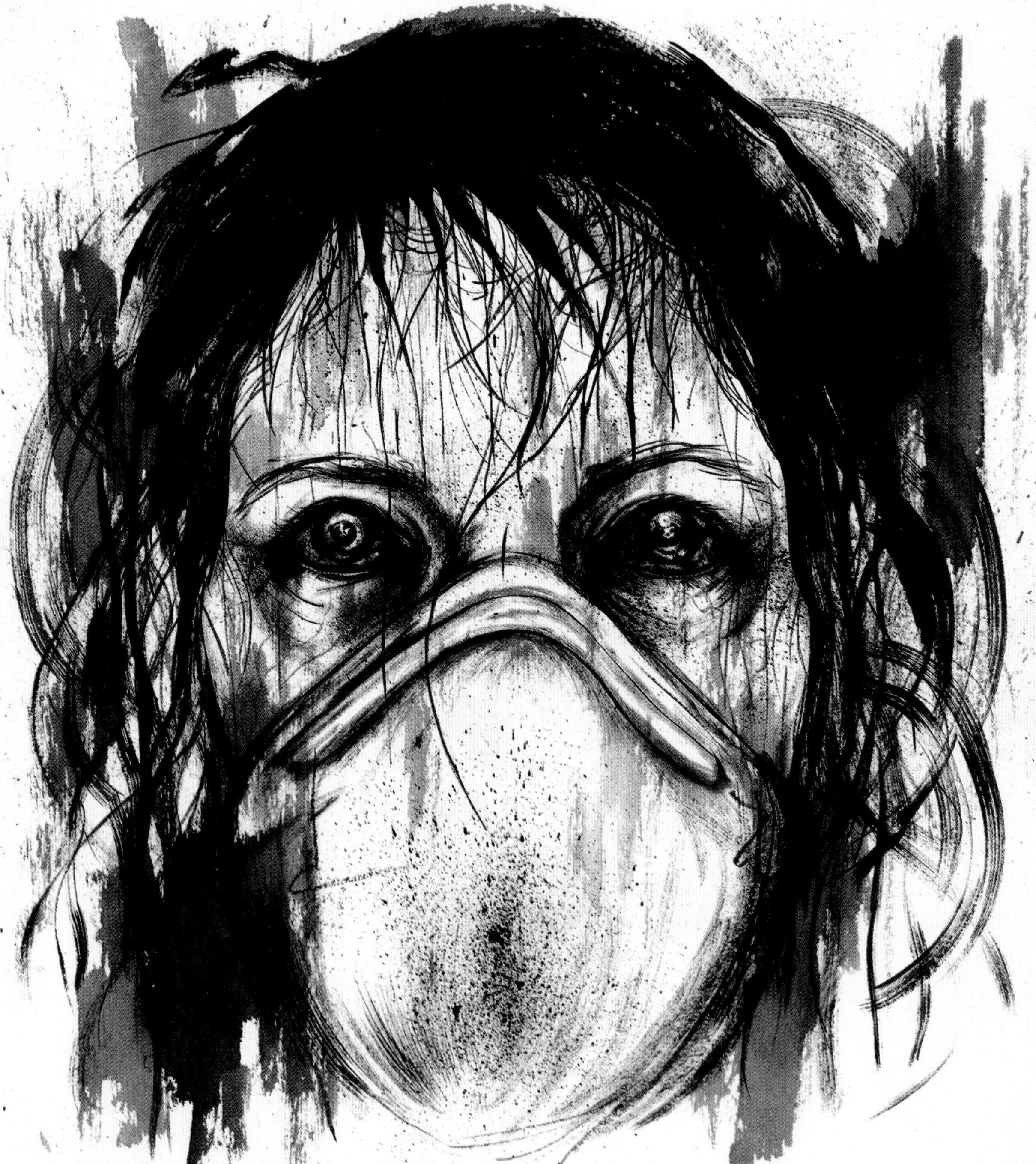

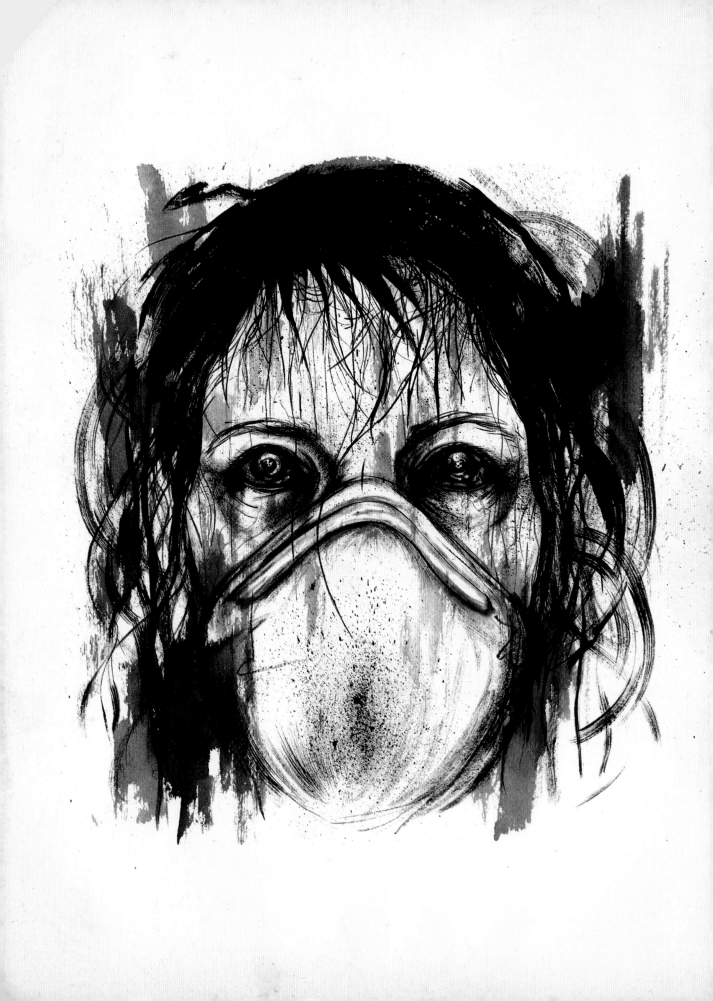

Hospitals have been at maximum capacity since day one, with patients spilling out into the streets. Same here in Seattle. What caused this? Doctors like myself have been working around the clock to find out. Blood samples from infected patients from Harborview were rushed over here and we've been running all known tests, but the results are coming back negative for everything—no identifiable bacteria, virus, or parasite. Yet people are stricken with severe aches and pains all over their bodies—"like knives sticking into every muscle." And then things got worse.

My lab is down to a skeleton crew as many of my team have been hospitalized, or are in line waiting to be. I feel helpless. At this point we're doing such research as we can, but I've also just been making up tests out of thin air, figuring if I get a result I'll backtrack to the scientific method later. Like stick an electric wire in a blood culture. Anything? Nothing. The power's out now, backup generator too. I ran a paperclip from a 9-volt battery. What does that prove? Nothing.

Everything's falling apart.

In the first few days of outbreak, horrific instances of suffering were
   broadcast on television and the internet, but mostly just short of the last stage
   of infection. But I've witnessed all of the following stages firsthand among
fellow colleagues. Physical symptoms at the onset of illness
   can be categorized as follows:

Onset: Physical Symptoms

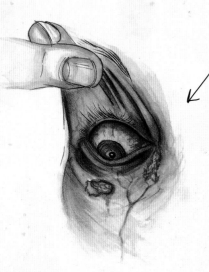

Eyes: The sclera become
enlarged and bloodshot.

Ear canals swell shut,
creating a tremendous
pounding sensation.

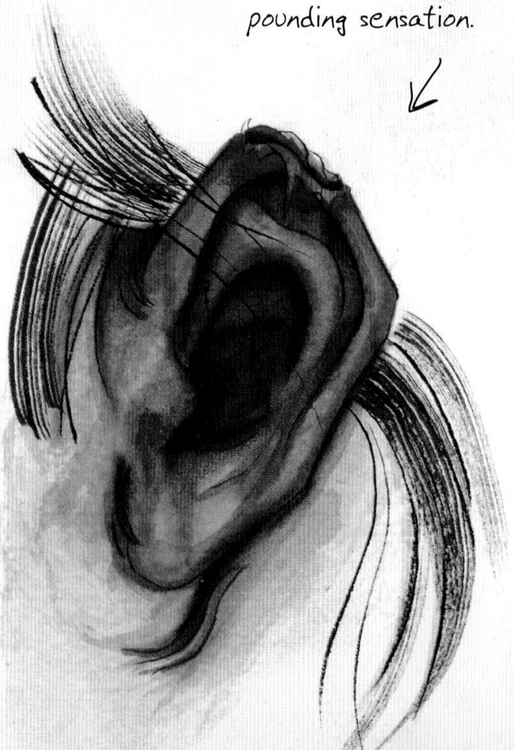

Nose and mouth:
Tissues engorge
with fluid. Severe
constriction of nasal
passages and throat.

Chest: Chest area "feels tight, like a squeezed sponge." Breathing becomes short and rapid. Lungs struggle for oxygen.

Stomach: Severe stomach cramping and constipation reported. Subjects are unable to digest more food, experience vomiting and diarrhea.

Arms, legs, back: Complaints of muscular aches similar to flu symptoms. (No evidence of viral infection.) These symptoms accelerate acutely, causing intense physical pain.

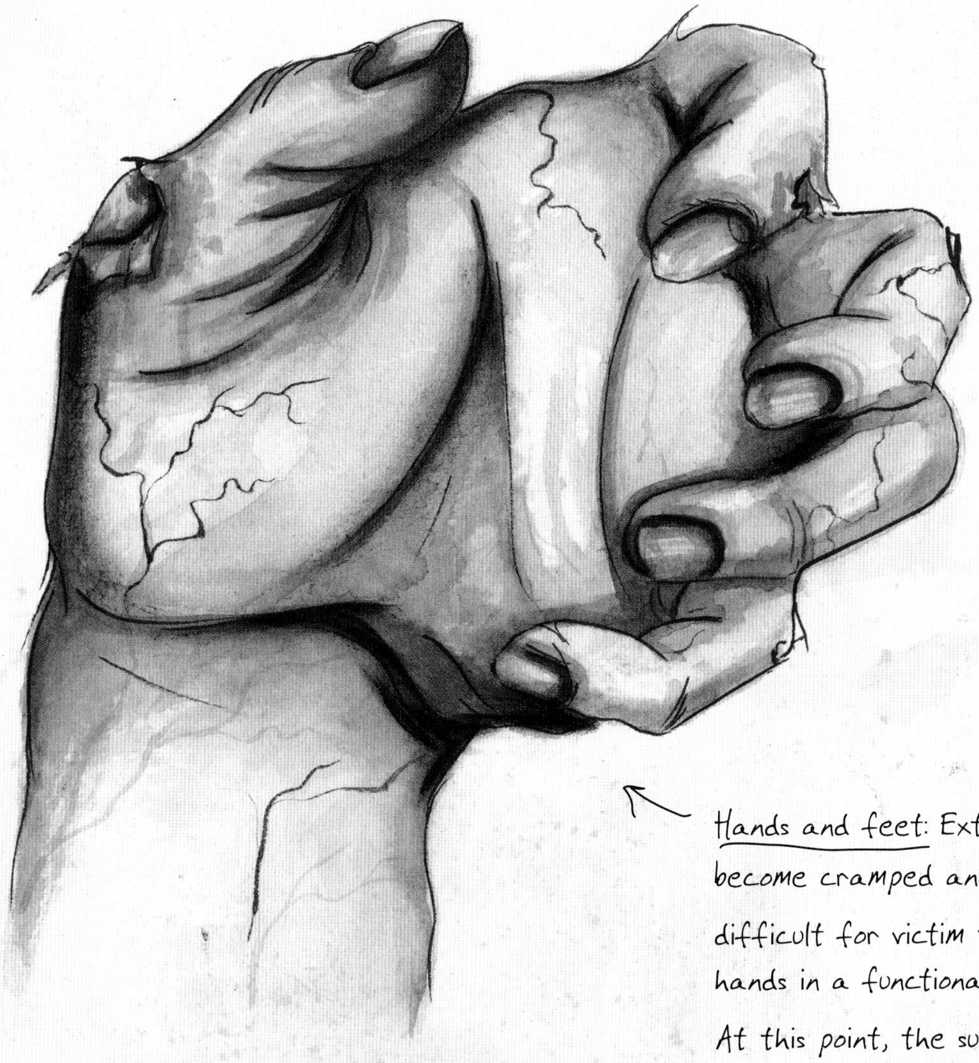

Hands and feet: Extremities become cramped and it becomes difficult for victim to walk or use hands in a functional capacity. At this point, the subject becomes bedridden and immobile.

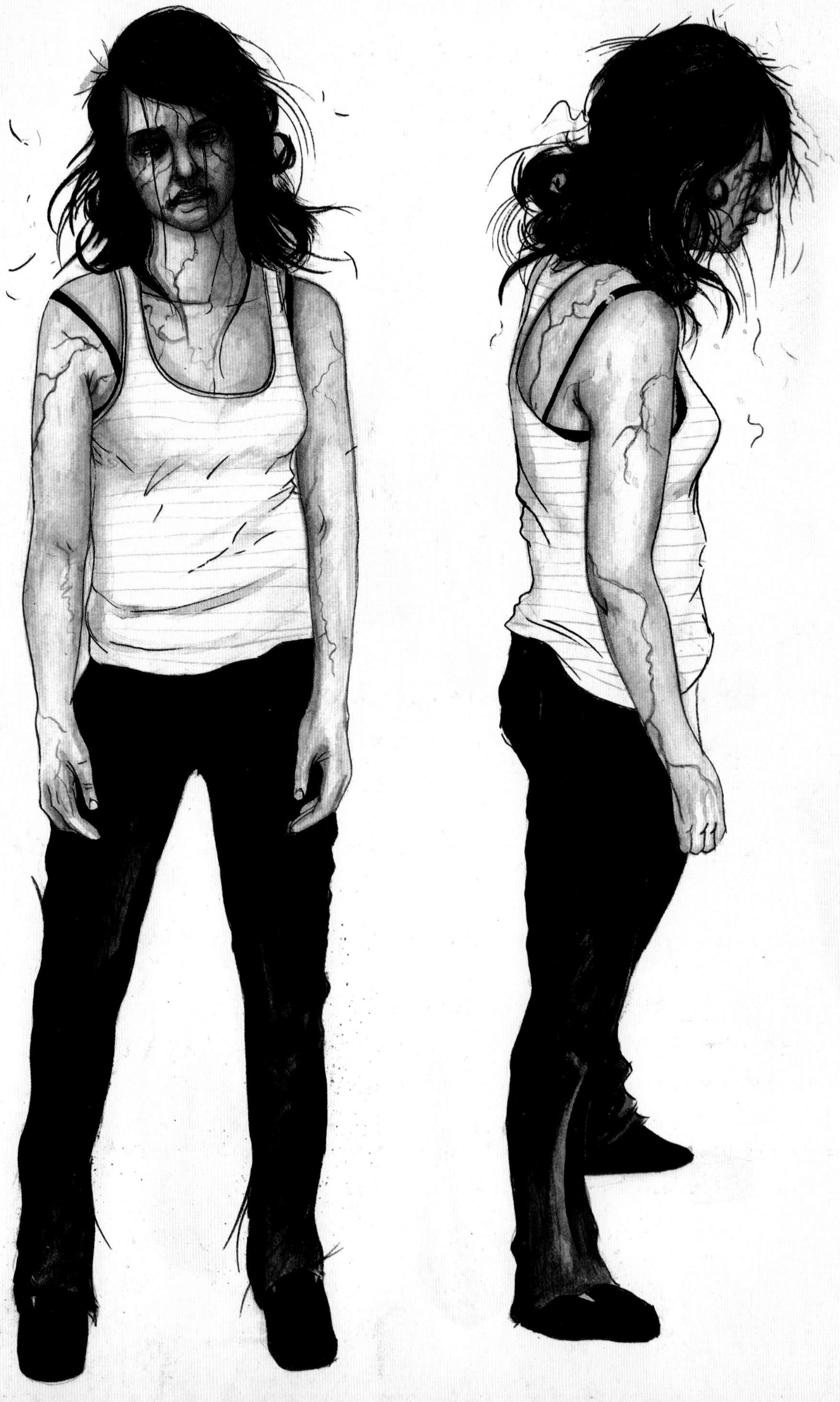

Illness was only the beginning. People succumbed. And died. But within moments of death, really, just shortly after "death" was noted, the bodies snapped back into "life" as though ~~something someone?~~ a switch was flipped. The bodies didn't even get to the morgue. Patients went from <u>flatline</u> to animation, though completely deranged. There is no scientific explanation. There may be a religious explanation, but—look we're going to have to figure this out, I think we have to try to stick to the science.

Once there is brain death, a person is—should be—dead. Yet function, I guess that's what it is, is reported to return among the "risen." The corpse becomes animated.

Post-Mortem: Physical Symptoms

<u>Eyes</u>: Red sclera darken further, then blacken over time.

<u>Nose and mouth</u>: No visible respiration. The mouth is drawn wide open, in what looks like a biting—or an anticipatory biting—position.

<u>Chest</u>: No physical change, but no rising or falling of the breast. No heart activity.

Reanimated subjects hooked to cardiac machines display terminal flat line.

<u>Arms, legs, back</u>: Movement returns to the muscles, albeit with a jerky, random rhythm, as if the dead subject is impossibly fighting against something, some organism?, animating him/her from within.

<u>Hands and feet</u>: Basic, primal function has been restored to the extremities: the dead subject can again walk and grasp things . . .

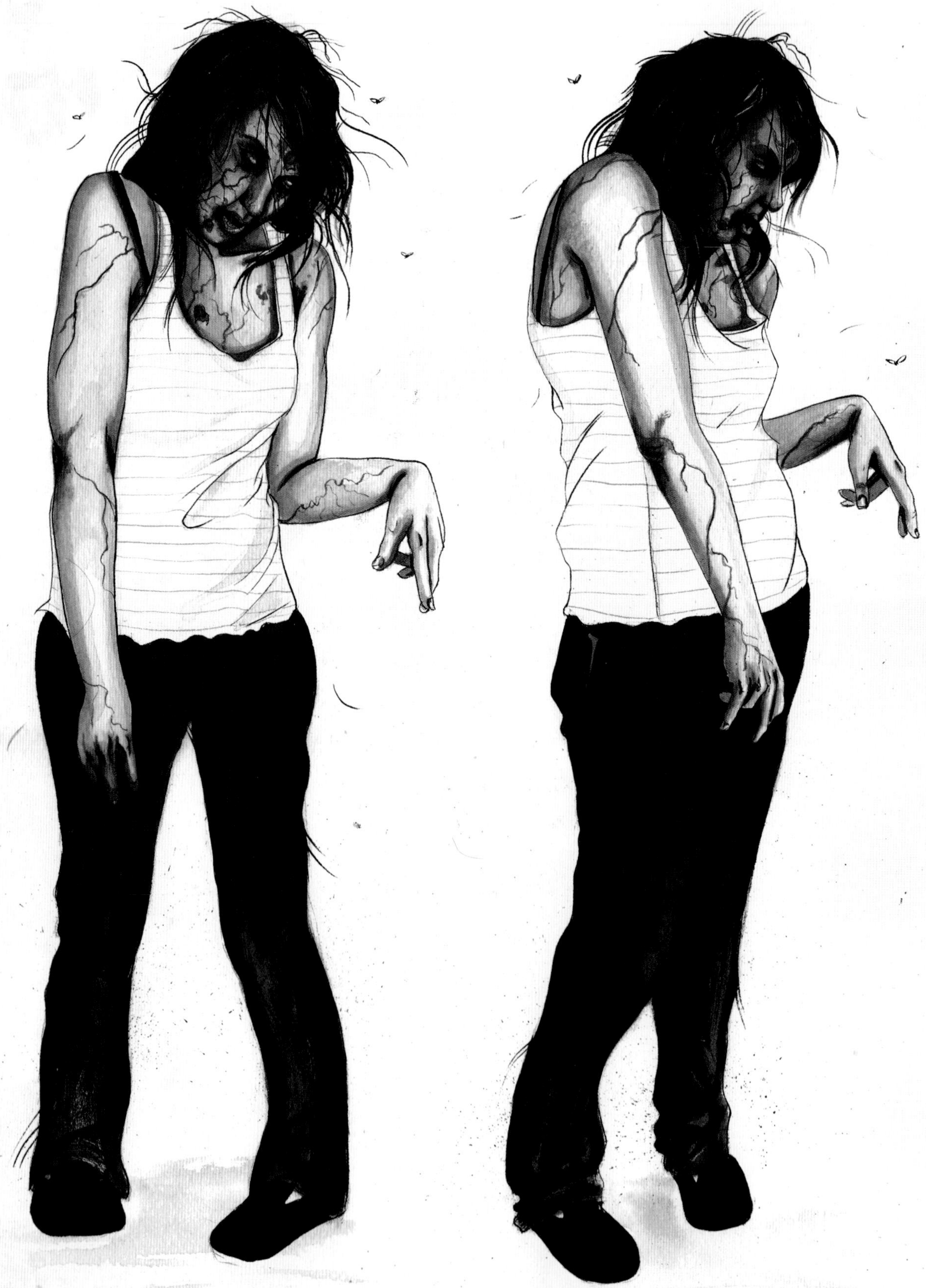

Once reanimated, the infected patient shows— I almost wrote "a single-mindedness," we really don't know what if any brain activity is happening in their "minds." No one can get close enough to one of the dead to really understand much because they seem . . . angry. Violent. It was hard to accept this from the last broadcasts before the blackout—the reports that the dead weren't just attacking, but actually trying to ~~to eat the living~~ to eat the living. And then I witnessed it for myself, and I can't deny what I've seen, even though it's almost too awful to believe.

Our power's out and judging by how dark the city is, it seems like the power is out on every grid. Internet access has been down for two days, along with cell phone reception. I can only guess that the same thing is occurring worldwide. We take for granted how much we rely on technology for information. I suddenly feel blind . . .

Only three of us remain in the office, and for all I know the entire building: the head of our lab, Dr. Carla Wilkins, my assistant, Paul Jenkins, and me.

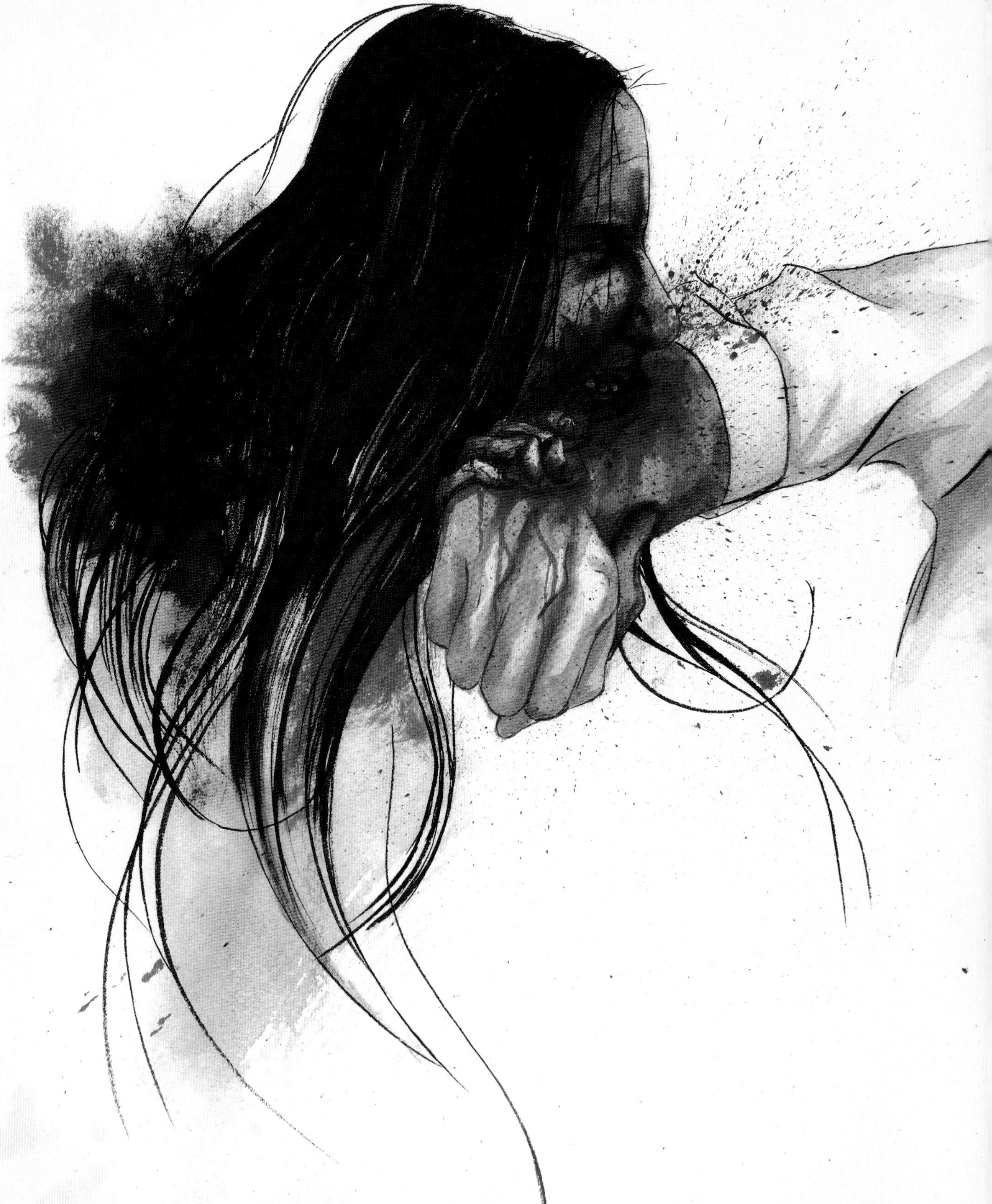

January 13, 2012

Paul and I had to lock Dr. Wilkins in the cold storage locker.

She attacked us. I have known Carla for three years. Wife, mother, excellent researcher. She's been with us here 24/7 for several days now, as long as Paul and I have. She'd left early on to check on her husband and son but came back within hours. It happened suddenly. She hadn't been sick. I don't know if she was infected, or how.

Paul and I had to repel her with the only thing we had—chairs. We pushed her back into the locker and wrangled the door shut on her flailing hands. I can still hear her pounding. I don't know how much of this I can take. Paul's downstairs, looking for something to treat the bite he sustained in the scuffle.

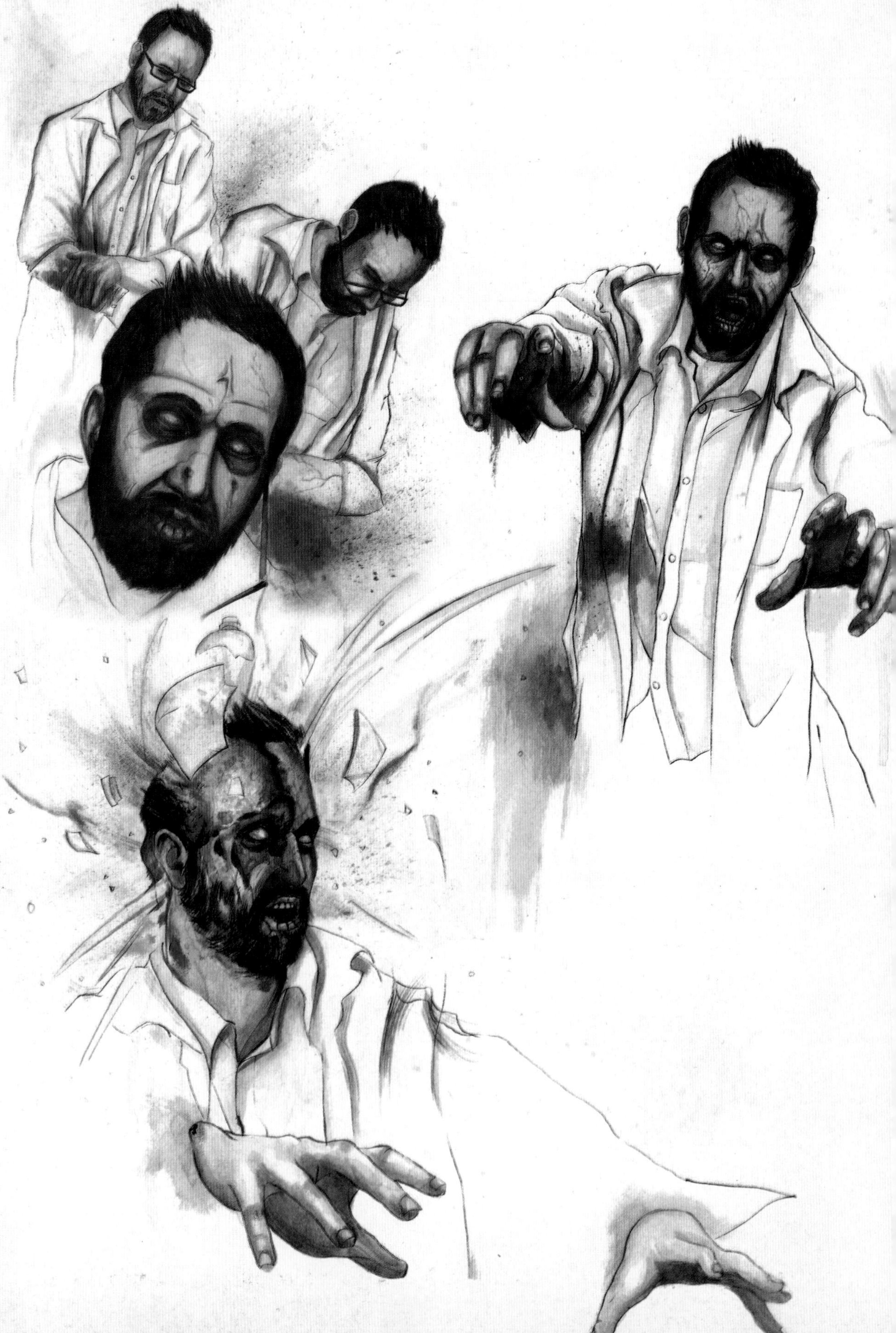

January 14, 2012

Paul's dead. I killed Paul.

We tried treating his arm, but didn't think about what we were actually treating it for. It's clear now that the bite communicated whatever had infected Carla to Paul.

His "zombification" took a matter of hours.

He—whatever I killed, it was no longer Paul. ~~Zombies~~ It came at me fast. I fended it off with a chair for long enough to look around the lab and grab a bottle of Hydrofluoric acid, which I shattered on its face. I don't know if it has brain function, but it seems as though a strike to the brain will kill—deanimate?—it. I'm drawing this in case the nature of the wound I inflicted on it is of any use later.

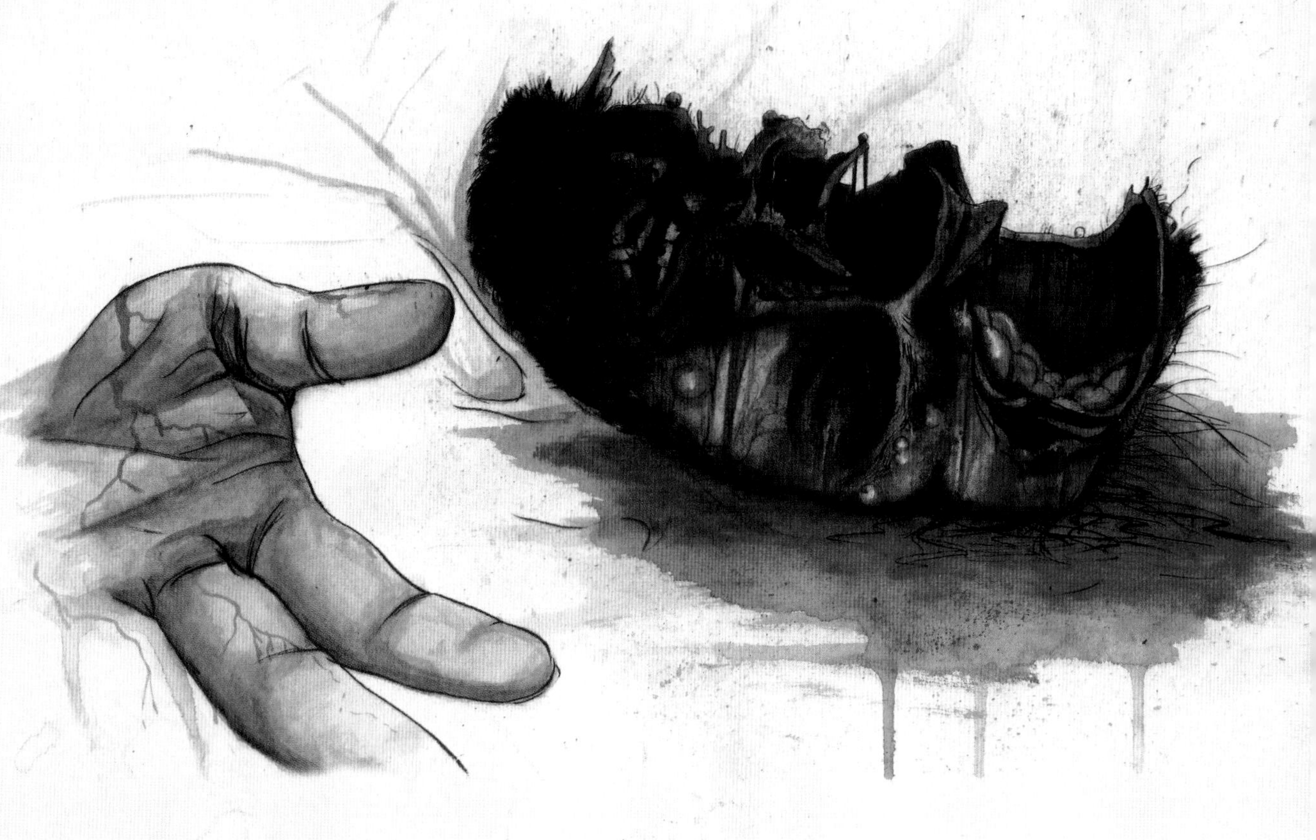

"Carla" is still pounding on the locker door.

January 15, 2012

Climbed up onto the roof today. Since the lab is on the top floor, I only had to go half a flight up to reach the service entrance. I am purposely avoiding accessing any lower floors, as I have no idea what could be waiting for me. I also have reinforced my barricades of all seventh floor doors. I have heard no signs of life from below, but that's little comfort.

On the roof, I was able to get a view of the city. Quiet like a Sunday morning. Debris everywhere. Smoke in the distance. At first no signs of life other than a lone Pine Grosbeak calling. Then the sound of a car approaching, an SUV with what looked like several people inside, some supplies strapped to the roof. I tried to shout and wave at them but couldn't get their attention.

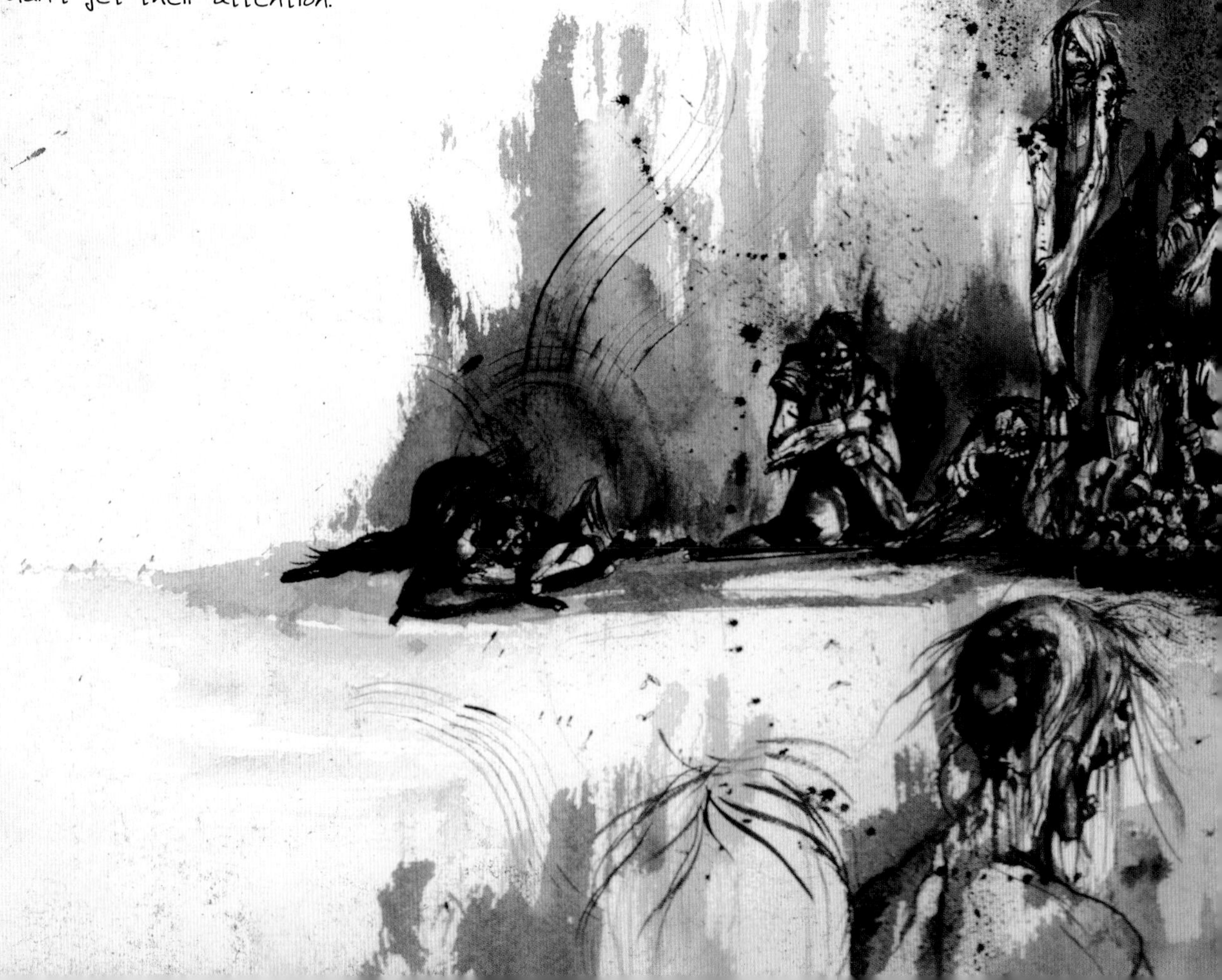

The car turned the corner of the building and I heard it driving away, then accelerate hard, then I heard the crash. I ran to the other side of the building and saw that the SUV was on its side, it had flipped—or they had flipped it—and the passengers were being pulled from the car and being attacked, eaten, by a crowd of the living dead. The screams were horrible, echoing. I can't get the images out of my head.

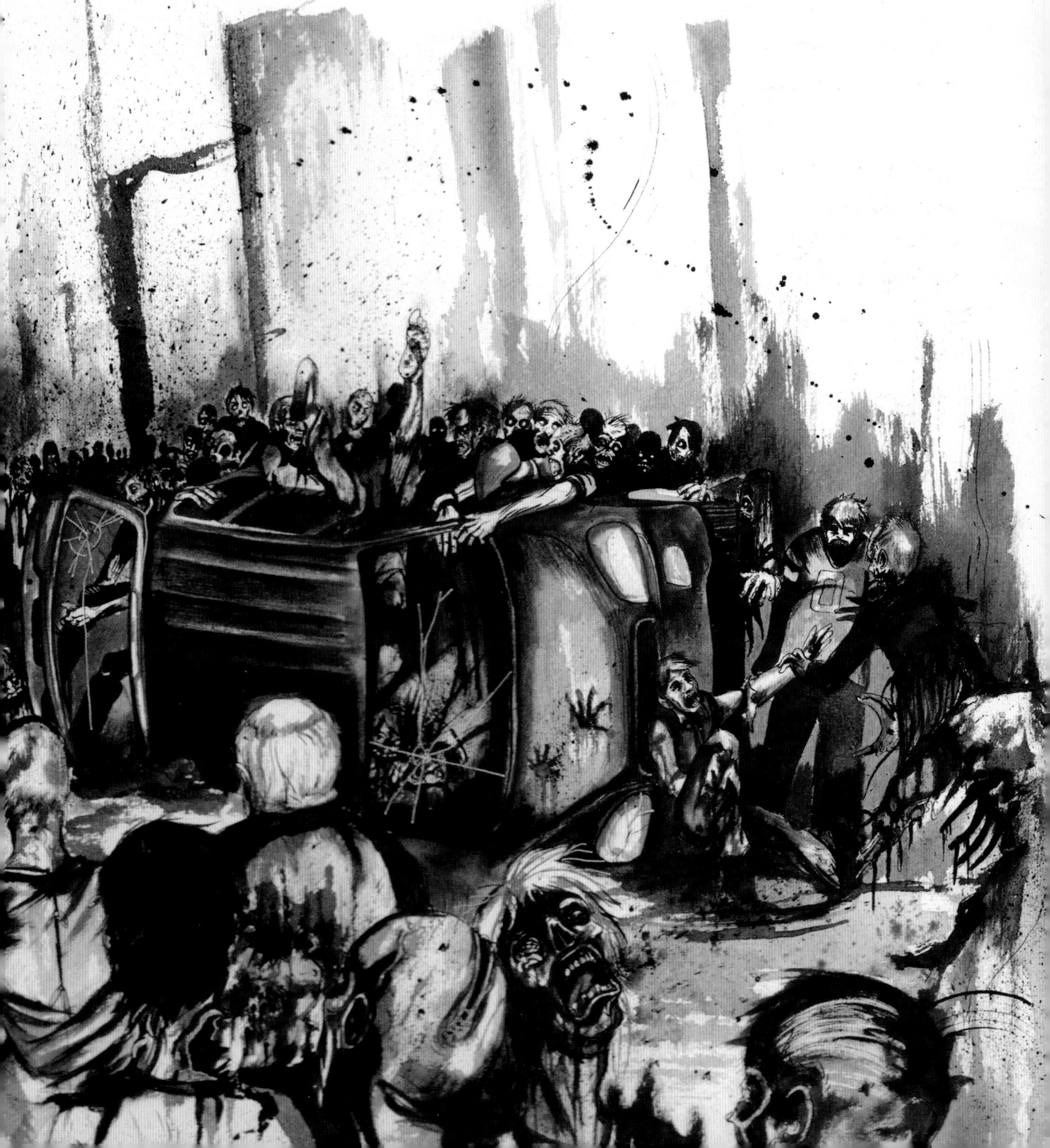

January 16, 2012

Details and observations about the creatures' capabilities:

Strength: The dead seem to possess less-than-average strength. With no heart function there's presumably no blood flow, which must decrease muscle ability. But being DEAD should decrease muscle ability 100%, so I don't know what applies anymore. It's unknown if the corpses go through a rigor mortis period, though that might account for some diminishment of ability. However, with enough of them—and I've seen hundreds on the street below the lab—they possess enough strength among them to overturn heavy objects and smash windows.

Speed: Decreased muscle function results in slower speed of movement. I haven't yet observed them running. This may or may not be within their capabilities.

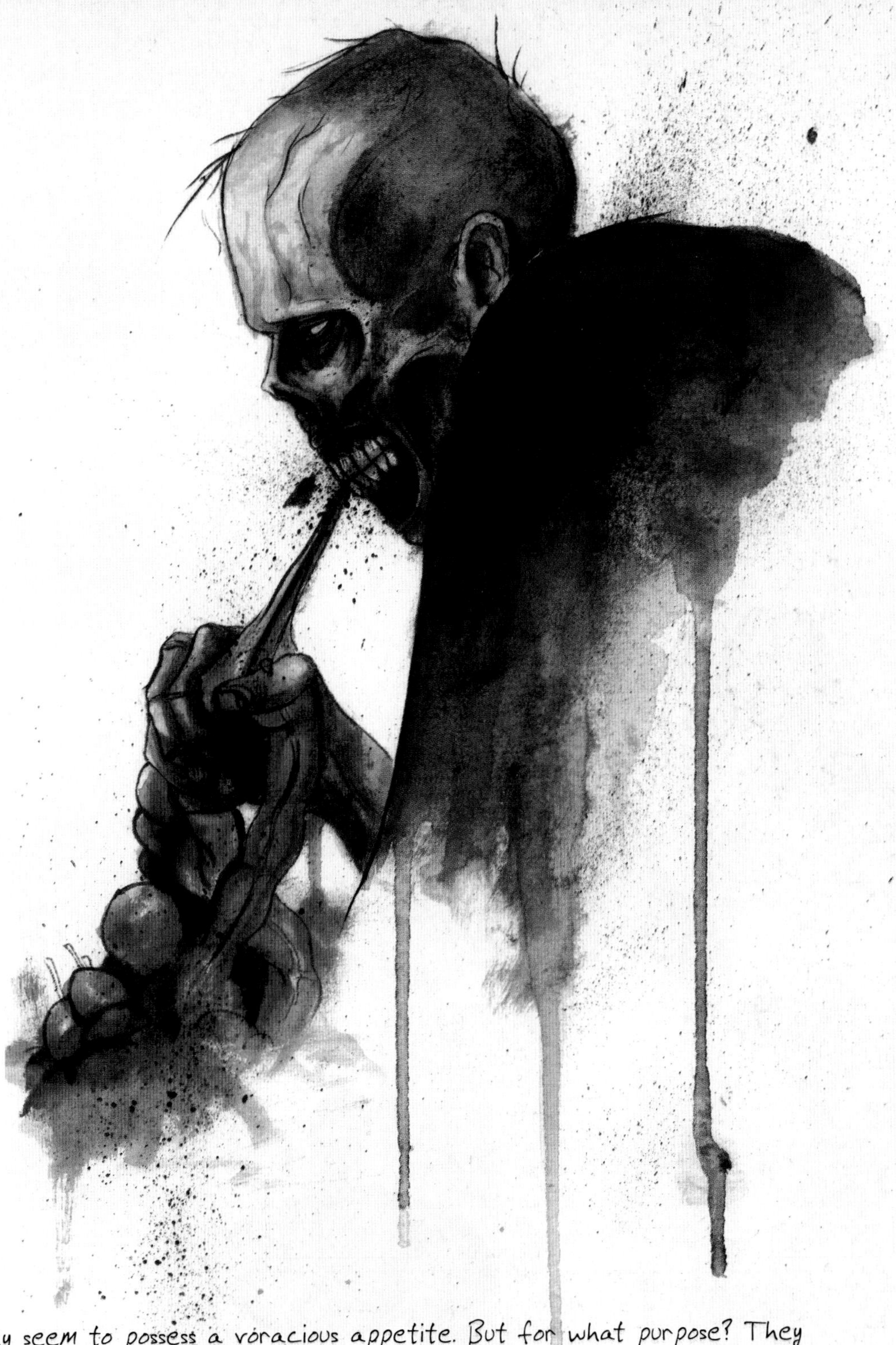

Appetite: They seem to possess a voracious appetite. But for what purpose? They are dead and need no nutrition? Yet they seem driven by this hunger. I watched six of them tear the stomach out of a struggling woman. Almost like lions would a gazelle. Many predators first tear open the stomachs of their prey, as it is soft flesh that leads to vital organs. Is it the same with the undead?

Socialization: I'm not sure what draws such a group together. It's a bad sign.

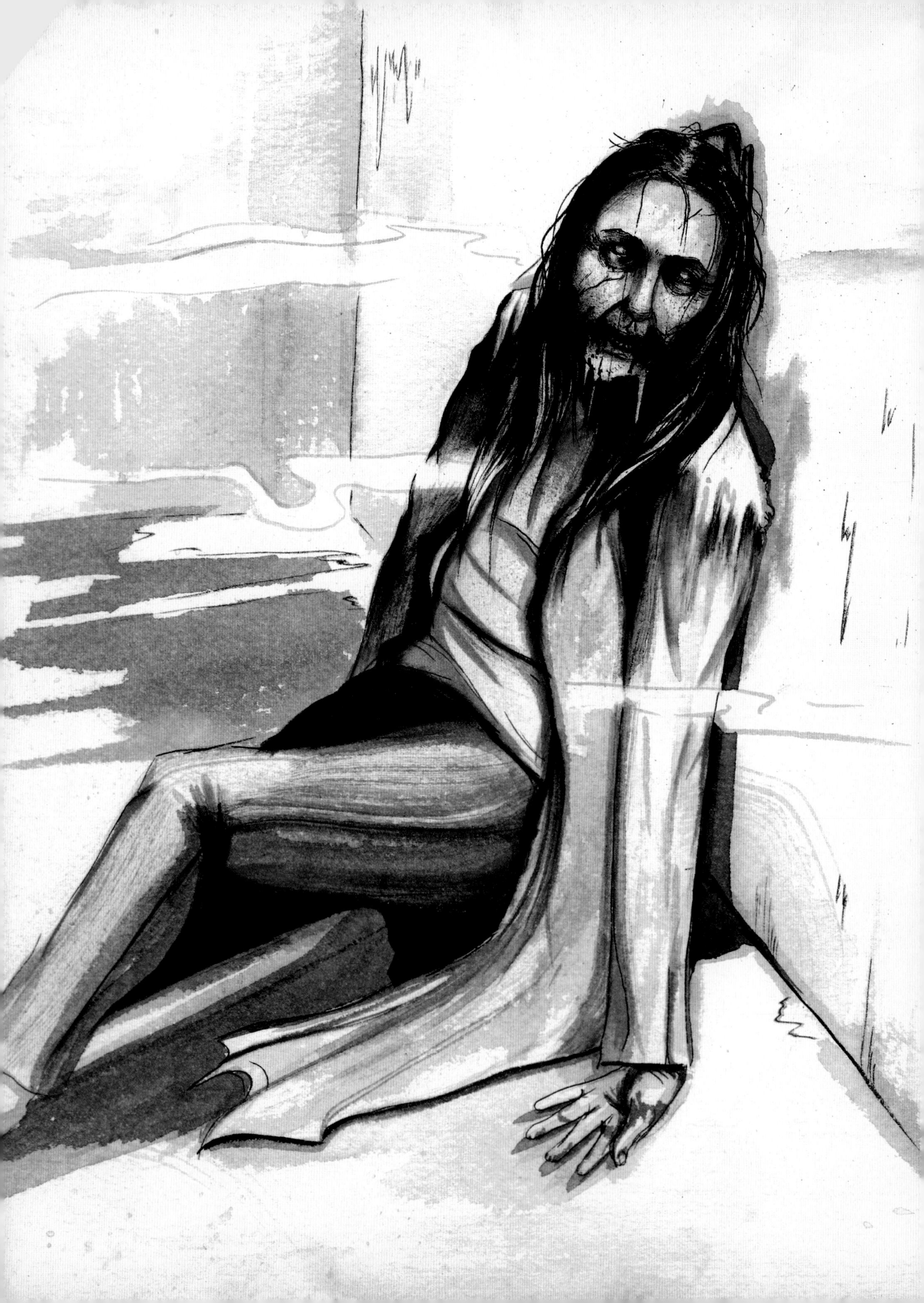

January 17, 2012

Cold and dark in the office. My food supplies have dwindled. Since I
tend to "live" at my desk during the week, I keep a supply of nuts, dried
fruits, and some instant soups. They're gone. I have pillaged the desks
of my fellow coworkers. Considering they're doctors, their eating habits
are appalling. I don't know how long I can make it on their cache of
gummy bears and fruit roll-ups. I could really go for some baked beans.
The office kitchen doesn't have much—mostly condiments and coffee
creamers. A few cases of bottled water . . . I won't go thirsty.

 I'd used a can of paint that I'd found in maintenance to
 write HELP on the roof, and hung a HELP sign out of windows
 on each side of the building, but I don't think help is really on its
 way. So I can stay here, and eventually starve, or I can try and
 leave and fall victim to a flesh-eating horde. And go where?

 "Carla" stopped pounding on the door of the cold storage locker.
 I didn't notice exactly when, I'd basically just accepted
 the sound as part of the new reality. When I went down
 to check, I found her still animated, and definitely still
 interested in attacking me, but ~~she~~ it could barely move—its
 muscles and joints seemed to have stiffened. So cold seems to have
 a similar effect on the dead as it does on the living.

January 18, 2012

I woke up to the sound of banging. At first I thought it might be coming from the storage locker, but that specimen was slower still than the last time I'd checked. I followed the low, rhythmic sound to the break room down the hall from the lab. Not about to stick my head around the corner of the doorway, I used a compact mirror that I found in a coworker's desk.

Mitch Parsons, a security guard at the lab, or whatever now passed for Mitch Parsons, was thumping on the front of the vending machine. I once saw Parsons do that—while living—after he paid for some licorice and it had gotten snagged on the wire coils inside. Why would a flesh-eater attack the machine? Surely they don't crave candy. Do the undead retain behavioral traces of their former habits? The elevators have been out since the power went, but I saw the door was open now. Is that how Parsons go on the floor? Did the door just open, or did Parsons open it?

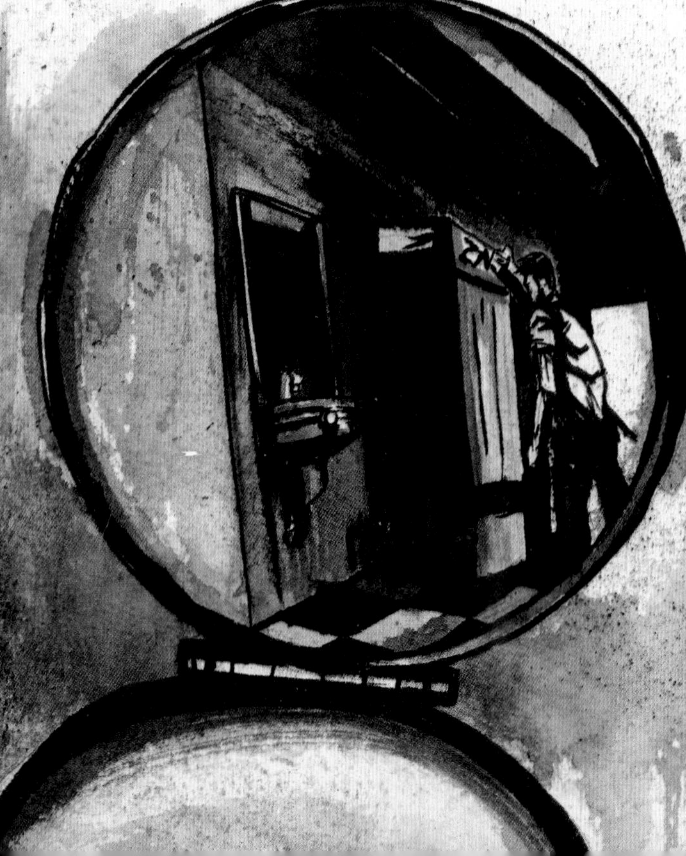

I was able to barricade a door between me and the break room. Parsons didn't seem to hear me. I'm not sure about their aural function. I checked the barricades on this side of the break room but can't really check the others.

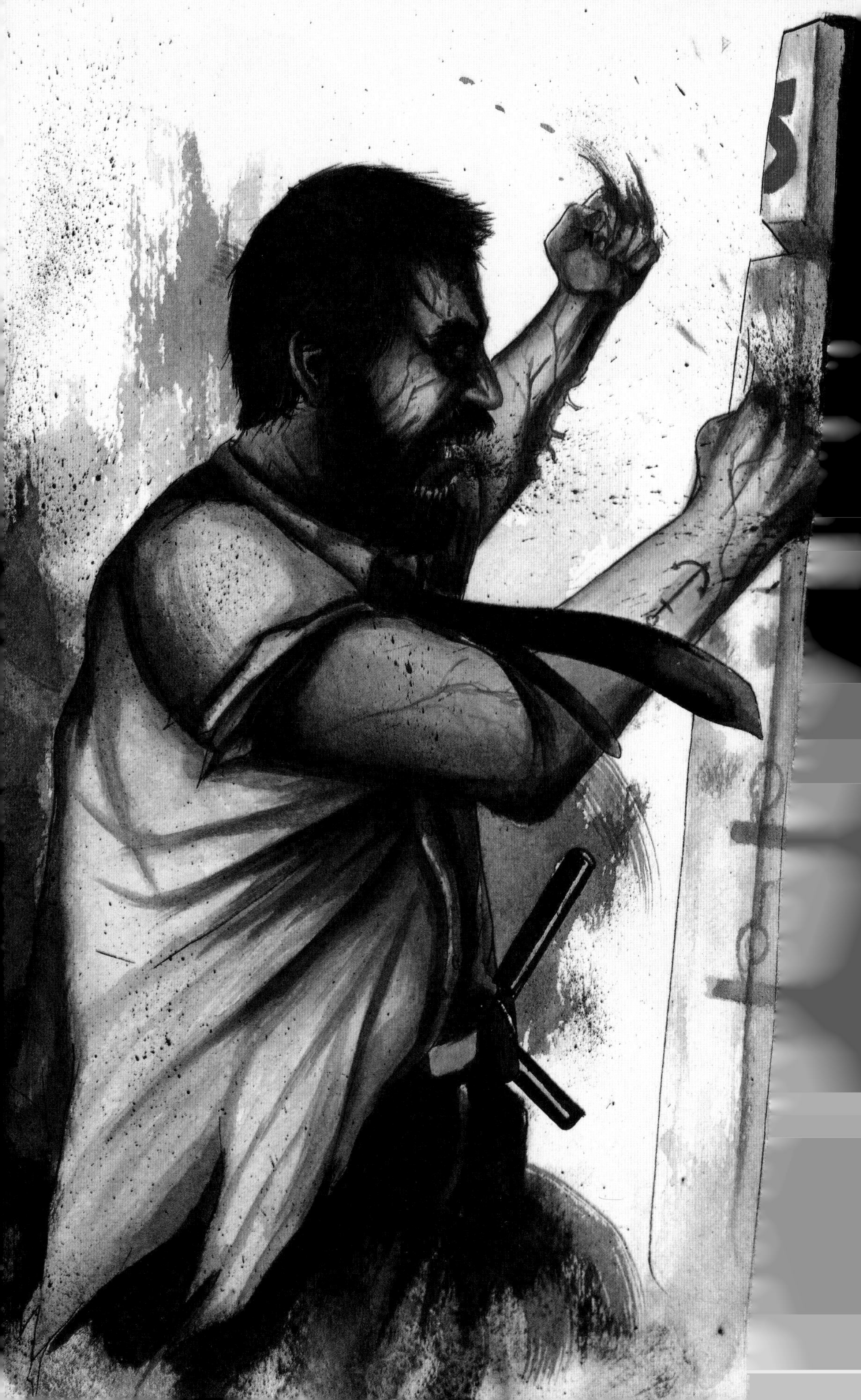
5

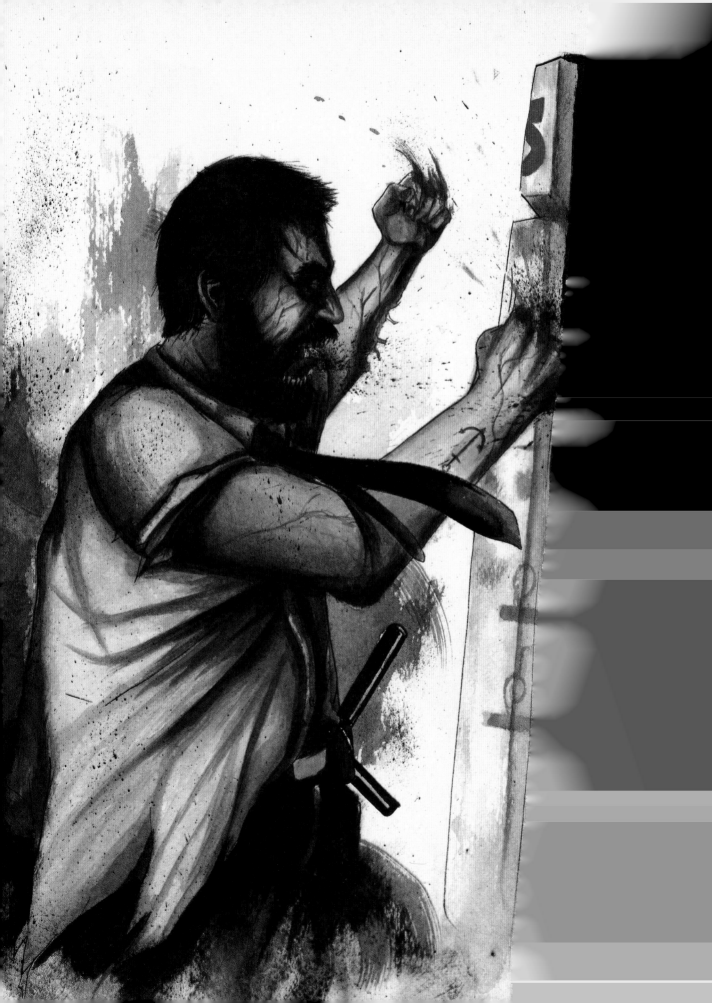

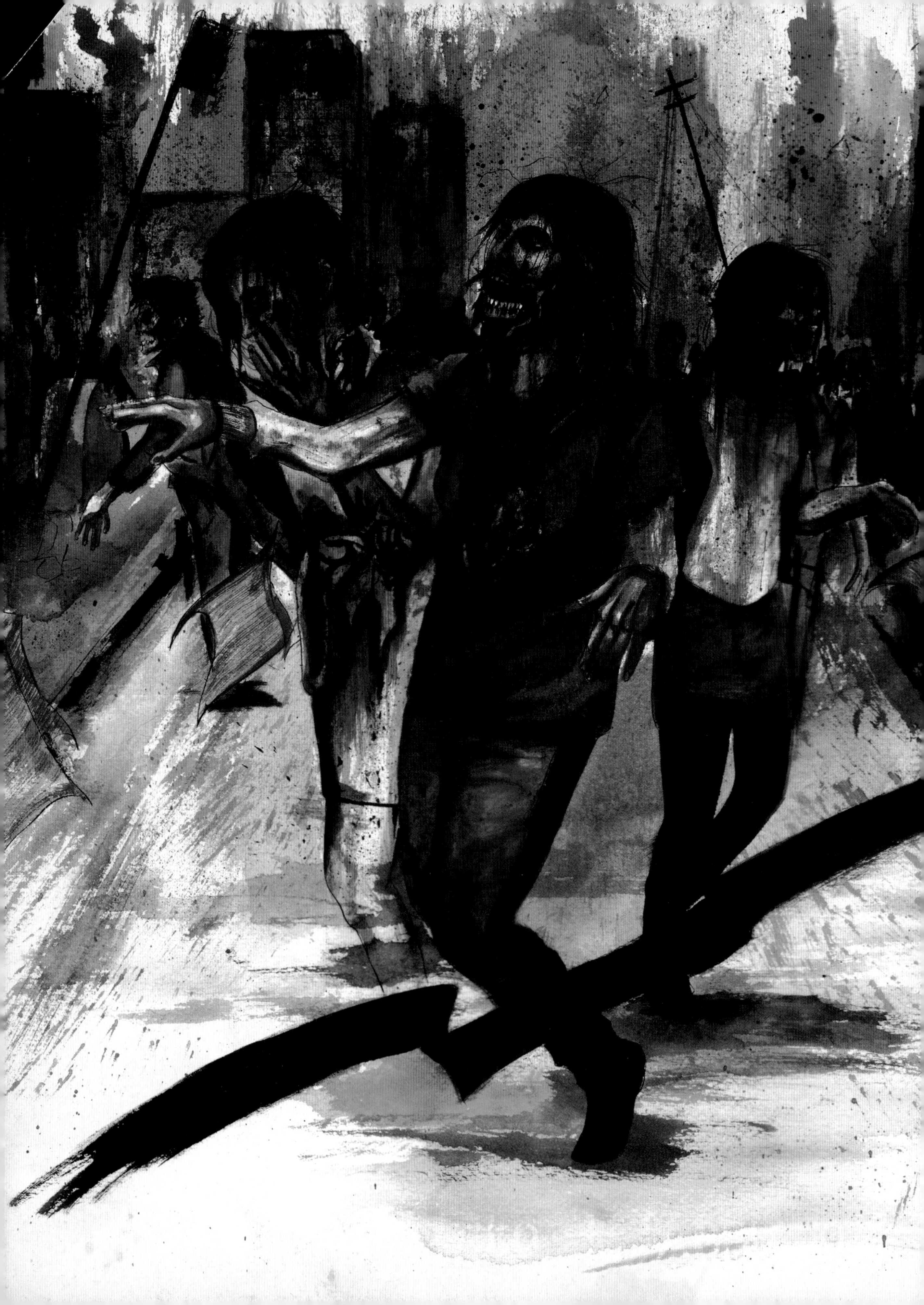

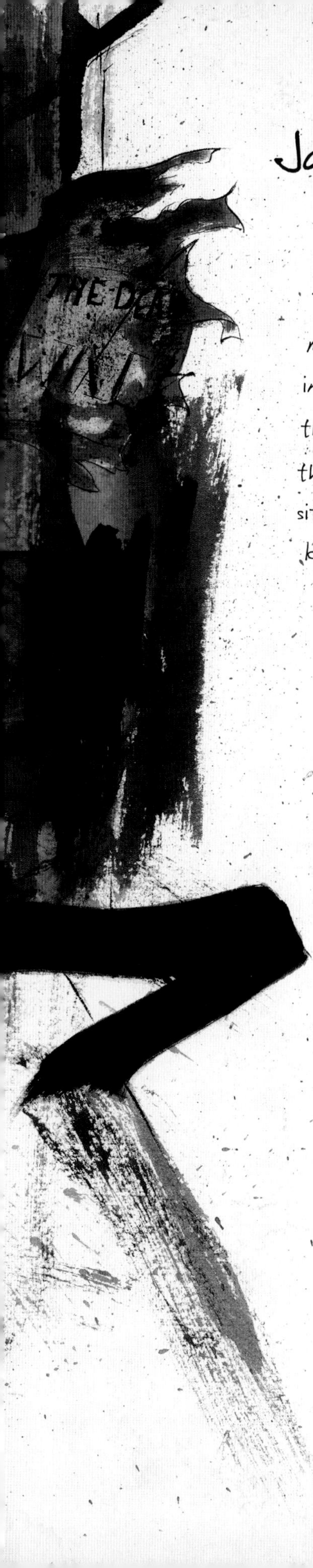

January 19, 2012

Food's gone. Up on the roof today trying to plot an escape route out of the city. Everything's smashed. Abandoned cars. Bodies out in the open. The dead wandering in larger numbers, generally in groups of several or more. A somewhat larger group is in front of the lab's main entrance intent on getting in. They can't be after me—suddenly? How would they know? I'm thinking, okay so this is what it's come to, I'm thinking that my best hope for finding a car is to look for a situation below where someone had been pulled from their car and killed—the keys would probably still be nearby.

Running. There's running in the stairwell.

So the group in front of the lab wasn't after me, they were after Ryan Frances, a 27-year-old intern at the Seattle Mercy Hospital on Capitol Hill. He had seen my sign on the window and made it here. We think he managed to barricade the doors downstairs after getting in and it's holding. The dead still seem to be milling about outside, like hungry sharks. He seemed (seems) clearly human and I let him in based on his running and shouting, something they don't seem to be able to do. I'm recording his story here:

"A day before the outbreak, we were swamped with people coming into the ER. Everyone had the same symptoms—aching joints and muscles, burning eyes, stomachaches, rapid heartbeats, and shallow breathing. None of our treatments worked. There wasn't much we could do but try to calm them. We were on a skeleton staff as many of the doctors and nurses were now patients in the hospital, too. We had some medics from the National Guard, but it wasn't enough. Then the dead started coming back to life.

The hospital was just about the worst place in the world to be since it had the most infected people in one concentrated place. I hid in the cafeteria with two coworkers. Juan left after a few days to try to find his family, something we were all thinking about. Nancy and I finally decided to leave a few days after that—gotta do something. We hoped the dead had moved on and thought we'd try to get to my houseboat. I share it with my girlfriend on Lake Union. We found what was probably Juan scattered outside the hospital. The dead found us pretty much right away. As we made our way down the hill, Nancy was attacked on the corner Bellevue and Denny. There was nothing I could do. I hate to even say it, but that gave me a chance to get to here. There are a lot of them roaming around out there, but they're not that fast if you start out with some distance between you and them. If they're right up on you though . . ."

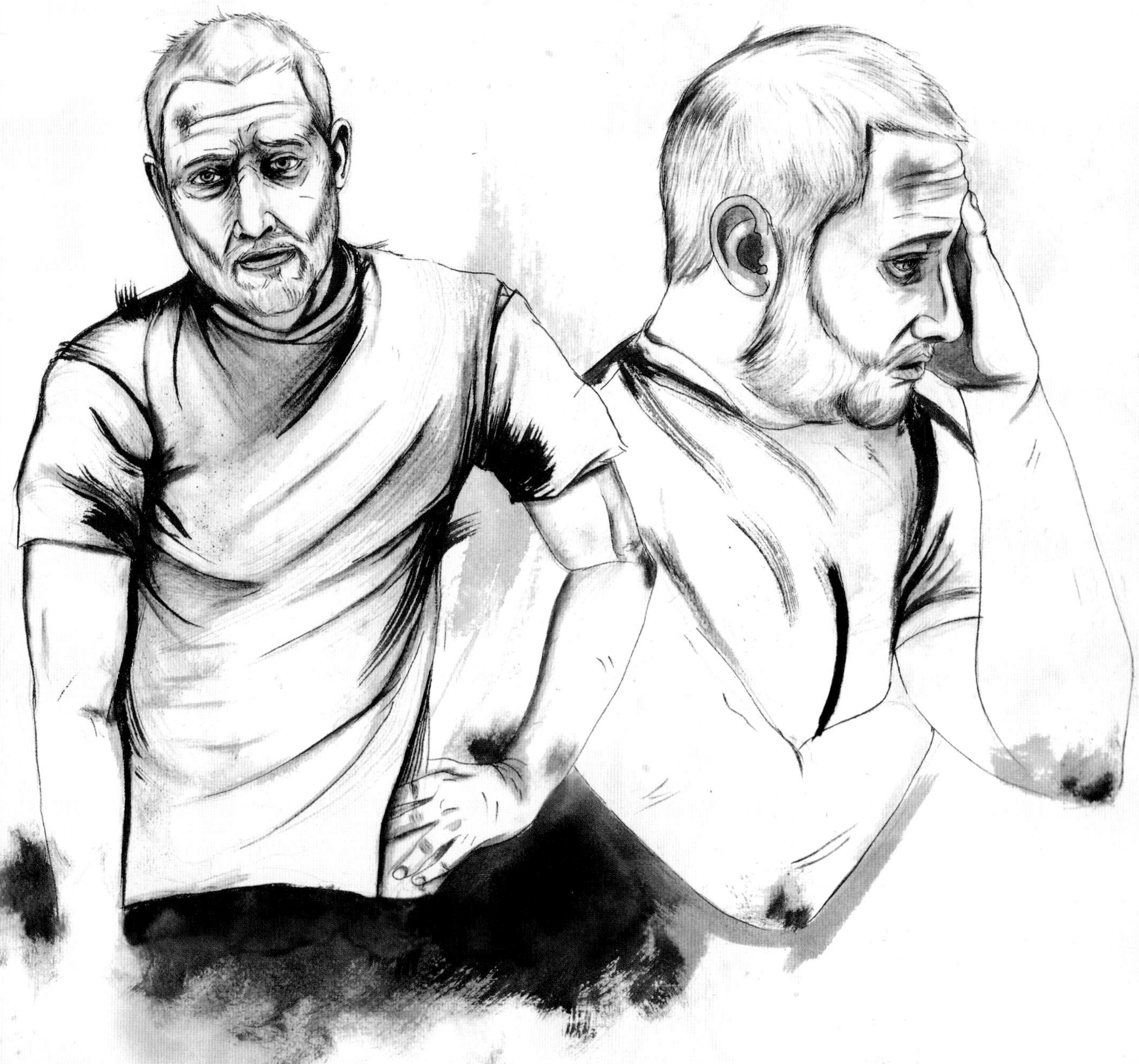

We'll leave for the boat tonight just after midnight. Ryan says he thinks that the zombies' eyesight is hampered by darkness. I don't know. I guess we'll find out. He hasn't heard from his girlfriend since the cell reception went out almost a week ago. We have no idea if she's alive. He's distraught. There's no reason to stay here. He found me, but neither of us thinks anyone else is going to show up and bring us any better options.

ESCAPE Route
US
PARKING LOT
HOUSE Boat
gas WORKS PARK

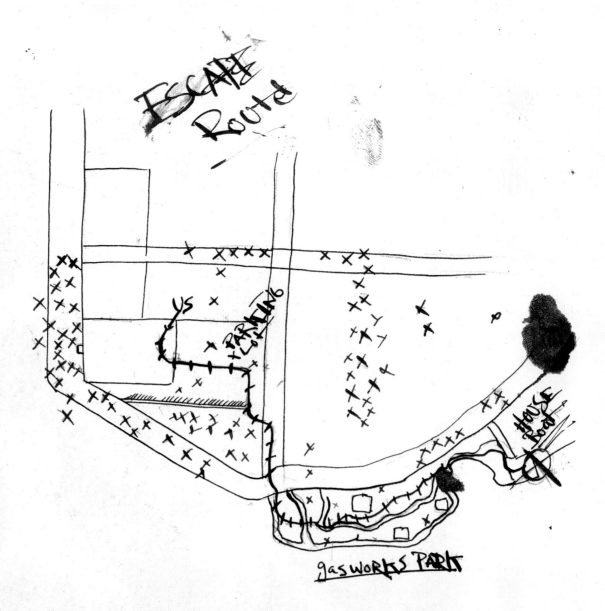

January 20, 2012

Made it to the houseboat. It's a bad scene here. Blood in the cabin and on the deck, dried. Not clear whose blood. There's no sign of Ryan's girlfriend. The useless cell phone is here. That's bloody, too. Ryan's a wreck, hysterical.

The marina is quiet, but the creaking of the boats, the ropes, the docks, the sound of the tide makes it hard to dial down my nerves—expecting the sounds to mask an approach by the dead. We don't think they followed us here, but unsure if there are any around. Hard to tell if they see worse in the dark than we do. In any event, that would cut both ways. We've been using a flashlight, trying to mask it from view as much as we can.

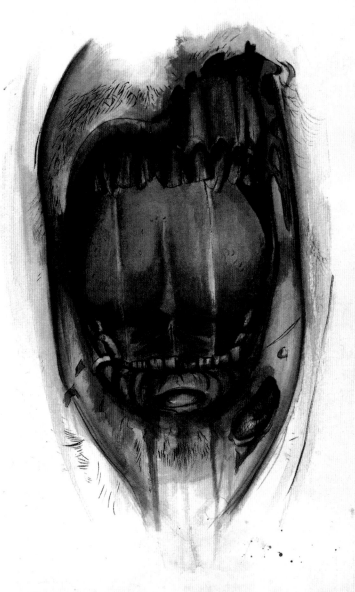

We made it downstairs from the lab and out the side door of the building and onto the street, and they were on us quickly. We'd armed ourselves with homemade clubs, furniture legs, and fought with everything we had. Clubbing them in the head seems to work best, it seems to stun them, body blows are less effective. Horrible. Their jaws are just gnashing, always, even if you're taking its jaws apart with a club.

There's food here, and bottled water. No weapons to speak of—Ryan's old baseball bat. His neighbor has a handgun that he knows of. That's where we're headed next.

Need to sleep. It doesn't feel safe but it can't be helped.

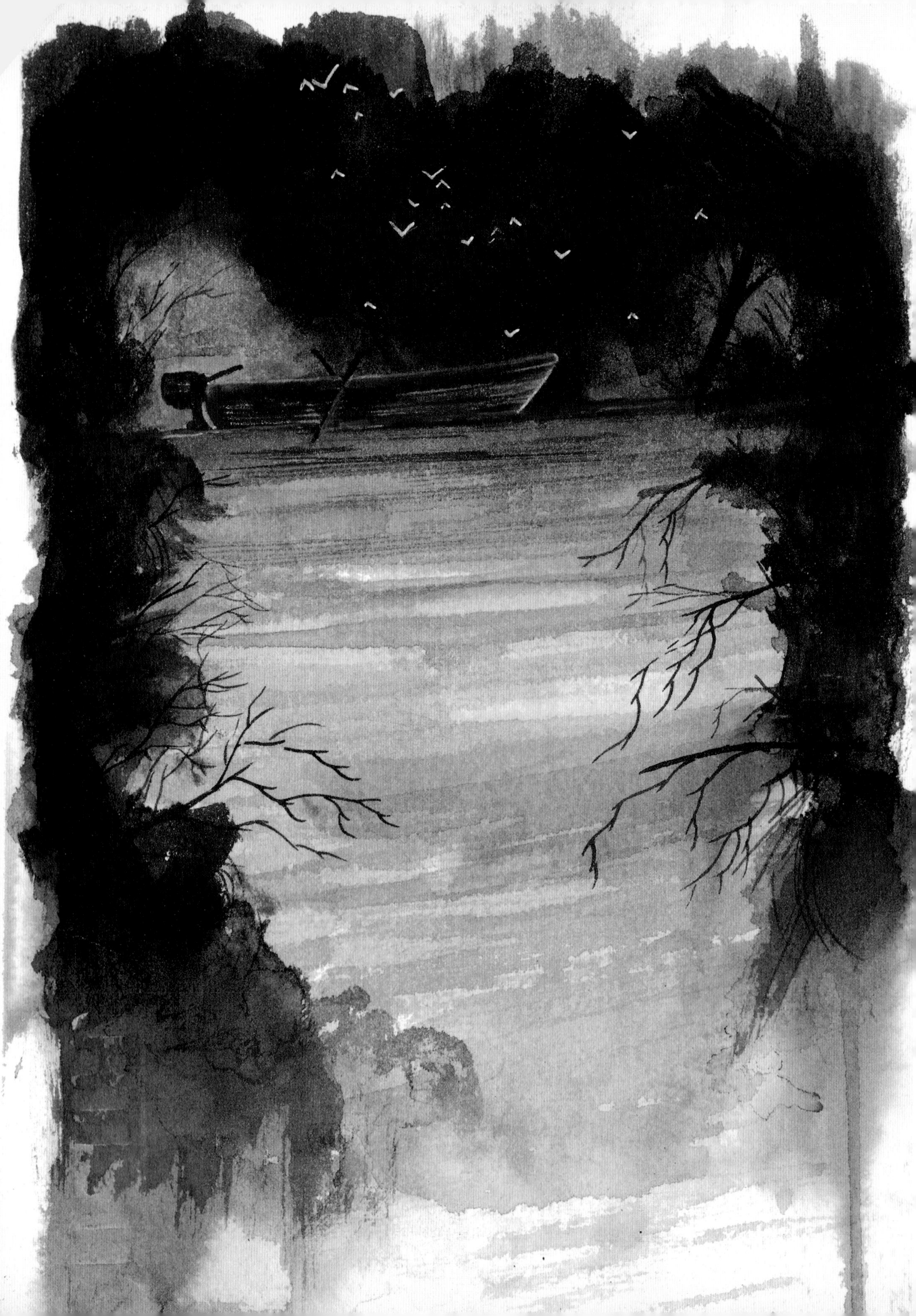

January 21, 2012

The neighbor had two handguns, some ammo, a couple boxes. Between his place and Ryan's we have: flashlights, batteries, food and water, extra clothes, some camping gear—a handheld GPS! From before everyone had them on their phones—a first-aid kit and a couple backpacks, and the baseball bat. We got all this into a motorboat and pushed off and away.

They came as soon as we fired up the engine, which means they can "hear", at least the roar of an outboard. Ryan has some experience with guns. I concentrated on steering. Bullets don't really seem to stop them. Body shots do nothing, their physiology doesn't make any sense. The force of the shot slows them but that's about it. He nailed a couple in the head, but they kept coming. When I killed ~~that thing that~~ killed? Paul or whatever it was the acid had removed either a crucial part of the brain or enough of the brain to stop it.

Ryan's ranting—we need higher caliber weapons.

We have a 9mm and a .22.

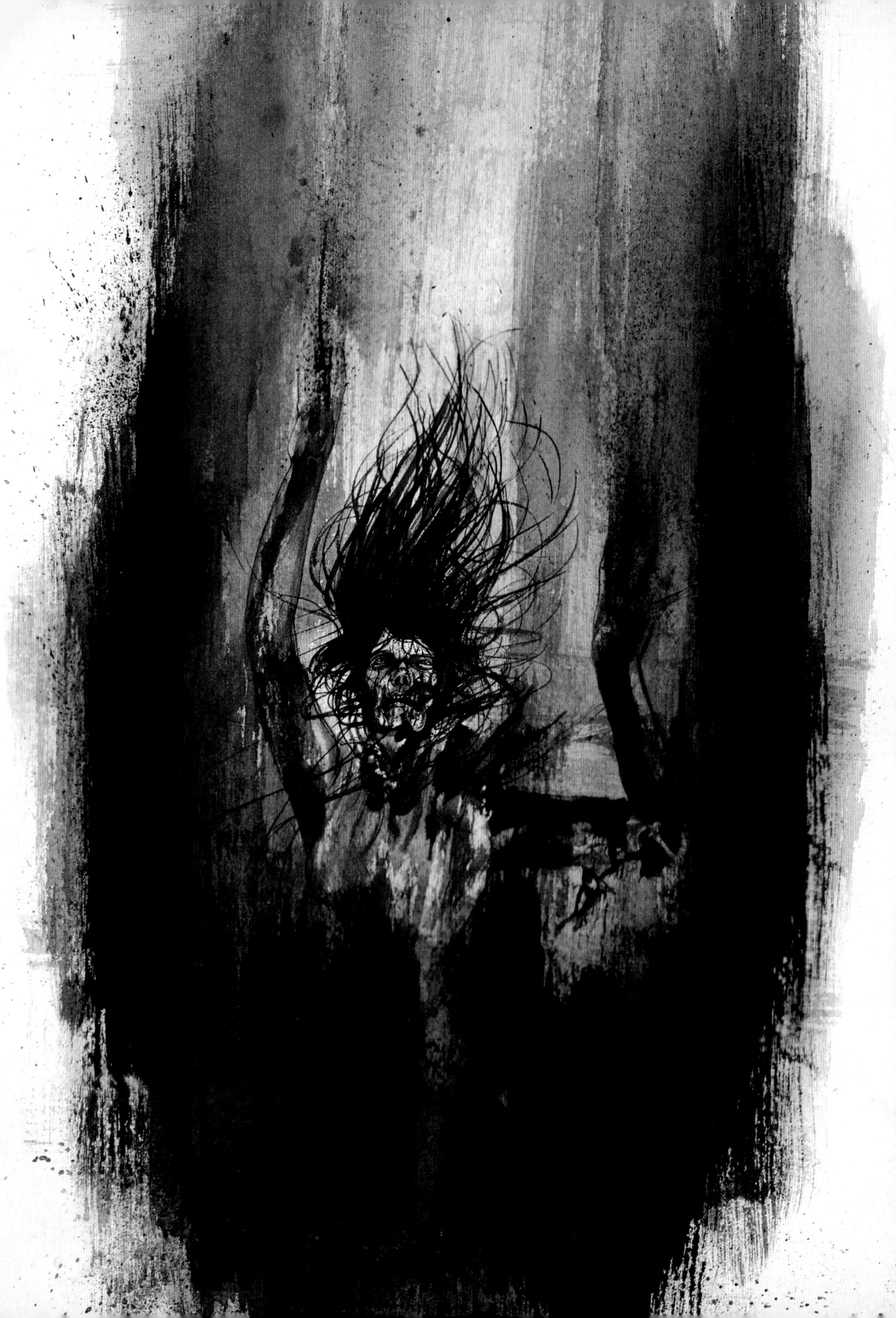

Zombies and water.

In their attempts to attack and eat us a whole bunch of them fell into the lake, or walked into the lake. They can't move fast enough to tread water and, due to a lack of air in their lungs?, they sink. For the same reason, I don't believe they actually drown. Somewhere at the bottom, hungry zombies lurk. Even from a "safe" vantage here in the boat, the thought gives me the chills. I keep thinking this is going to make sense. Anaerobic effects should be, they shouldn't even be moving around on land. How long can they live underwater?

We could see them come out onto the banks as we steered out into open water of Elliott Bay. You can tell they're dead rather than survivors because of the way they move.

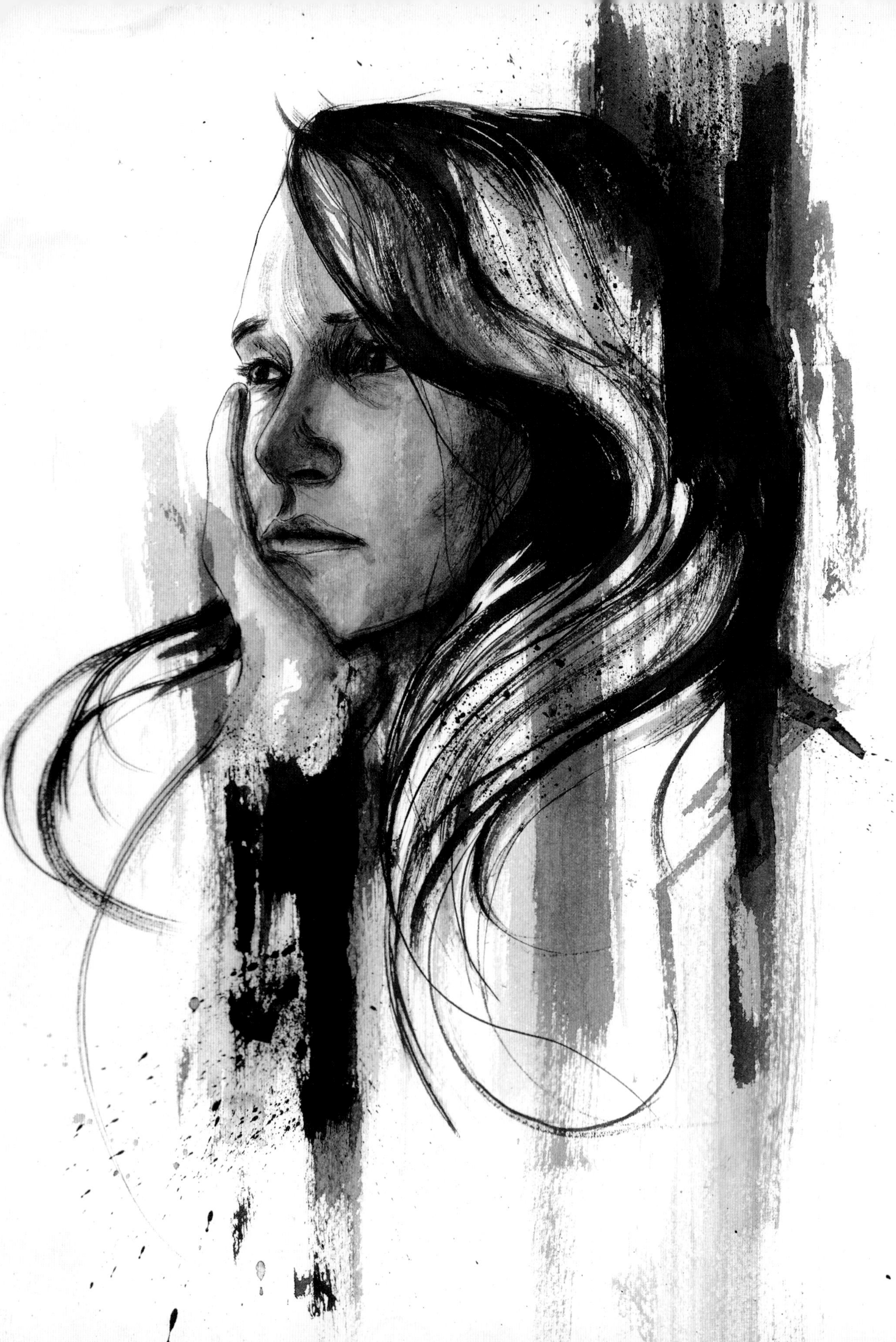

January 22, 2012

We've met survivors. A woman named Jeri and her dog, JoJo. We'd run out of gas. Stupid! There was gas at the pier, we just didn't think! 10 or 12 miles out the engine sputtered and Ryan and I picked up the oars and were scanning the shoreline when we spotted another small boat in the distance. We were thinking gas at the very least, maybe people. When we got close we could see movement, and hear a dog barking.

No gas. Jeri said she'd been floating for two days. We tied her boat to ours, waiting until dusk, and then rowed to what looked like the most zombie-free spot? on shore. What's zombie-free?

It looked woodsy. Jeri has a map. We think we're somewhere in Snohomish County.

We're in a craftsman-style house that we found up and in from the shoreline. No one inside or around. No car, maybe they got out. We checked the house carefully, room to room. Drawers and closets ransacked—left in a hurry. When it was cleared for zombies, we shut all curtains, locked and barricaded the doors, and lit a few candles that we found in the pantry alongside what was left of their canned and dry goods. No baked beans, but they left chickpeas, coconut milk, that can of water chestnuts everyone has but never uses, some other stuff. Food rotten in the dead fridge. Should probably board up the windows but worried about the noise, just moved some mattresses and tables to block the candlelight somewhat.

Crashing together on the couches and floor downstairs.

Ryan is wired, he gets the first watch.

January 23, 2012

JoJo is clearly an asset. He growled a few times last
night—whether due to a passing zombie or what, a raccoon?
We don't know. No one is going to investigate. Worried though if
he barks. A few panicky moments. Breakfast was corn flakes,
coconut milk and water. Bowls and spoons, weirdly civilized.
Jeri told us her story, which I'm recording here.

"I live in Poulsbo. My parents and I were staying at a cabin we have.
They turned into those . . . When they died, they just woke up and
attacked us. JoJo and I just ran.

My dad had been having chest pains, my mom too. I put them to bed and
was trying to take care of them the best I could. They couldn't breathe
and I called an ambulance that never came and then they died. Then
they got up. JoJo and I ran to the neighbor's house, but they were
already . . . the neighbors and my parents chased us and we ran
to the boat and just left them, they kept coming into the water
after us. What's happening? I don't understand why nobody's helping,
what's happening?"

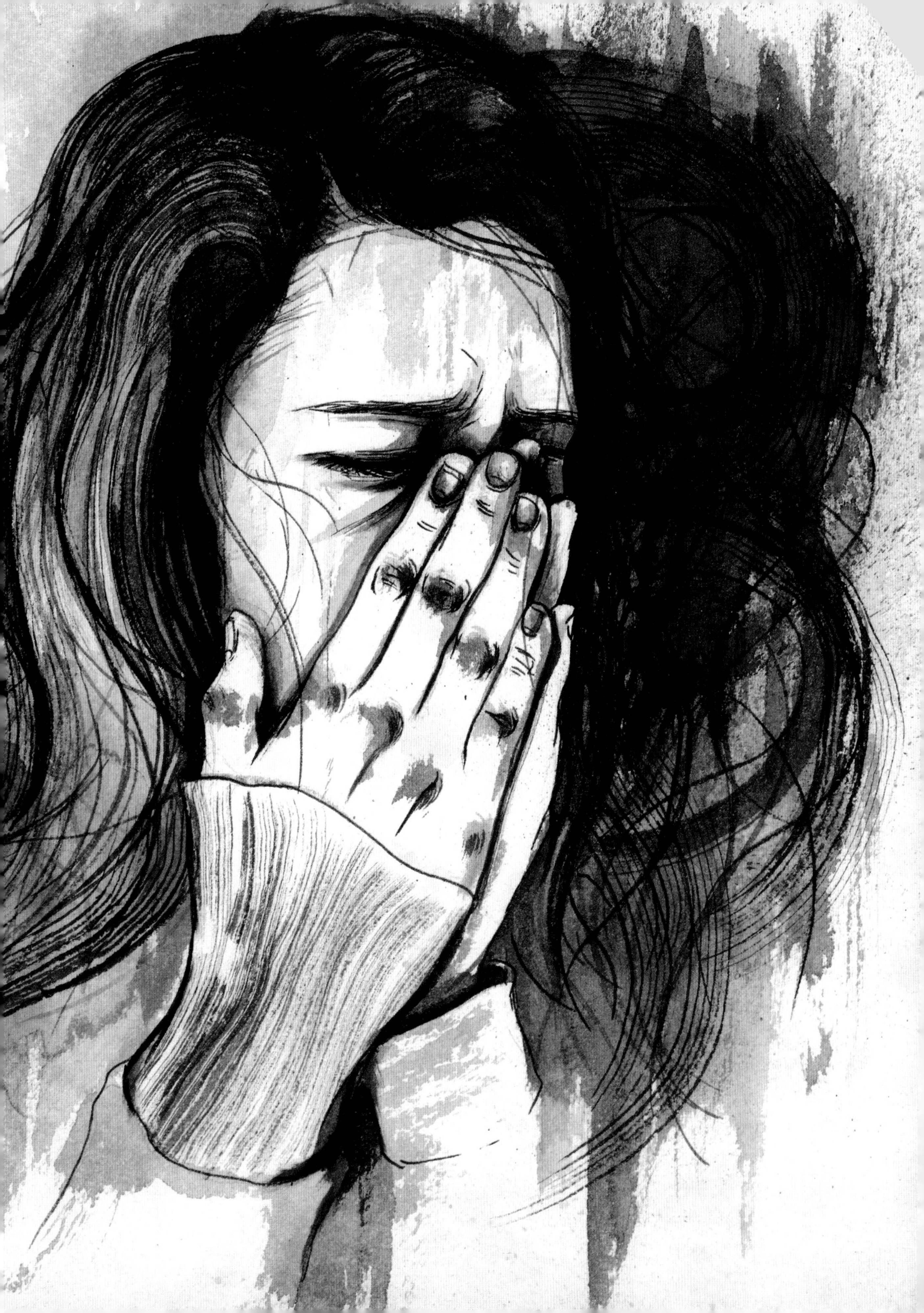

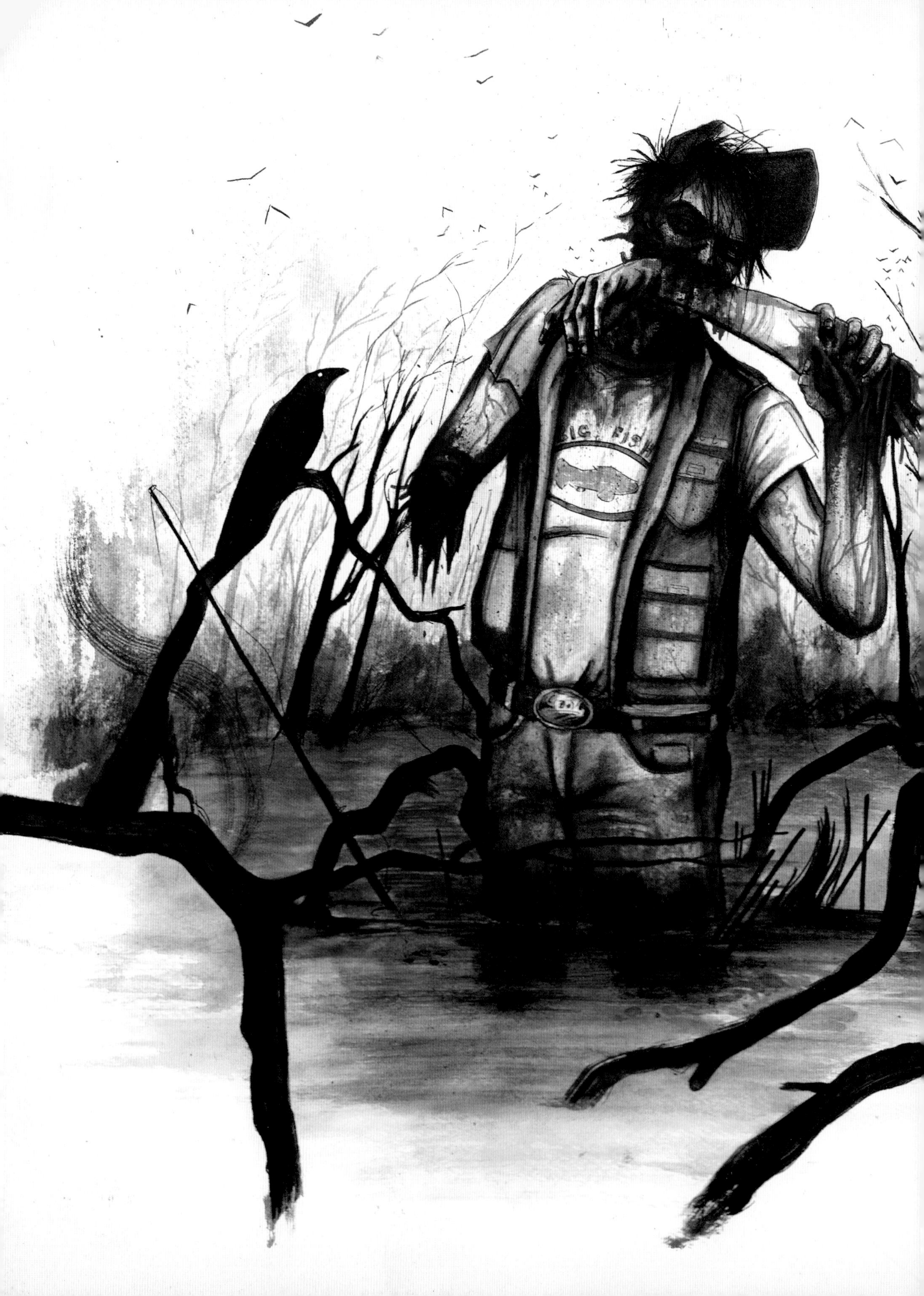

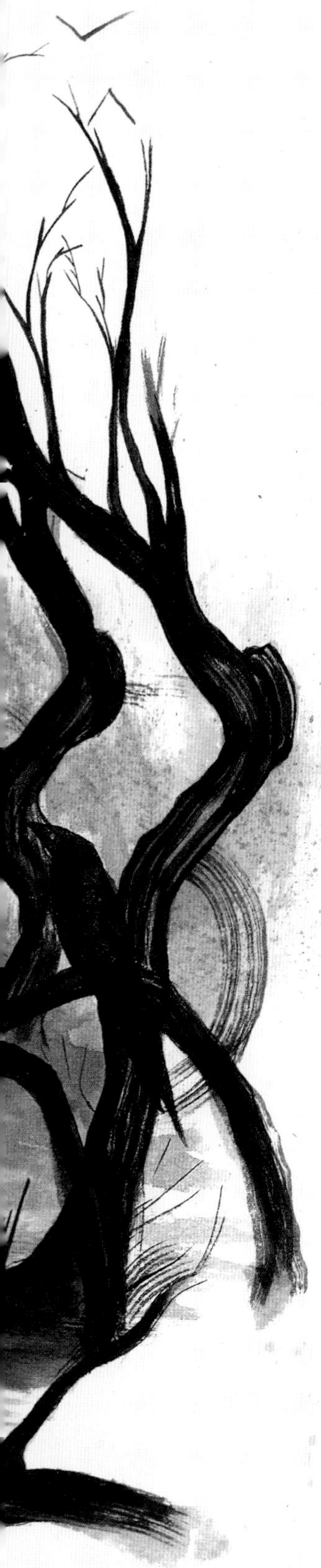

The house is freezing and we've been burning wood in the fireplace to keep warm. No firewood left at the house and the furniture is barricade material, though also perhaps not good to burn treated wood in a closed space—maybe that's the least of our worries.

Half reconnaissance and half gathering wood I left the house today. At a good distance I saw a zombie down by the water in fishing gear, just standing there, swaying, and staring? out over the water. Do they think? Then it ripped off part of its own arm and gnawed on it like it was beef jerky.

We haven't seen any zombies preying on each other, let alone eating themselves. Was this zombie "starving?" If isolated from live humans, which they're definitely interested in eating, do they eat each other? Was this zombie recently dead enough to consider itself still "fresh"? Was glad to get back to the house.

January 24, 2012

Found a pair of binoculars in the house today—very useful for observing things from a safe distance. This afternoon, from a top-floor window, I was able to witness something that I believe is relevant to understanding the zombies' physical decomposition.

At different times I saw two of them shuffling down the road. The first one moved slower, looking more ashy, more "off", with veins and deep tissue layers emergent. The second one, a postal worker, looked "fresher"—visible decay but less of it, and moving at a quicker pace. My guess is that he had died within the last day or two? What stood out the most to me was the expression on the mailman's face. Like he was frozen in mid-scream even though he didn't make a sound.

I've sketched a progressive chart that features the breakdown of living tissue into undead flesh based on the two I observed:

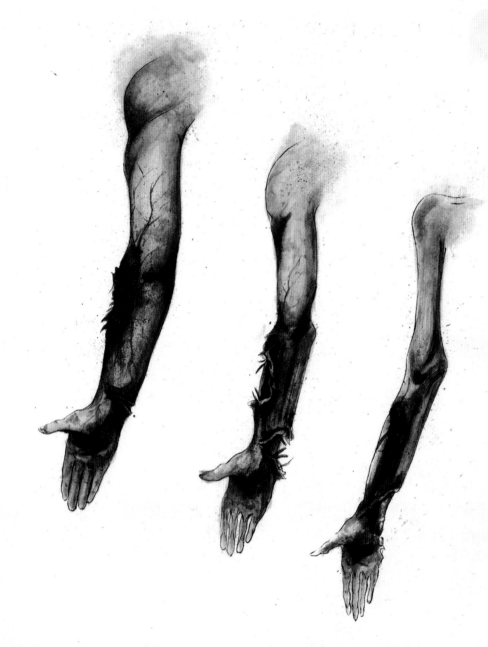

This might be both good __and__ bad news. The good being that natural decomposition is occurring in the walking corpses, which would mean that within a few weeks, they should rot enough to not be much of a further threat. The bad, however, as we know from Jeri's story, is that not everyone is affected at the same time. Need to make further observations on this.

A little freaked out that the zombies passed within sight of the house.

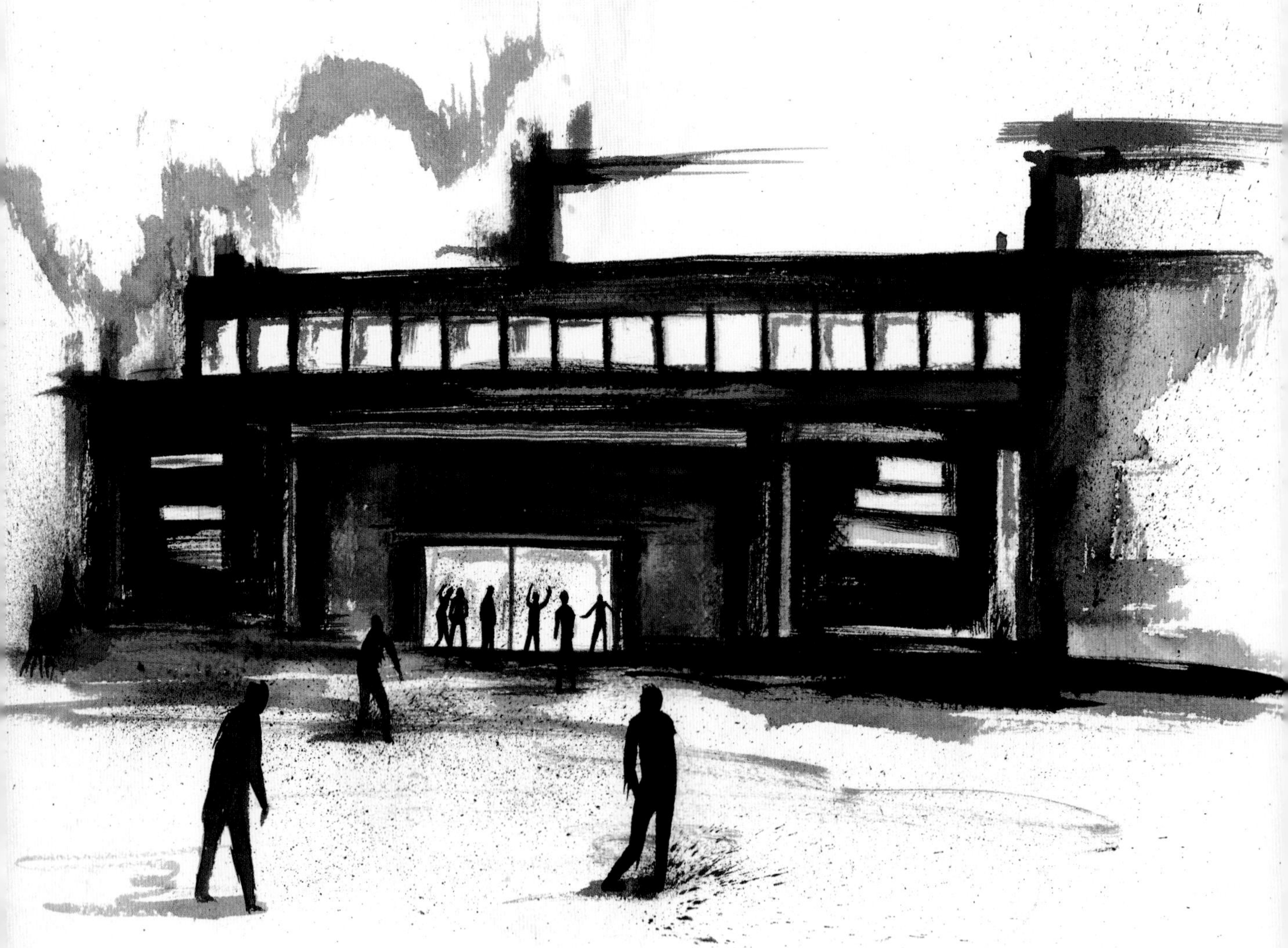

January 25, 2012

Took a bicycle from the shed today and rode out, I'd estimate 3 or 4 miles, and found a small commercial area in a valley past the edge of the woods. The dead of what must have been the town are still congregated here. Why? Cautiously, I've been observing and sketching it from a hidden vantage point. They're not eating each other, the fisherman must have been some sort of [redacted] aberration. They're not exactly interacting with each other, either, just sort of [redacted] they're just wandering aimlessly. A legless zombie just crawled over to butt its head against a glass door, now just sort of looking inside. There's one with a . . . purse? And their jaws are all moving, chewing? Through the binoculars, the raw areas around the mouths, lack of cheeks, tongues, suggests a gnawing of their own soft tissue, but not extensive cannibalism. I'm wondering if this activity parallels the living's preoccupation with the mouth—eating, smoking, biting nails, sipping coffee, whistling, speaking, chewing gum, grinding teeth, etc. Their systems can't need or process food. Is living human flesh some sort of connection with life, some sort of "comfort food" to the undead?

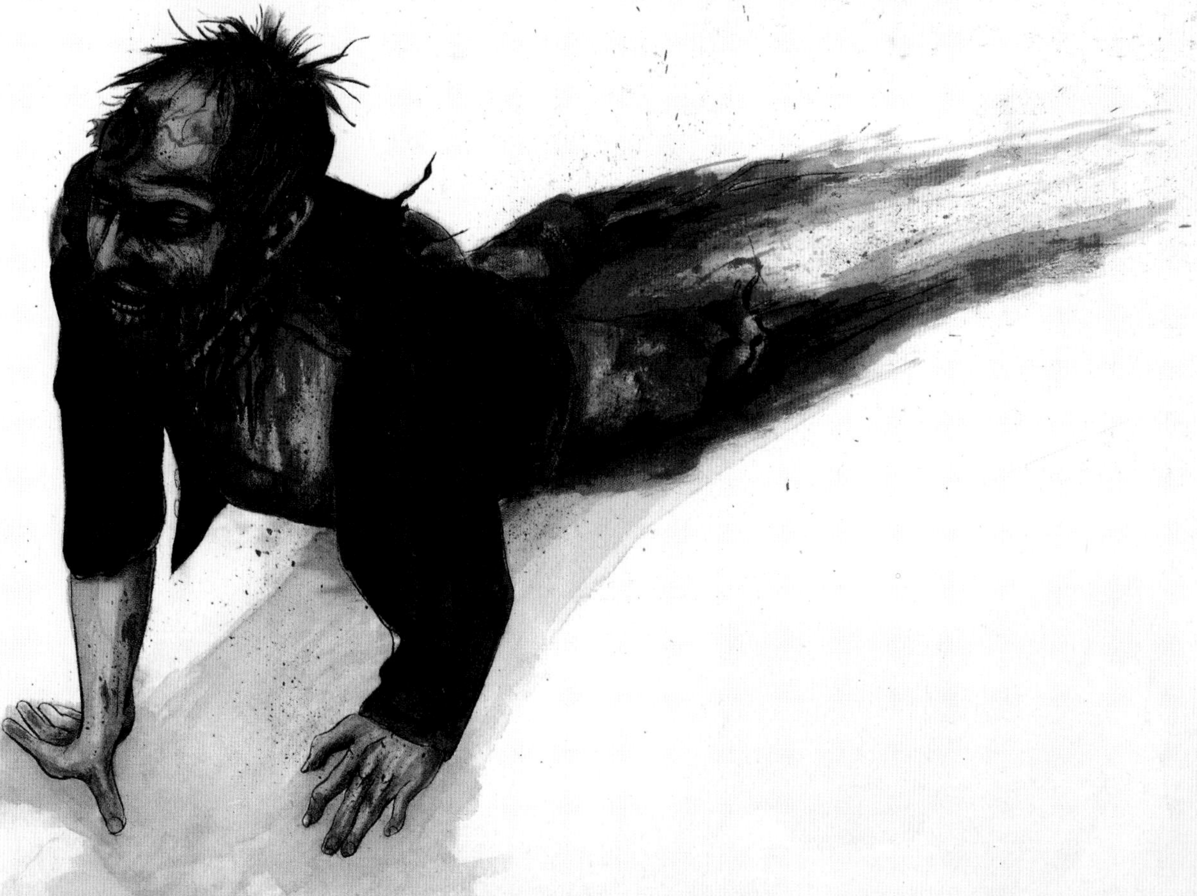

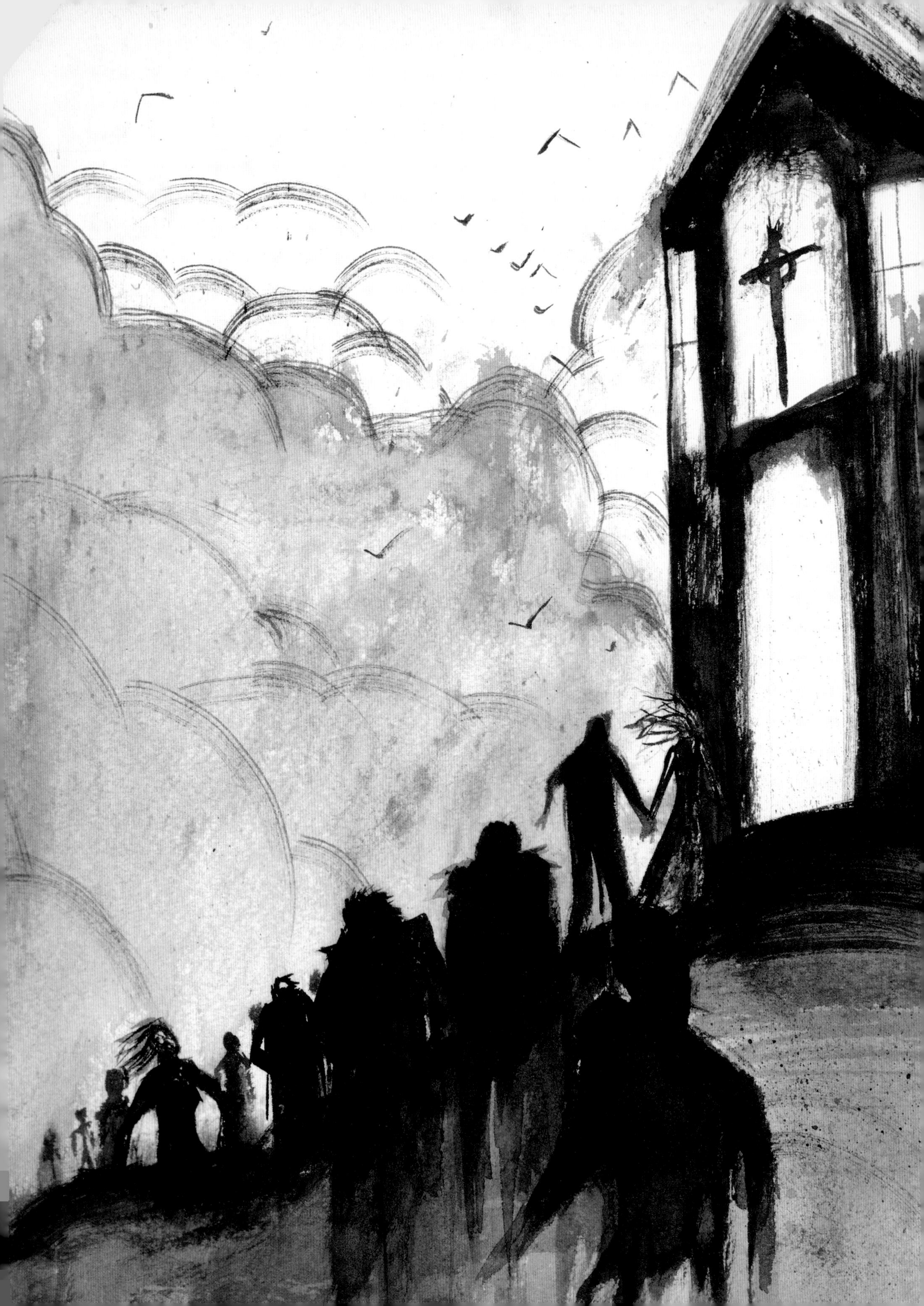

More evidence of zombies retaining living behaviors in death. I'm by a little country church and a [redacted] wedding party.

Did they succumb together and are now, sticking together? Out of familiarity? Are there zombie families "living" inside of houses in the area?

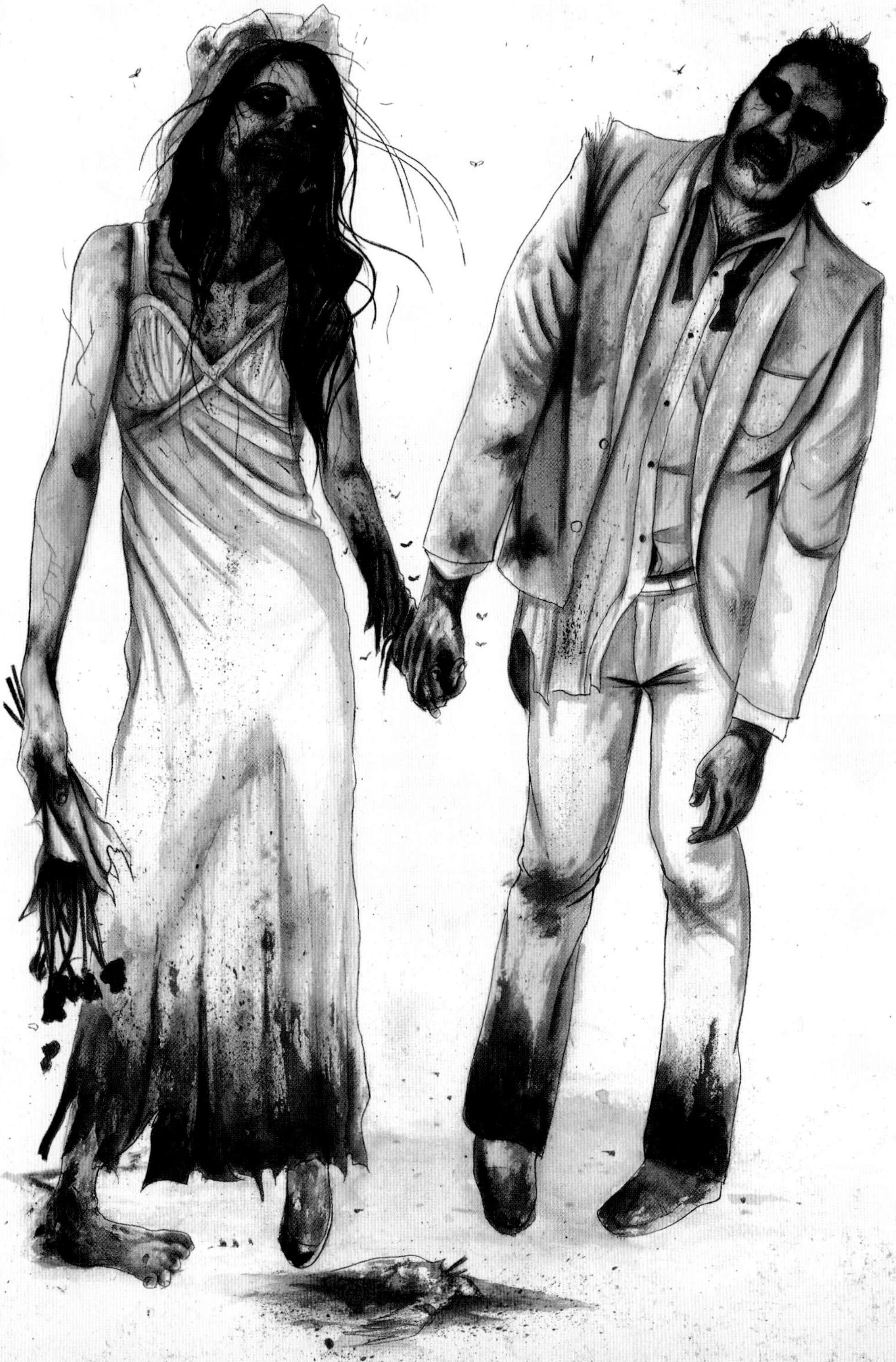

Are GMOs Responsible For Sickness?

By JEFF KRIEGE

SEATTLE, Wash. — Leading food additive manufacturer Primodine Laboratories was placed under quarantine Saturday, according to officials at the Centers for Disease Control. Compounds sourced from the Primodine facility are suspected to be responsible for the violent illness and deaths of an estimated 16 million people in developed countries worldwide.

According to the CDC spokesperson Kevin Byron, "While testing has proven inconclusive, indications point to the cumulative effect of an additive produced and distributed from the Primodine site. We do not expect this quarantine to have an immediate effect on the pandemic, but believe it to be a crucial measure."

Primodine, located north of Seattle in Bellingham, Wash. has been owned by the InfraNeuronics Corporation since 1998. INC chairman and CEO Michael Healy released a statement on

Continued on page 7

January 26, 2012

Noticing for the first time the contents of the newspapers
we're using for the fires. Ads. The sports section. Vestiges of
society we're not sure is ever coming back.

←——————————— And this

Primodine has a serious R&D facility up in Bellingham that hires all
the Chem grads from UW and Western. They should just give them lab
coats instead of caps and gowns. Regularly protested by the Poli Sci
students for its military contracts—the company's behind everything
from cleaning solvents to automobile tires to wonderfood additives,
like C88. "C88—Tastes Great! An All-Natural Flavor Enhancer That
Brings Your Favorite Foods to Life!" After seeing the gnawing
activities yesterday ~~that night typemerk~~ Here are ads for it in chips,
chocolate, instant soup, chicken nuggets . . .

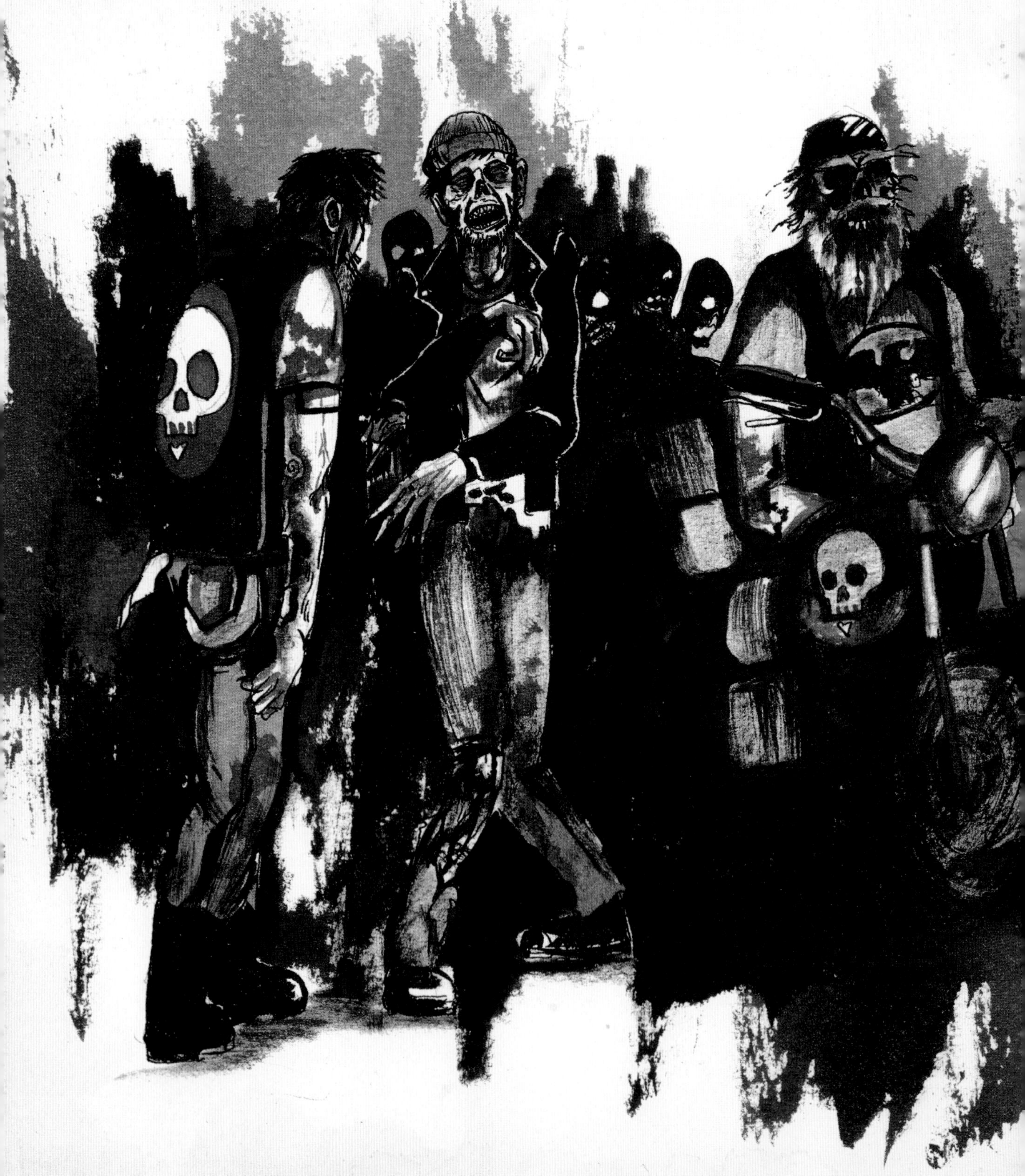

January 27, 2012

Approximately two miles northwest from the house today I observed a zombie biker group. NOT riding their bikes—luckily no evidence that the dead have any vestigial recollection of technology, what it means, what to do with it. But they do seem to have some recognition of social order or hierarchy, at least this group did. Maybe I'm projecting my beliefs about bikers, but they seemed to be milling around a central figure. Not that he, or they, were actually doing much of anything. Not actively hunting for food. They all appeared to be at the same stage of decay, which I would theorize means they were afflicted at the same time. Likely endemic among tight-knit groups.

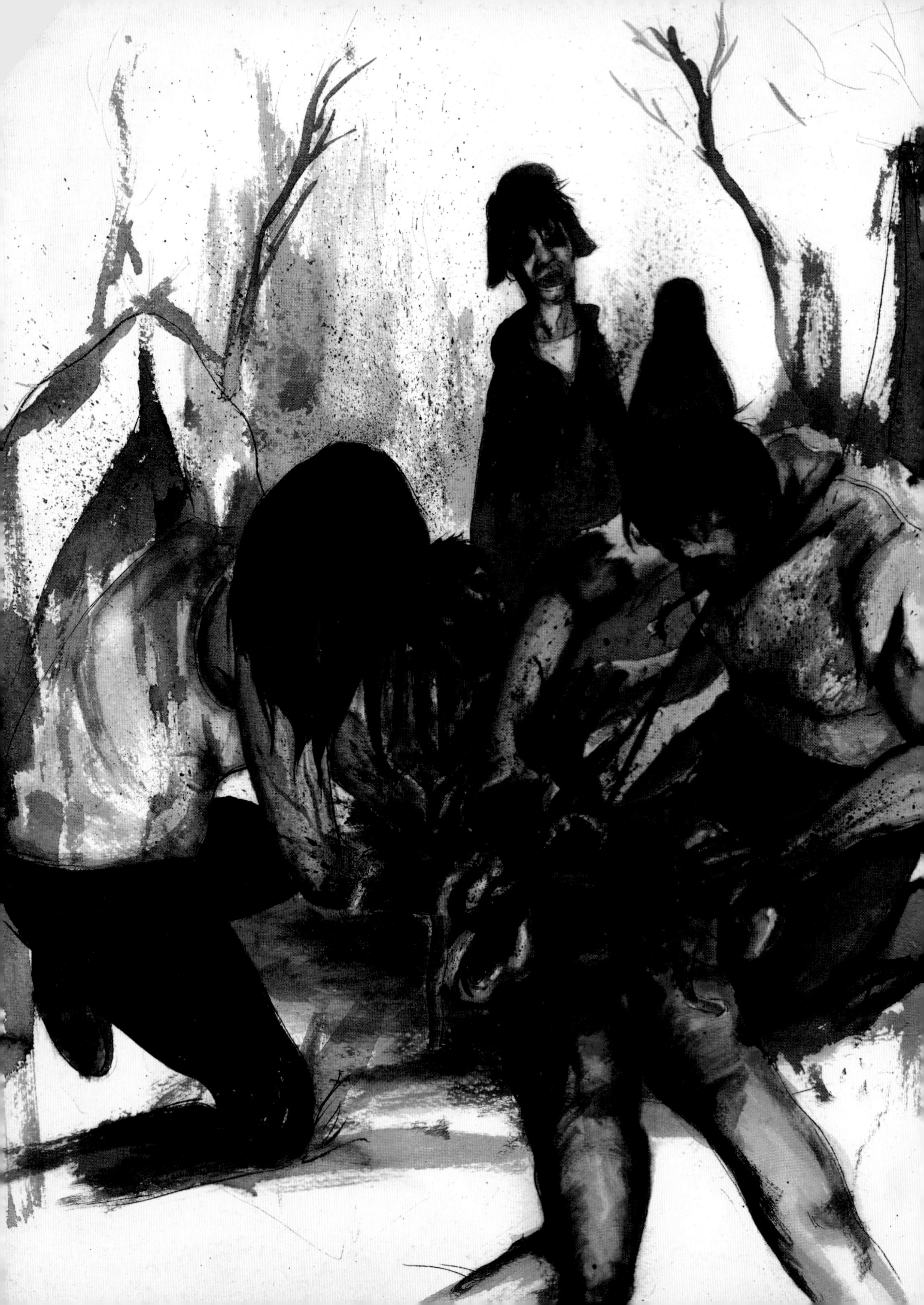

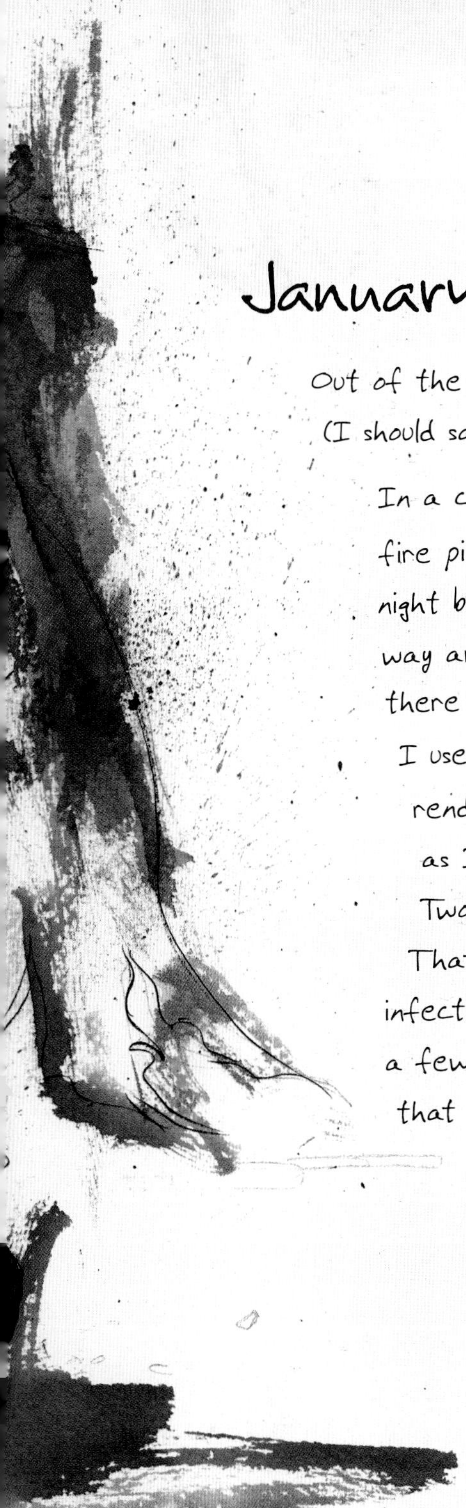

January 28, 2012

Out of the house again in the early morning hours. Went out alone, again. (I should say, Jeri and Ryan think I'm nuts.)

In a clearing, I came upon a small campsite with tents and a fire pit, still kind of steaming in the mist, probably burning the night before. I almost called out, but thought better. Working my way around to the other side of the tents I heard there was a wet gnawing sound, some snapping. A little further I used the binoculars to see a hunting party, three or four, rending another one of the group apart. Watched for as long as I could stomach, a few minutes? Couldn't let myself vomit. Two of the zombies seemed to be just kids, 13 or 14. A family? That they'd turned on each other suggests a different rate of infection among them. This is not far from the house. We'd passed a few days without direct incident and I'm understanding now that the sense of security we've been enjoying is false.

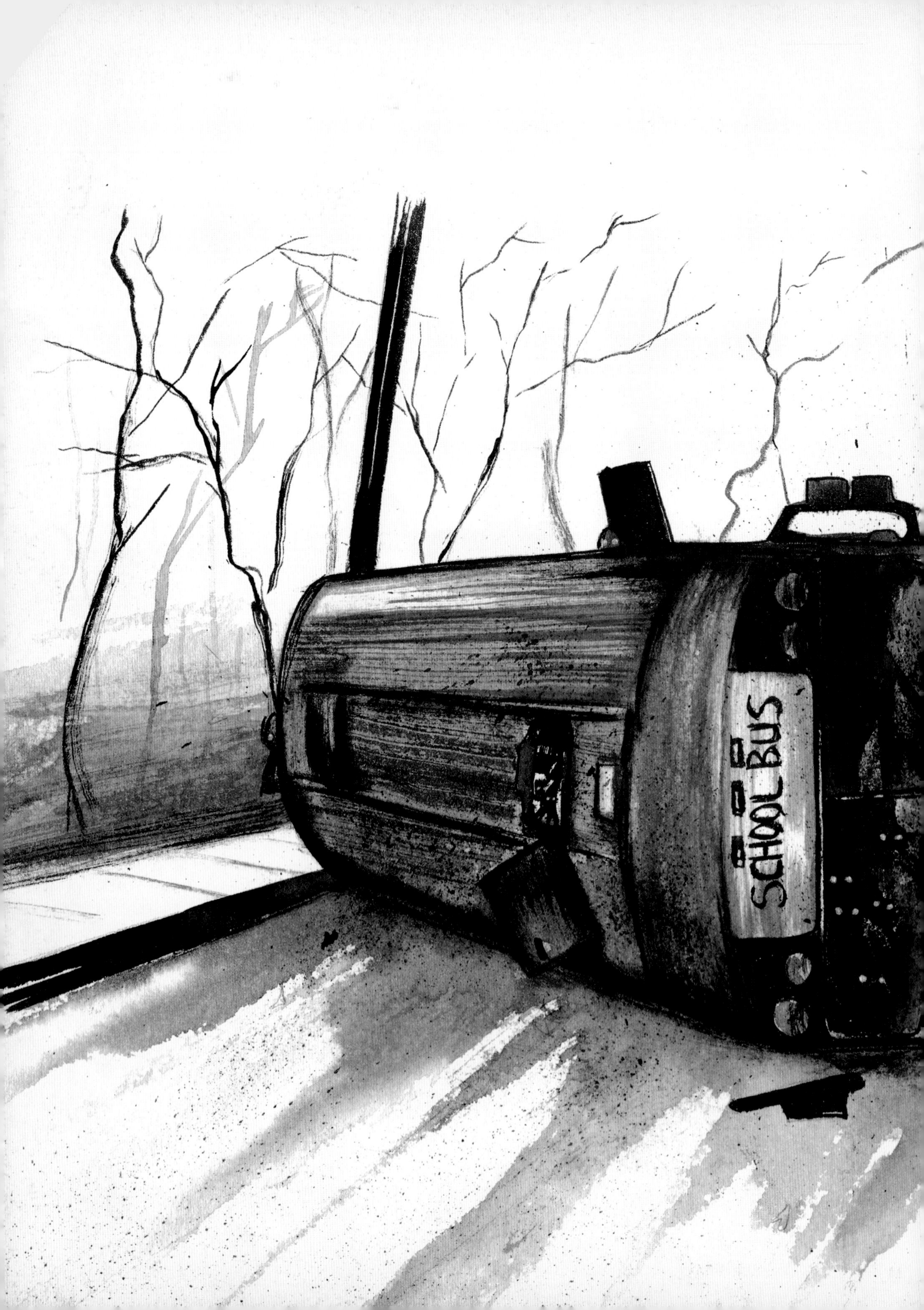
SCHOOL BUS

January 29, 2012

A bad day. I headed off in a different direction and came across an overturned bus. As I approached, they came out of the woods. Were they hiding? Can they plan? Faster than I'd expected, maybe because of their youth, a class, maybe a dozen 8-10 year olds. Not children.

I ran and they followed. I made it to the house, Jeri, Ryan, and JoJo were outside poking around in the shed.

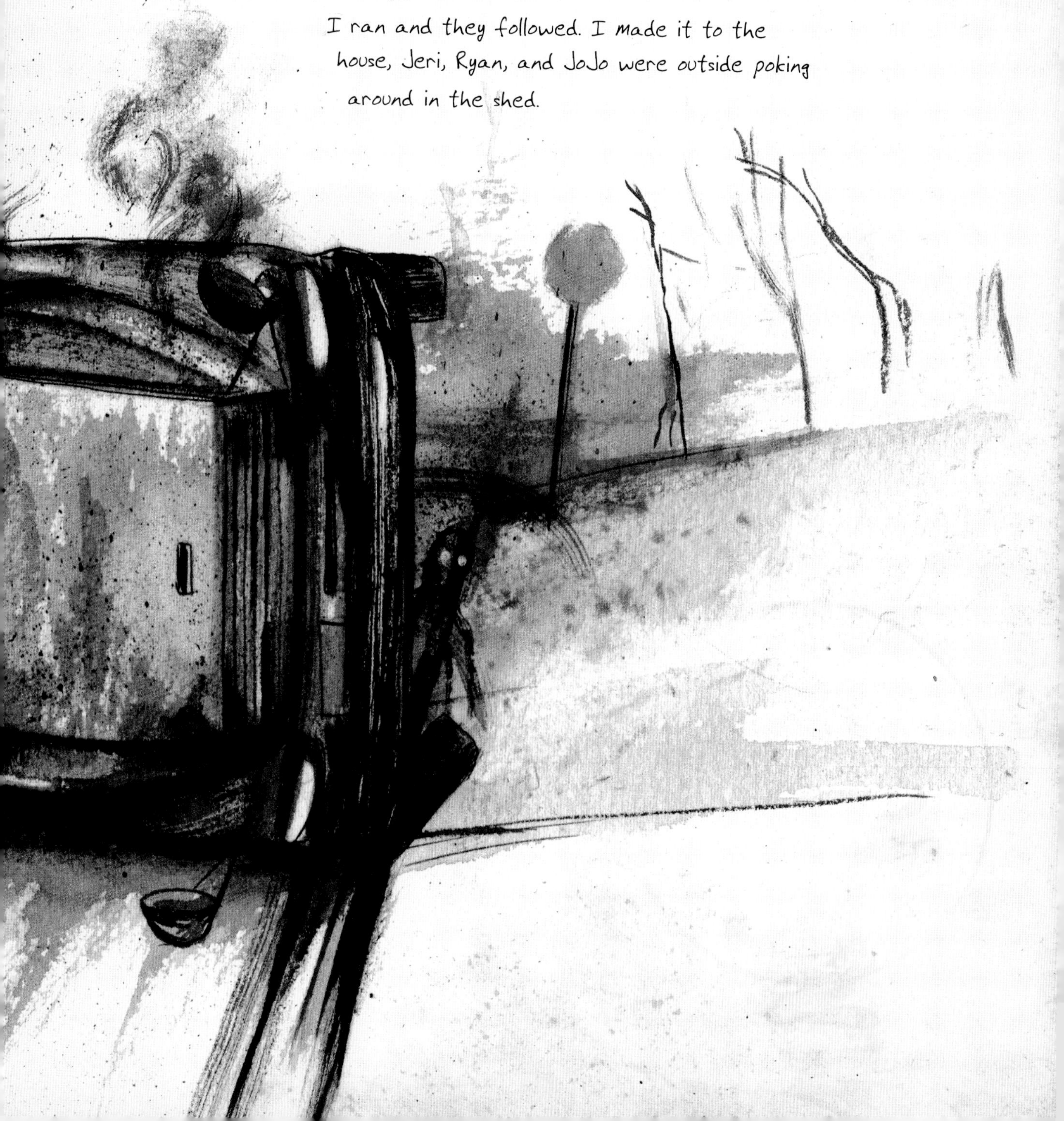

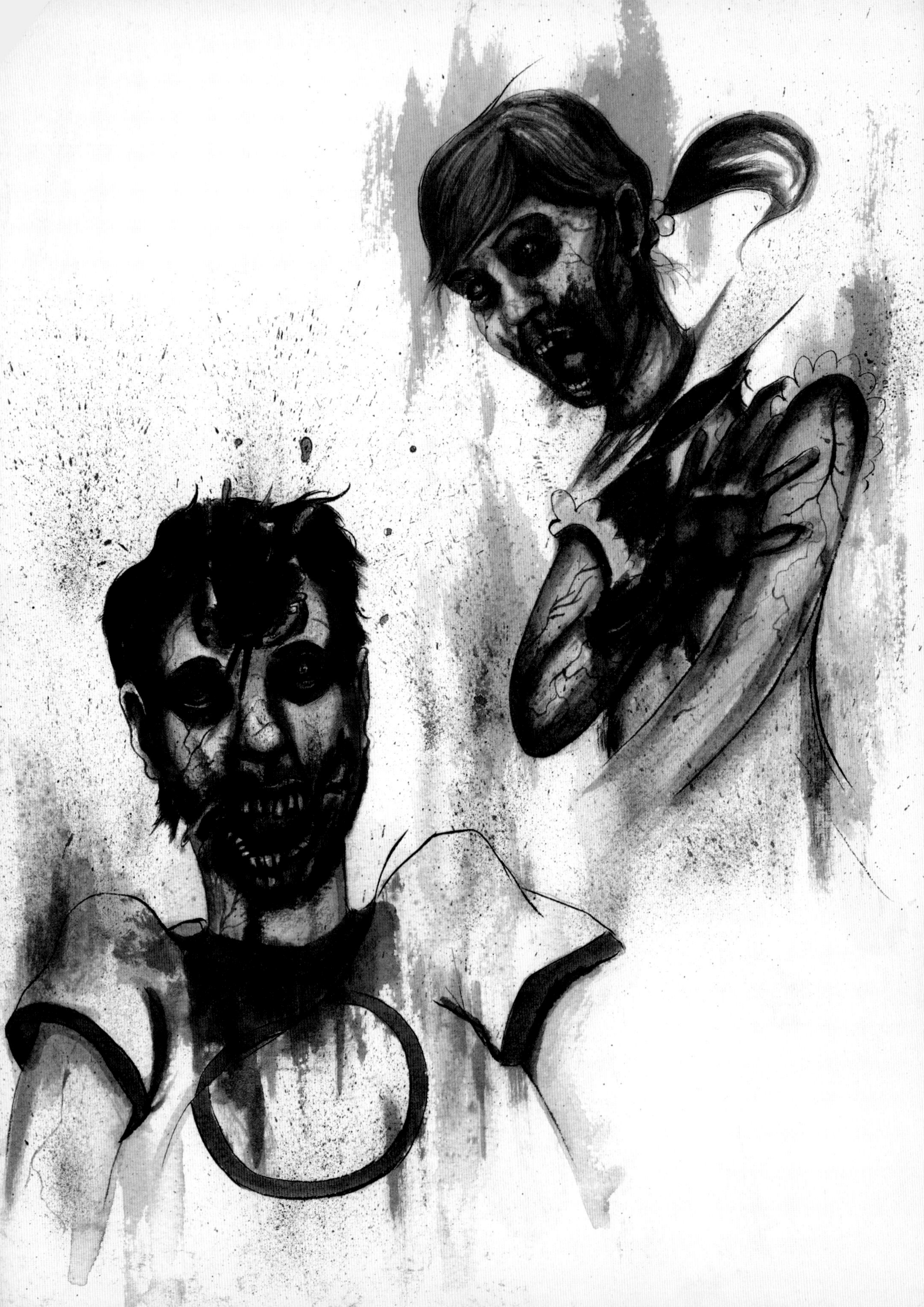

JoJo charged, barking, and leapt on the "boy" closest to me, knocking it over and coming away with part of its arm in his mouth.

Ryan had luck with the gun on that one (a center shot in the forehead) but head shots only slowed the next one. Kerosene and the lighter worked, but not immediately—they would stagger and struggle before being consumed in fire and falling to the ground, flesh bubbling.

Jeri had the bat and I had an axe. I took the head off one. Whatever passes for a nervous system kept it in motion for a moment before it fell. Bashing the cranial area, repeatedly, puts them down. If we couldn't get heads, we went for limbs to drop them and set the writhing little bodies and their hungry, decaying faces ablaze.

Inside now. It's not safe.
We made a lot of noise.

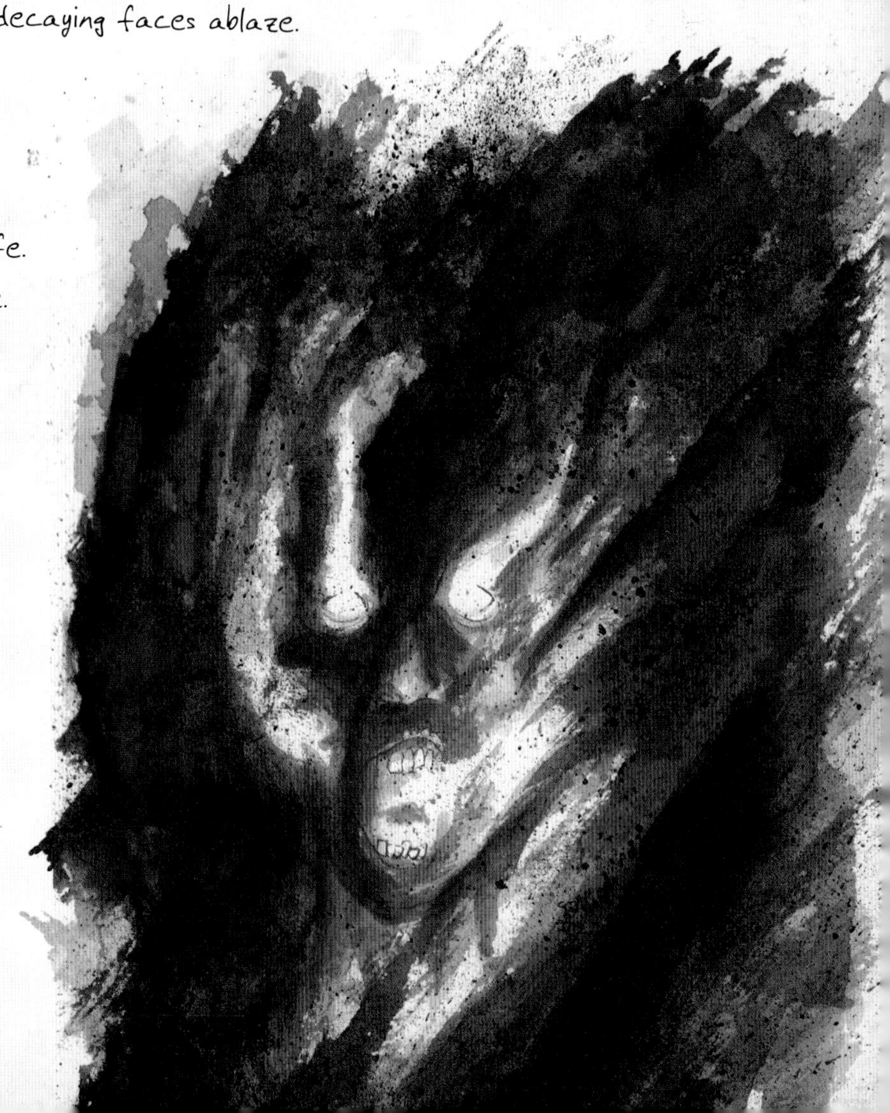

January 30, 2012

Everyone's dead.

Jeri was bitten in the attack. For a short time she was able to hide it from me and Ryan. We took her symptoms, pale, sweating, rapid breathing, for the aftermath of the attack, and didn't resist when she wanted to sleep upstairs while we kept watch downstairs. JoJo stayed downstairs with us. Later that night she turned on us.

She bit Ryan on the neck and tried to tear him apart. I took a shovel and got her in the head and she fell off Ryan. JoJo tore at her. With another swing I knocked her in front of the fireplace. I was able to get a clean slice at her gnashing mouth, cleaving her jaw, before the rest of her caught fire. Then the house caught fire.

Our packs had been ready in case we had to flee an attack from the outside and I managed to grab mine and Ryan's. We stood panting out on the lawn. We knew what the bite meant. Ryan turned and ran away from me, into the woods. The fire was already drawing zombies. JoJo growled at them, barking and snarling, but he would also not leave the vicinity of the house. I couldn't convince him to come with me, and I ran.

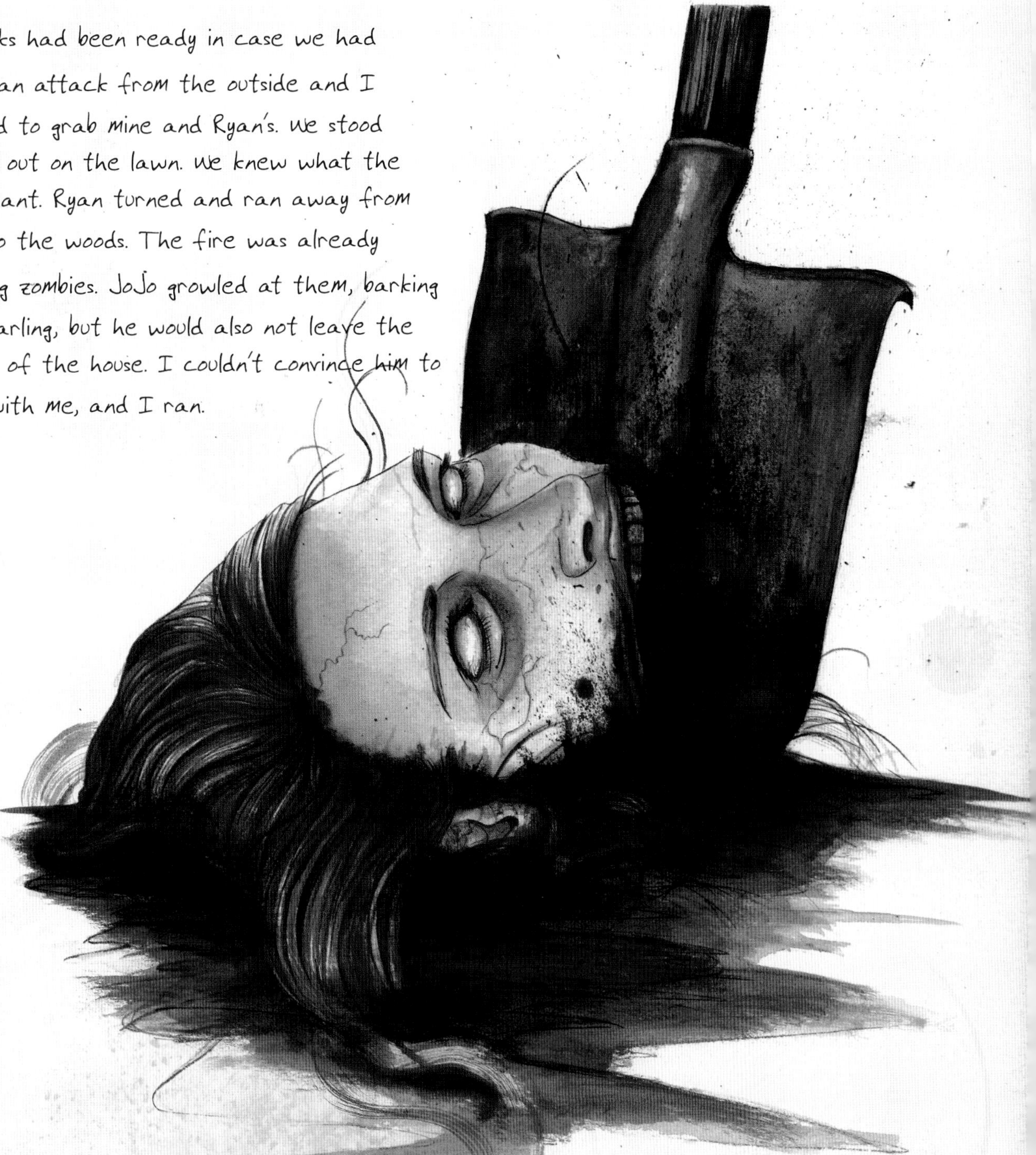

January 31, 2012

DEFENSE AGAINST THE LIVING DEAD

Guns: Mostly useless. "small caliber" (9mm and .22) are only effective with a perfect shot or at close range. Aim for the frontal lobe. ~~Bigger guns~~ Bigger guns might do more damage, I don't know. Ryan would know. The impact of the bullet anywhere can slow or knock them down. That's something.

Hydrofluoric acid: Any acid corrosive to human tissue could be effective, but it would HAVE TO BE APPLIED TO THE HEAD. They seem to have at least primal cognitive ability? And the center of that ~~whatever~~ drive seems to be whatever animating force is still functioning in the brain tissue.

Axe: Dismemberment is THE WAY TO GO in slowing them down. Off with the head.

Bludgeon: Blunt force is more effective than firearms are in terms of keeping them back at close range. You can bash whatever brains they have in but I can't ~~~~ I mean, you get tired. They don't get tired.

Extreme cold: Cold seems to adversely affect their physiology. I haven't actually touched the flesh of one of them, but without function of human systems, they must it stands to reason already be at no warmer than ambient atmospheric conditions? Reduction of that temperature seems to hamper a zombie's capability for motion, tightening tendons, muscles, and ligaments? A living person might take advantage of this in relocating or already living in extreme northern or southern regions.

Fire: Effective in that it destroys tissue, but the infected retain mobility for an unpredictable length of time until fire has done a fundamental level of immobilizing damage. They keep coming.

OTHER FACTORS

Birds: Species that feed on carrion as a natural part of their diet—crows, hawks—seem to have a taste for undead flesh. Species that would normally feed only on a carcass seem to have some sort of innate understanding that zombies are "already dead" and don't seem to be put off by motion. Still, they prefer zombies in what seem to be later stages of decay, when mobility is decreased. With great satisfaction, I've firsthand seen a crow pluck rotten tissue from reanimated dead.

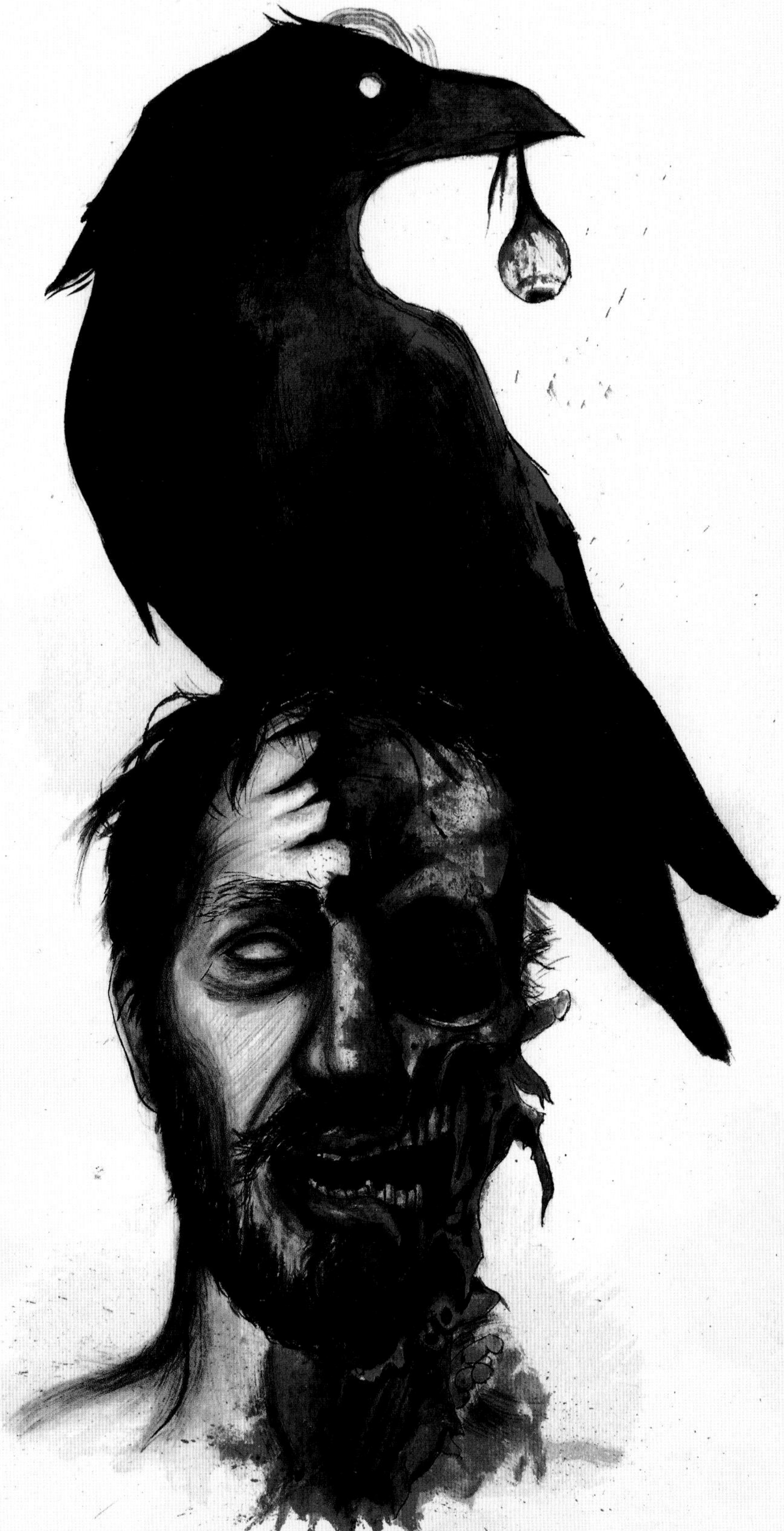

Dogs: Highly socialized to human contact and interaction, dogs are particularly freaked out by the presence of the undead. They will bristle and bark in their presence and even willfully attack a nonhuman. It is unknown if animals are infected—as are humans—by contact with zombies. None of the wildlife (squirrels, birds, a raccoon) or dogs that I have seen have shown any outward signs of infection or derangement, but I am not sure what those signs might be. In any event, contact with the dead by animal species might render that animal a carrier of the unknown element that has infected humans.

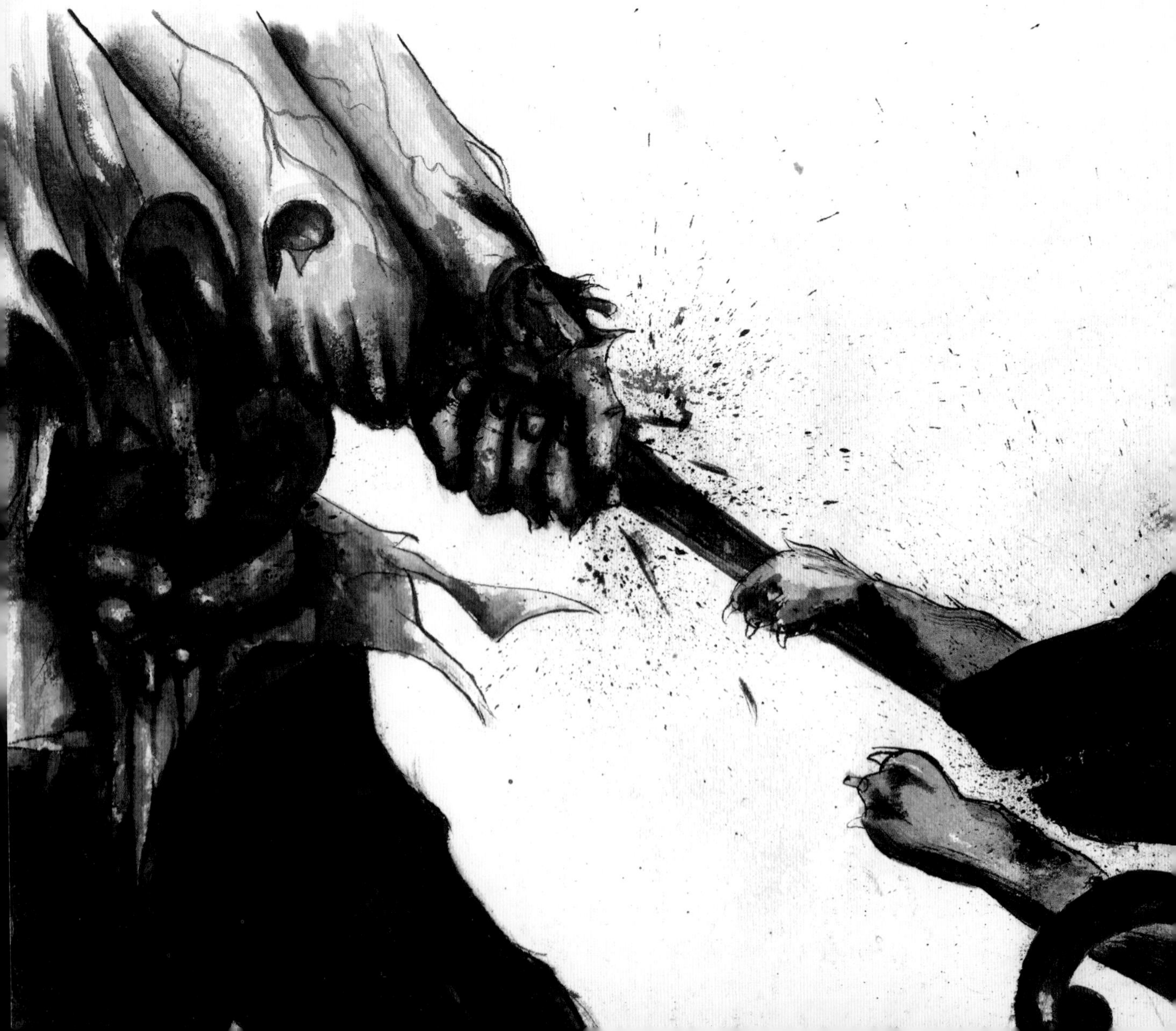

February 1, 2012

I'm alone. I'm not sure why I'm even keeping this notebook. There doesn't seem to be much point. Death is everywhere. Even the living are dead. I may be as good as dead. What I have, I have this notebook, and:

The axe

Food (a week's worth?) and water

The GPS

A watch (why?)

Ryan's .22, ammo

Clothes (important, it's cold)

A lighter

A tent (terrified of using, can't risk being trapped inside if I need to run, wrapping it around me like a sleeping bag)

Flashlight, batteries

What I also have is the woods. Never sure if the next cracking branch or brush of leaves is an animal—a fellow survivor of the natural world—or something worse.

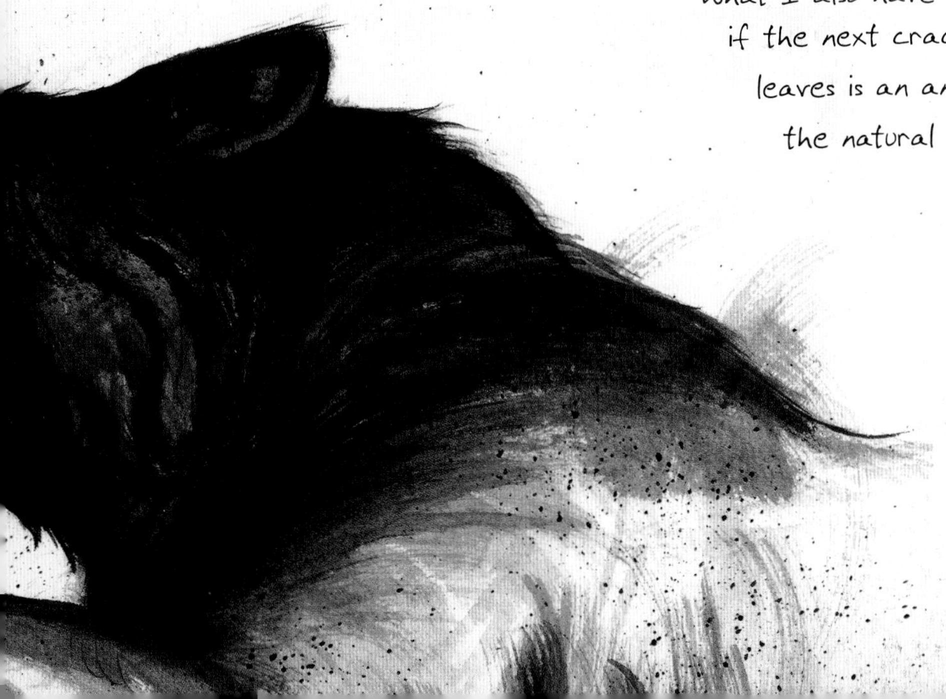

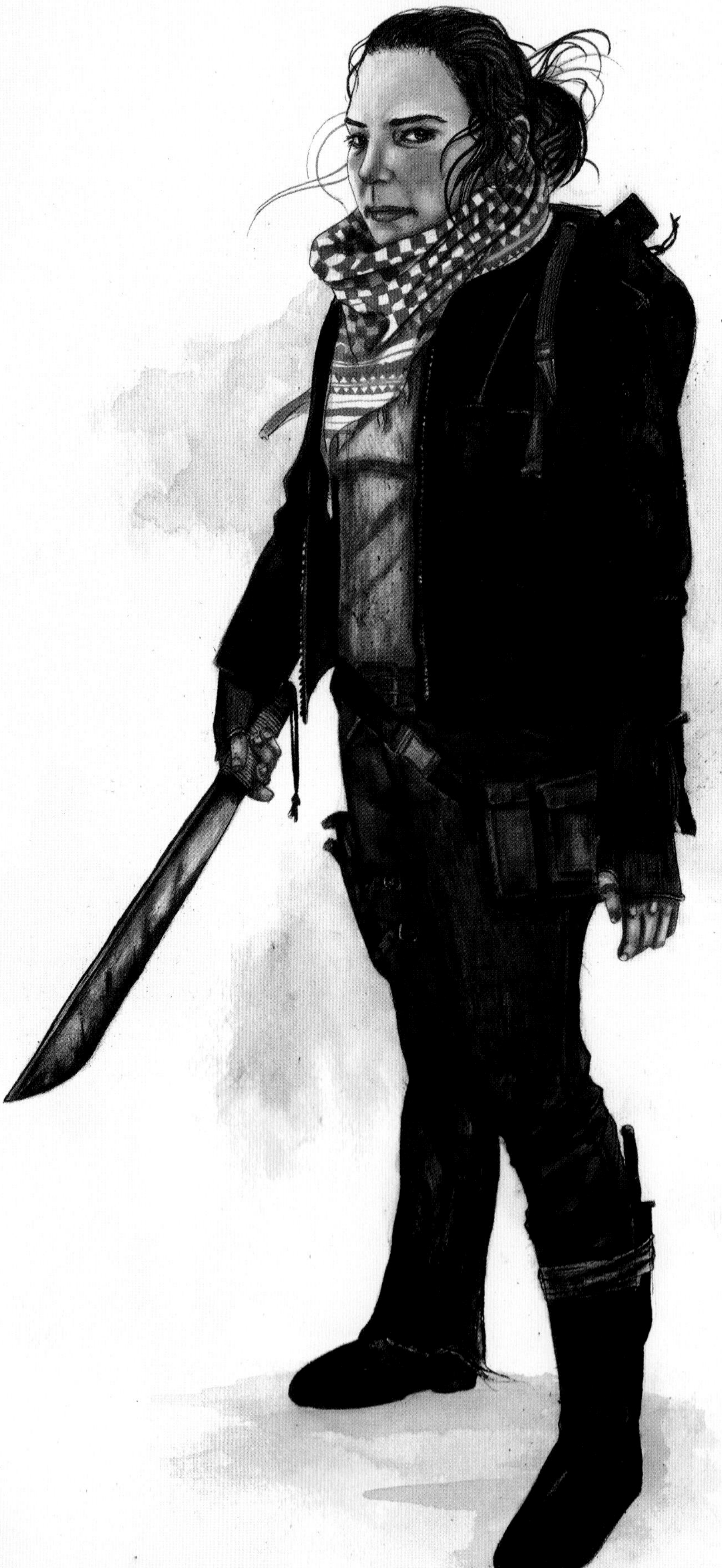

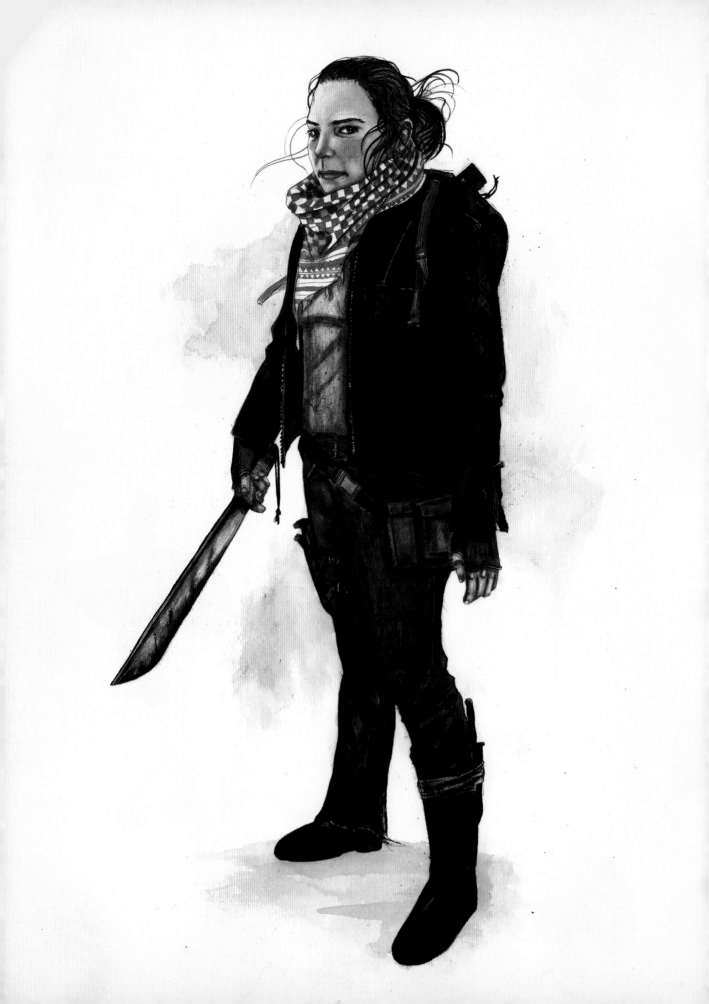

February 3, 2012

Woke up today to a sword at my neck.

"Breathe," I heard. I opened my eyes and jumped.

"Good."
Another survivor. Her name is Katherine.

"My story. Okay, sure. Everything went to hell."
She doesn't need any of my food. We compare notes on what works and what doesn't.

"Guns, yeah. Wait for them to jam."

Does she know what happened?

"Primodene, nobody knows, but the last news I heard was blaming the food. Like it even matters why now. You think?"

Primodine R&D isn't far from here. Like 20 miles. She's from near there, can point me. She's heading north. There's an encampment called the Farm in Canada broadcasting on 1031 AM. A radio—I'm realizing now I don't have one. This is good though—humans broadcasting. There's hope. I weigh whether to investigate what's happening now at Primodine or go north with her and she makes the decision for me.

"I make better time alone."

February 6, 2012

Headed for Primodine. Making slow progress, maybe 6-7 miles a day, when it's light. Using roads for short periods and then back off them into the woods. I'll make some distance, then wait, hide, listen, rest, and move along some more. Spent some of last night in a tree after hearing something moving nearby. Could have been anything, probably (hopefully) an animal. Along the roads so far, no cars, no zombies, no people.

Heard woodpeckers, saw an eagle. Peaceful, except for the constant terror. I can see attacks coming when I close my eyes. It feels strange to be alone again after just a brief encounter.

So many people dead, and still more dying. I've been incredibly lucky so far.

I don't feel lucky.

It's strange to have nothing but the natural world around. It feels especially empty with nothing coming down the road. The wind is terrifying, I keep freezing in place whenever it picks up to make sure everything else stops moving when it stops. I think I'm nearing Bellingham.

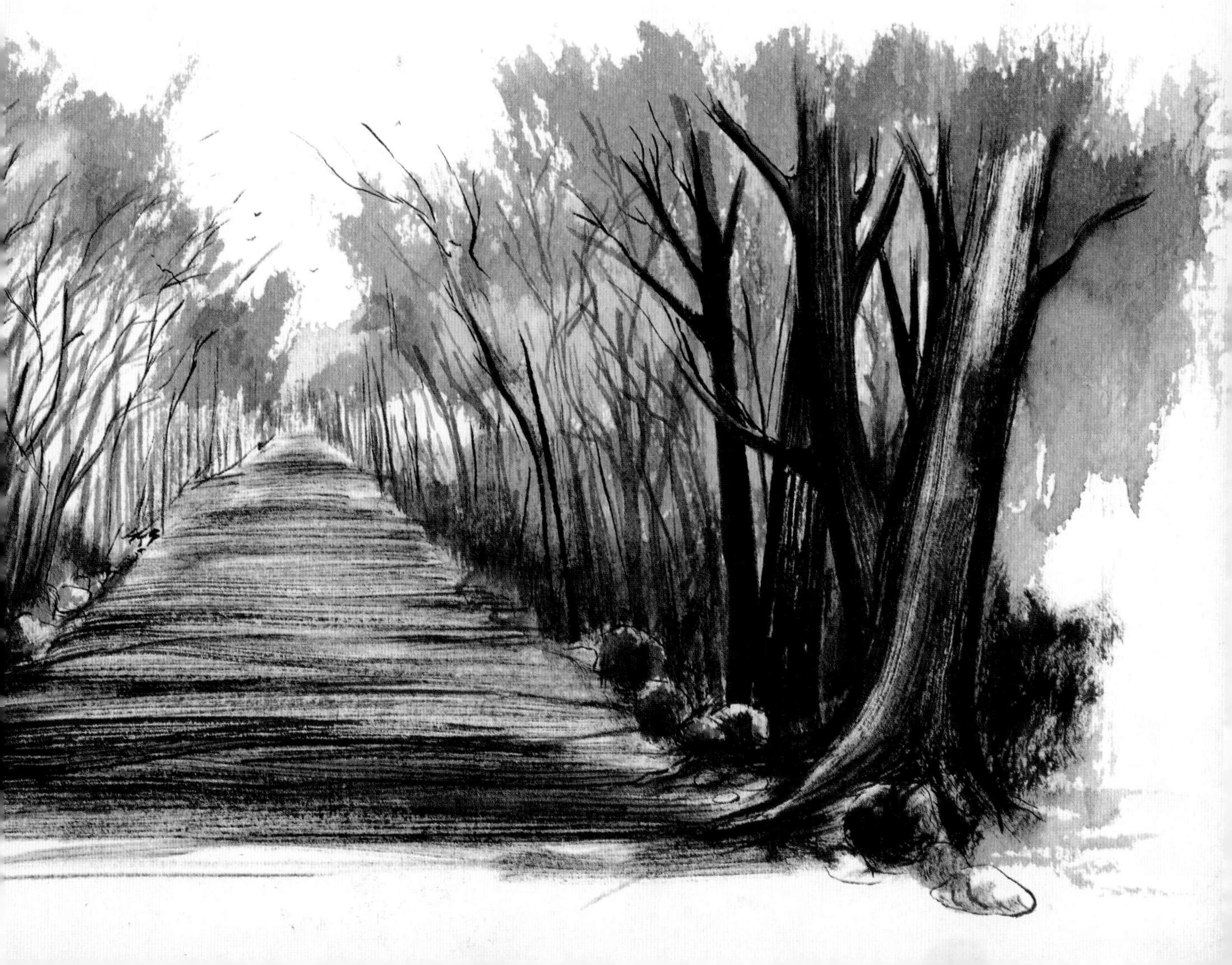

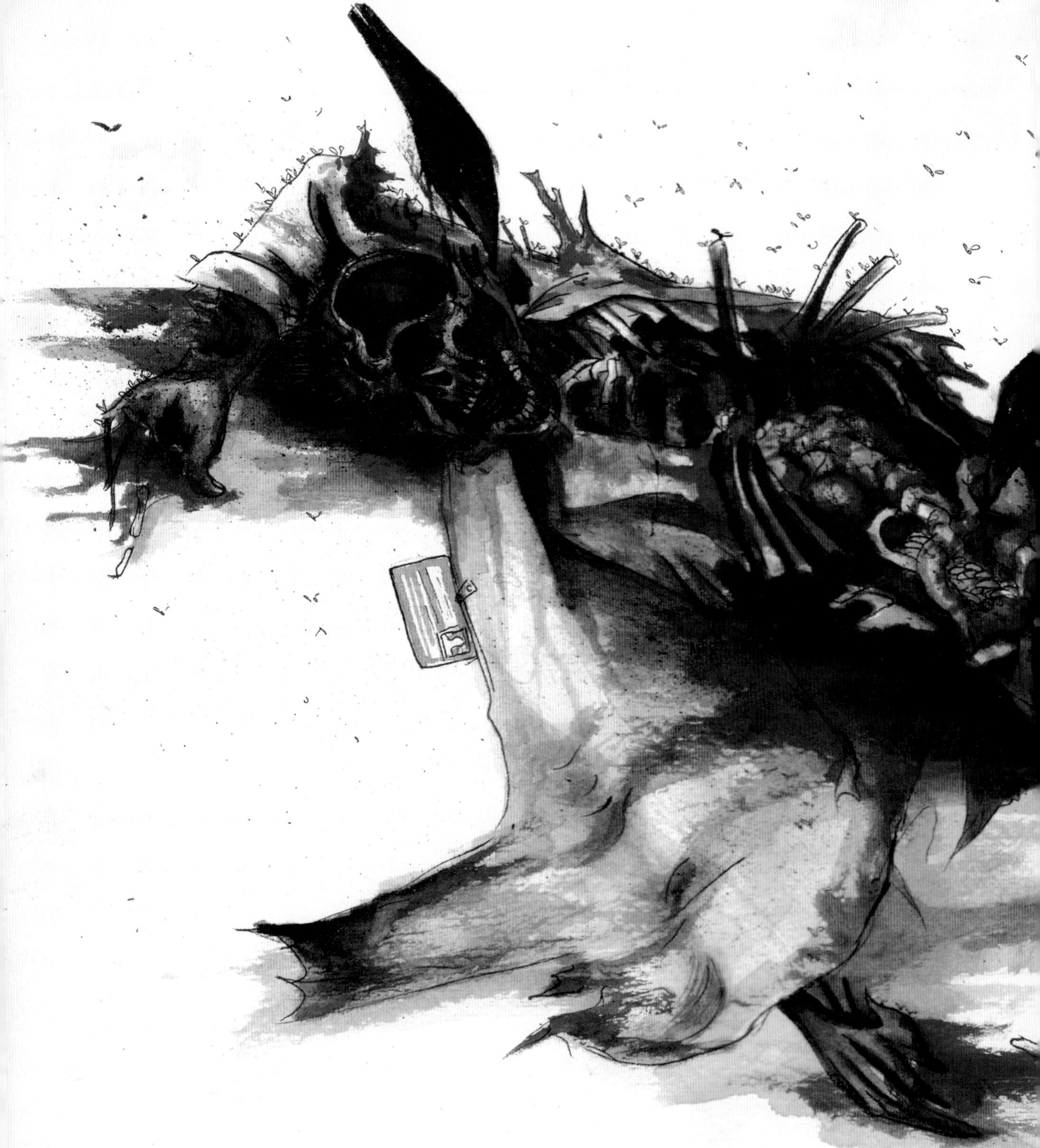

February 8, 2012

Zombies. I must be getting close to Primodine. Saw a few techie looking zombies wandering the road in various states of decay. Encouragingly, a few of them in pretty bad condition. Where are they going? And why?

Separated from the pack. They're using the road, too, same as I am. Sense memory? My progress is slower now. I'm not silent in my own movements, I'm too tired, but I haven't been noticed. They don't seem to be able to smell me—no sign so far that they have any sense of smell.

I can smell them, though.

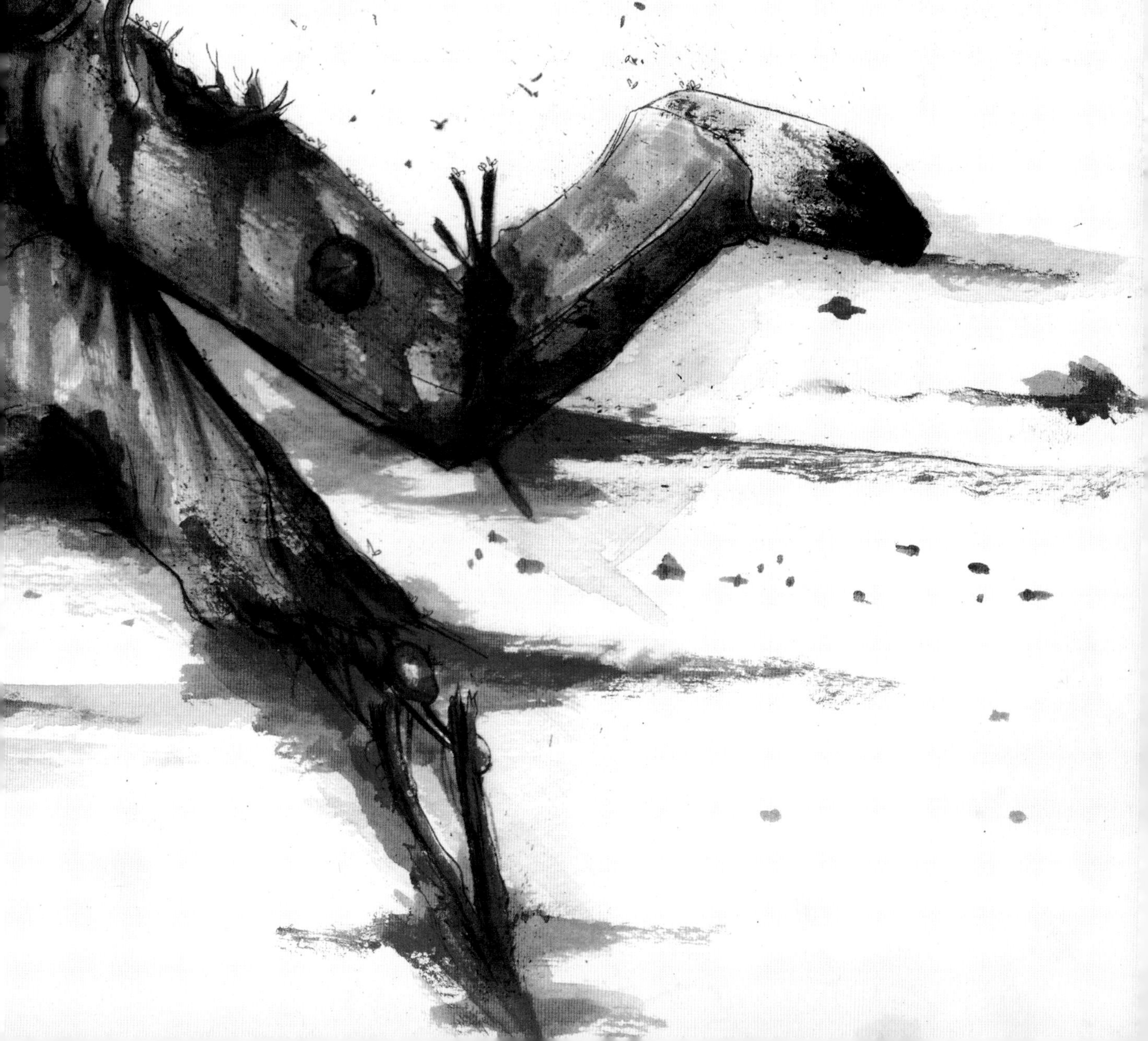

February 10, 2012

PRIMODINE. I'm in.

The R&D facility is sort of in the middle of nowhere, I assume to discourage the curious. The complex itself is surrounded by a high wall. The main entrance gate is open, but there are zombies wandering in and out, employees—or "former" employees. A car had driven up over an embankment at what must have been flooring-it speed, now sitting with the front end buried in the guard's kiosk. Some remains scattered. Crows. There are a number of zombies wandering along the exterior wall, occasionally walking into the wall, gnawing at the air. I've been moving along a culvert and was able to find another less infested entrance on the north side of the perimeter.

~~had to~~ had to kill two zombies that had noticed me as I moved along the inside of the wall. Using the axe. In a way the blunt end works better. My first swing with the blade split the head of a zombie in a lab coat down the middle but it wasn't a killing blow ~~and kept going~~ it just kept coming. Dropped it with the blunt end and took off the head. Another one rounded the corner and I used the blade sideways to get the head off sooner. I hid after that to see what would happen next but the fight didn't seem to draw any attention, and other zombies didn't pay any notice to the "dead" zombies. I found a keycard still attached to the once-white lab jacket of a half-eaten doctor, but didn't actually need it. The door locks aren't activated and the power seems to be fully down.

Inside, the smell is indescribable, literally stunning—zombies in an enclosed area and corpses of humans, some torn apart on or around their desks. I tied a t-shirt around my mouth and nose until I was able to find a filter mask. Still, my eyes sting. With the power out, it's pitch-black in here at night, and the exterior-facing offices are really the only thing I'm willing to brave during the day. Don't dare use the flashlight when moving around, but using it in moments when the coast is clear.

Zombies milling about, wandering the halls, walking in and out of offices. I'm hiding in an office with a desk against the one door, using the flashlight inside a supply closet. So this is home for tonight. There's paper everywhere, all around the building, just kind of strewn about amid the other debris. Sitting here reading sheaths of printed e-mails, reports, files. All just office tedium. Meetings. Financial reports. Some discussion about bonding polymers related to the pliability of rubber garbage can lids—stuff not worth caring about, if anyone was alive to care.

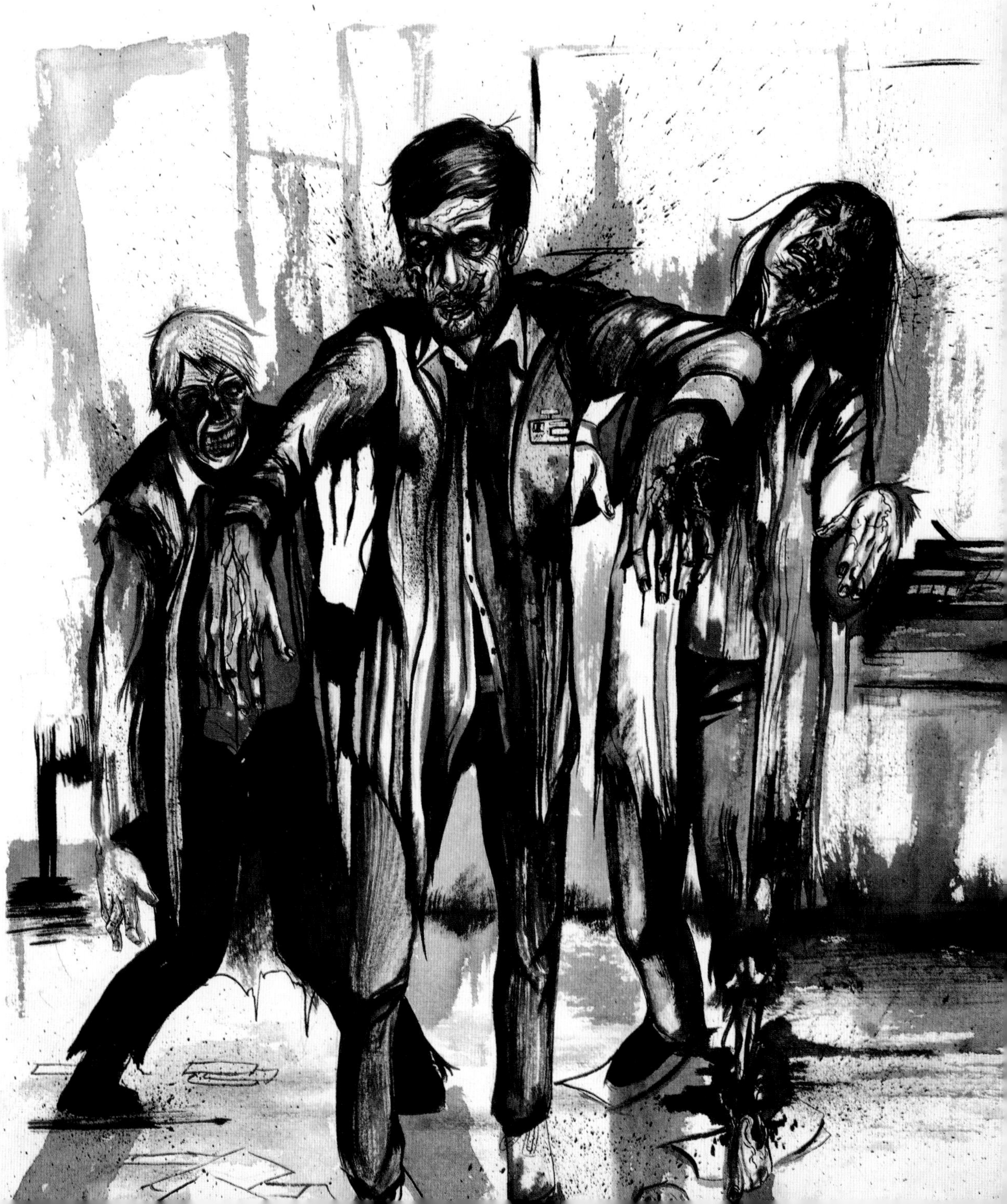

duration remaining in the body after ingestion. No negative reactions in human trials or in widespread consumption thereafter. Toxicity reached on average of six months after first exposure or (unclear) upon accumulation of unknown levels of the compound. Cause of reaction unknown as yet. Testing reveals consistent results as indicated above across batches of the compound manufactured at domestic and international facilities. Some subjects showing no signs of reaction despite high exposure levels; theorizing genetic factor in some cases. We may need to expand our research base to achieve inquiry results on requested timetable due to staff illnesses. Main staff is on NTK basis. Discussion restricted. Please advise.

— Tom

Please consider the environment before printing this e-mail.

February 11, 2012

← Found this e-mail in a stack of papers at one of the printers, went back but couldn't find the first page. It doesn't say what the compound is. C88 has been on the market pretty heavy since late summer. I eat pretty healthy but C88's in everything and it's hard to avoid, and I've been living on almost nothing but processed food for a month now. What's the toxicity point? Have I hit it? Will I soon? The compound didn't seem to be affecting subjects in the same way, and some maybe not at all. That's something to hold on to. Weird to think that, what with that 90% initial infection rate in the early days, that might leave a billion? people around the world, fighting off ~~xxxxxxx~~ ~~xxxxxxxx~~ 8 billion living dead, and that these are _hopeful_ numbers. But what are the people who are left eating? If the trigger was in the food, all the food containing the compound would have to be destroyed. What's left out there? Was anywhere unaffected? How infectious are the human dead, let alone the living dead? Do we need to just put a match to everything and start over, provided we get the chance?

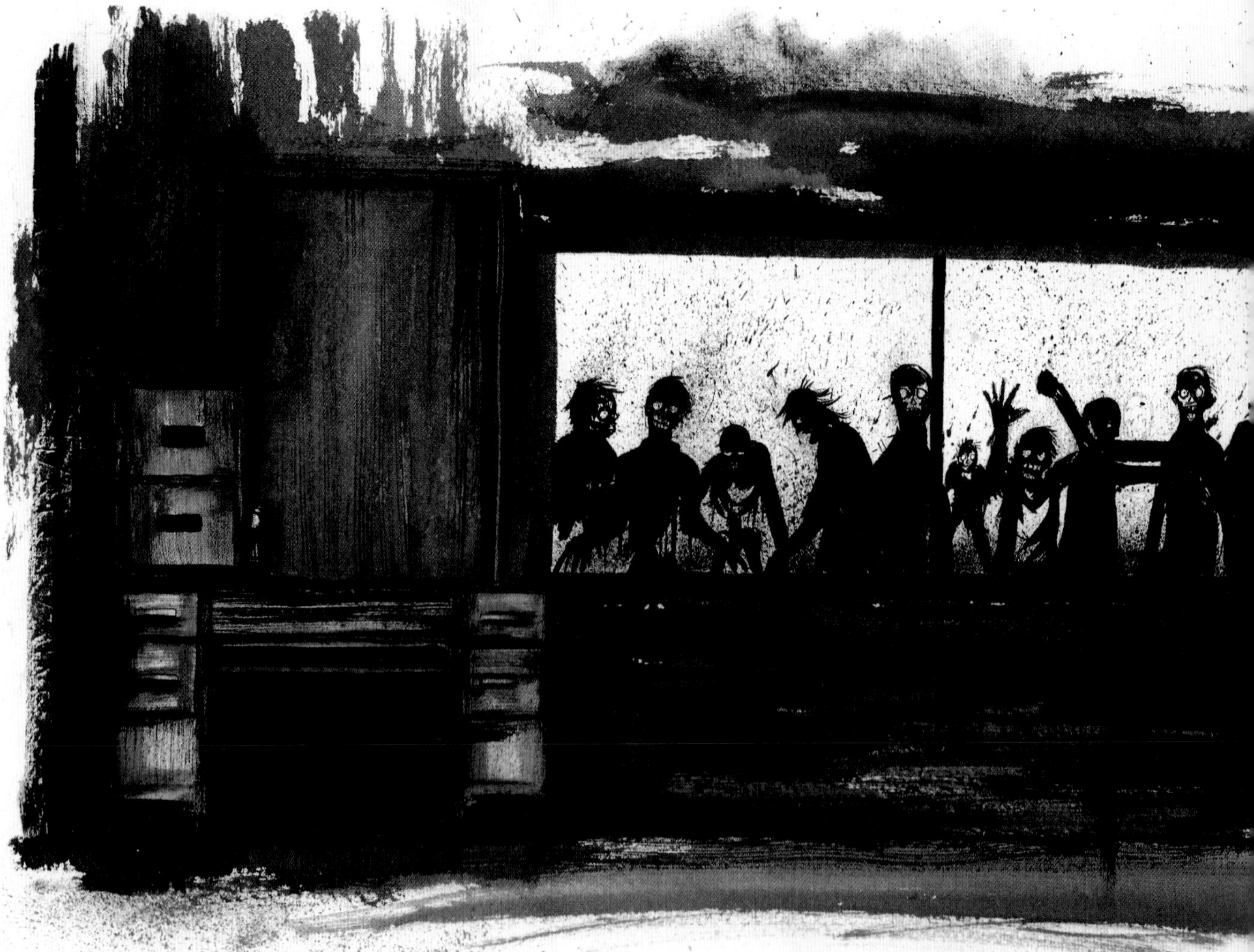

February 12, 2012

It's my birthday today. I'm 33. To celebrate I had a potentially zombifying nutritional bar from my pack (peanut butter chocolate chip) and a bottle of potentially zombifying nutritional water that promises calm focus, energy, and antioxidants (tropical breeze). I'll try to stay away from this stuff given the chance, but I don't have another option at this point, trying to limit my intake but feeling too shaky to not eat. Not finding anything else in the papers in the office. I'm not willing to risk busting into file cabinets because of the sound.

I've been undetected so far but I can't stay here. There seem to be more zombies in the halls, more shapes. The doorknob to the outside hall rattled about an hour ago and my heart stopped. The desk against the door held it closed. I couldn't tell if a zombie had bumped against the door or had actually tried the knob. I have to get out of here.

February 13, 2012

I'm out. There was commotion outside, whooping and shouting—human—and the halls mostly emptied of zombies. I got outside and a bunch of survivors, maybe a dozen of them, were shooting and torching their way through the dead. I came out waving my arms and yelling and just kept shouting and luckily they recognized me as human. One of them made me strip down to check me for bites and wounds and then sprayed me down with a can of household antibacterial spray, which hurt like hell. One member was going around spray painting skulls on the walls. The rest just killing zombies. They're traveling in an improvised armored bus painted with skulls, like a combination street gang and paramilitary outfit, and they seem to be having a good time. No fear.

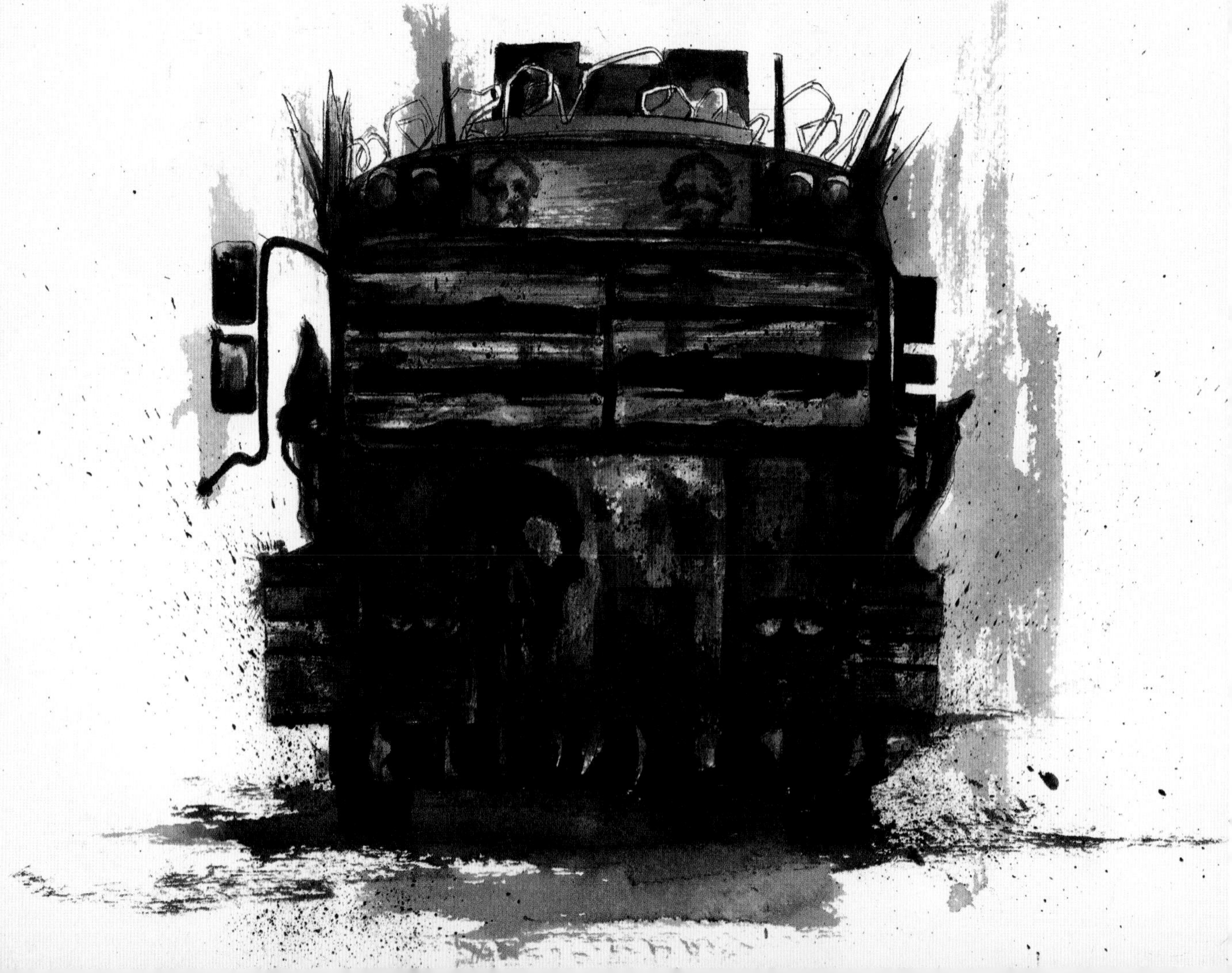

Angel seems to be the leader.

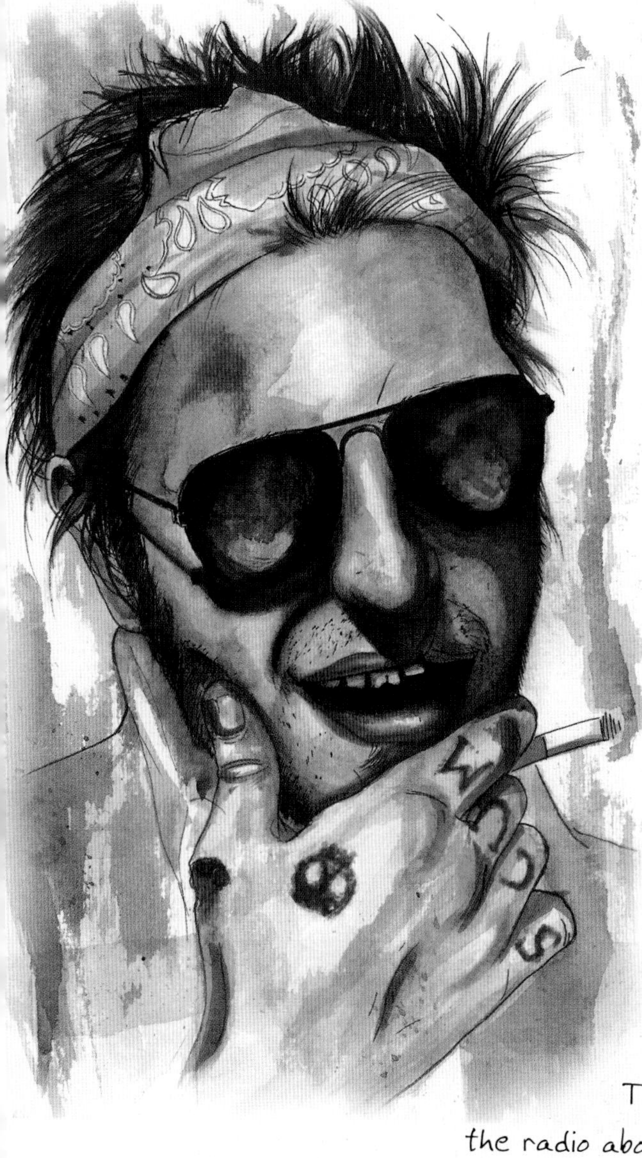

"You're lucky we came by, man. We're not finding too may survivors, you know? Lots of these dead freaks though. We're just killing as many of these things as we can, but they're like everywhere. Keeping us <u>busy</u>."

He laughed at that. This is the first time I've heard anyone laugh in a long time, and it [illegible] I don't like it.

"We find 'em and kill 'em and claim 'em, leave our mark. Nobody else is doing anything. Nothing else left to do. These here are the end of days, man. Things have turned and the low down have risen up. I was just a mechanic with some job just clocking time, work, home, work, home, but now it's all happening. It's here, and we're doing the Good Work. They're weak, and we're strong. Crap on the radio about survivor this and that up north but this is all too far gone. Look <u>around</u> you. When's the last time you seen an airplane? Think you'll ever see one again? You're the first person we seen alive in two weeks. It's all already gone. All this has to keep moving toward the end and we're just helping grease the wheels till we get to the next thing. There'll be a final tally in the end and we're working on our numbers."

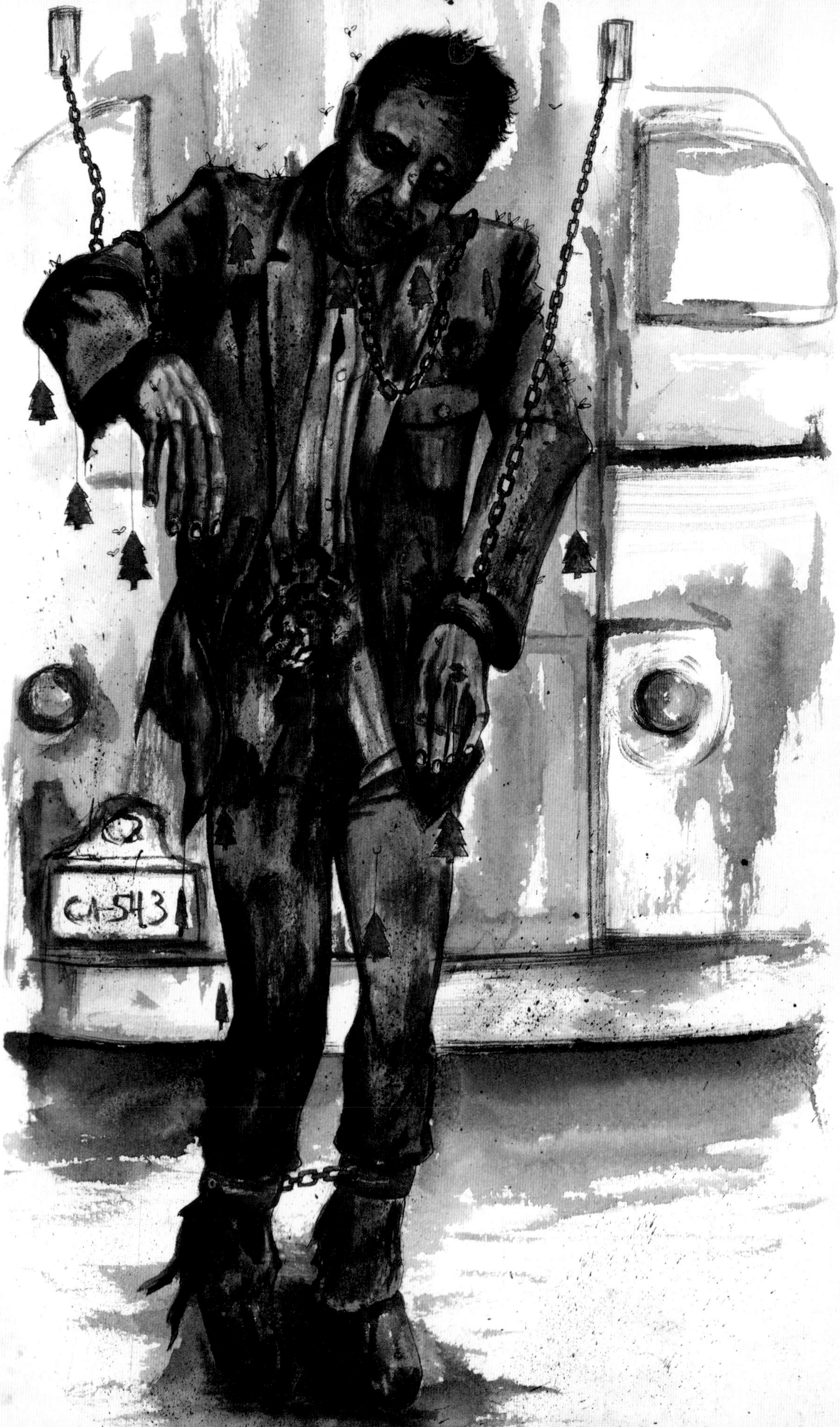
CA-543

They've got a zombie chained to the back of the bus, who they call "Clyde." He's in a caked, crusty Armani suit and tie. Occasionally they'll hand him something, like dead cell phone, and Clyde will hold it and sort of look at it? His movements are dopey, feeble. Dead maybe a couple weeks? They'll also occasionally shoot him, but not in the head. He seems to be around for amusement value, they don't seem to have any scientific interest in him. I don't like giving the zombie a name. It's been easy to forget that the zombies were people.

I am tempted to draw a blood sample from "Clyde" for future study, but I am afraid that my efforts might get noticed. I'm already treated with borderline contempt. I think they see me as weak. With a zombie up close here I'm more disturbed than ever by the suggestion of anything human left in them. Awareness is terrifying for what it means in dealing with the zombies that are left. It's also a sort of nightmare—do they know what they were, or what they've become?

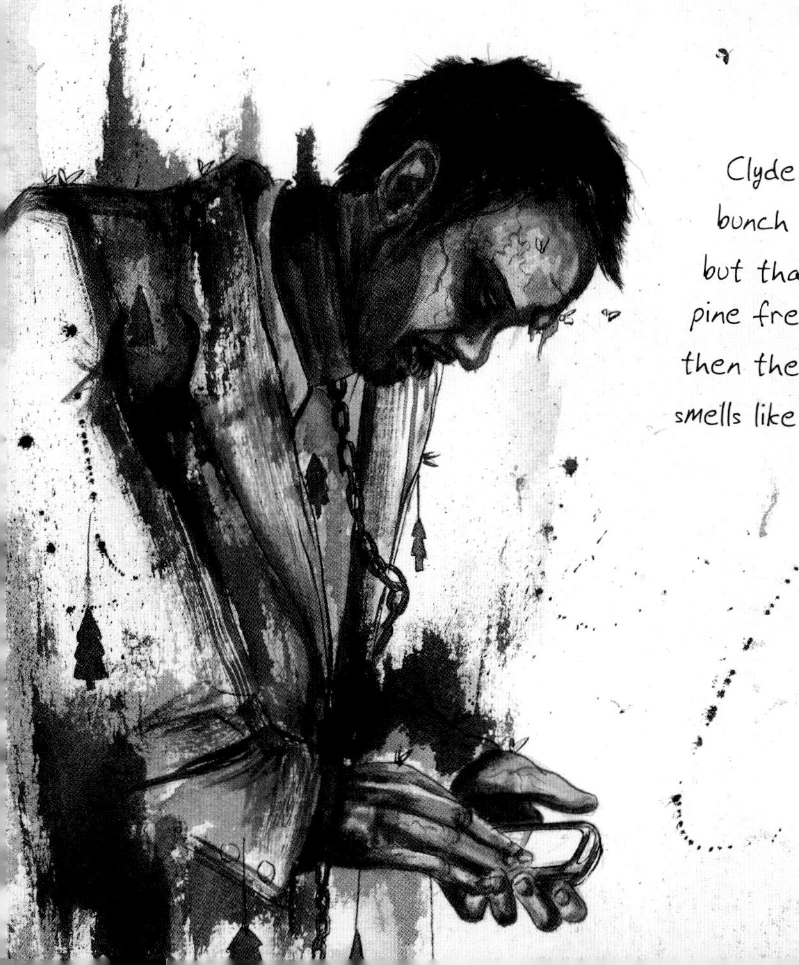

Clyde is pretty "ripe." They've hung a bunch of air fresheners off his suit, but that's infinitely worse. You catch the pine fresh smell, an old world smell, and then the rotten odor, what everything smells like now.

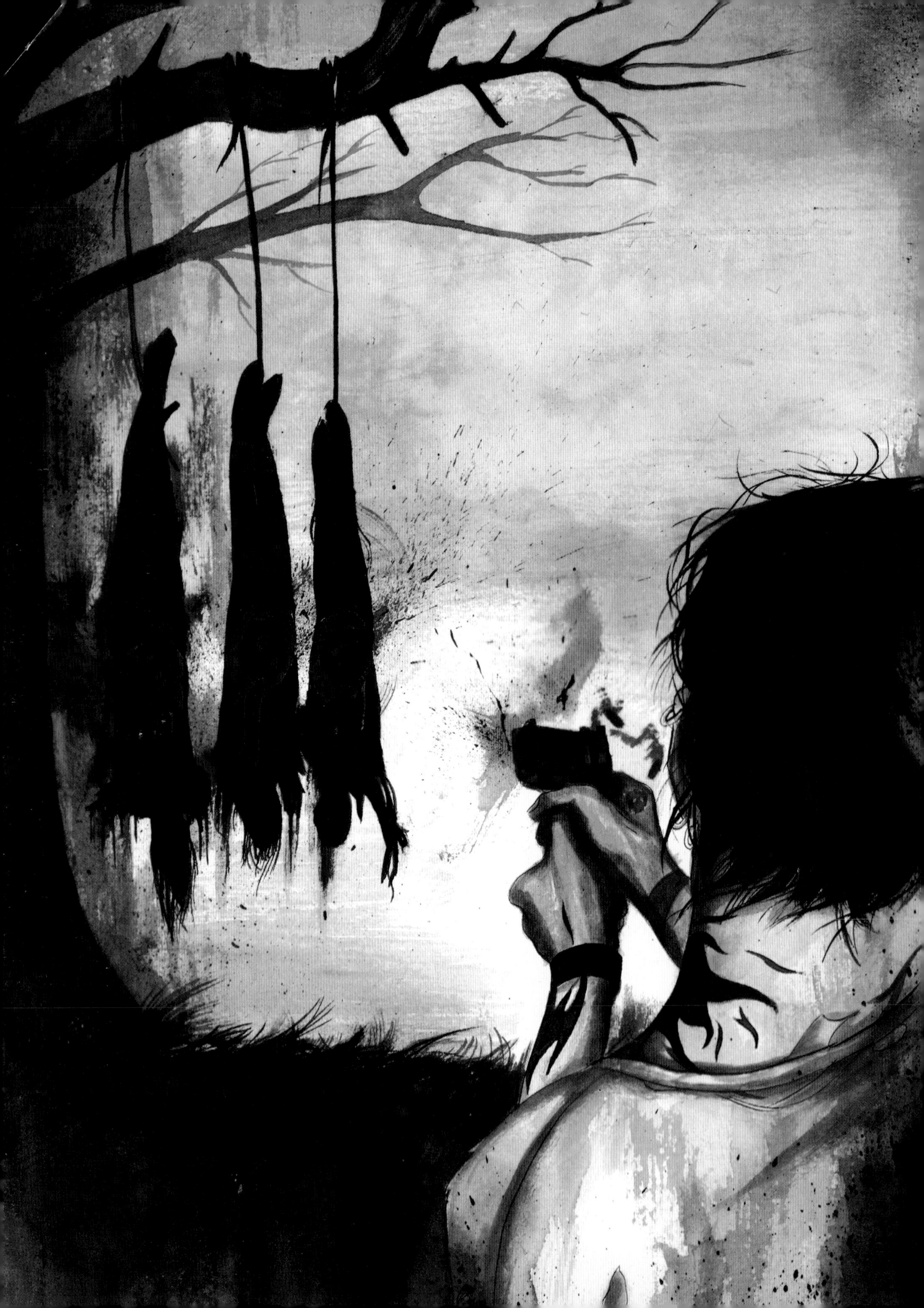

February 14, 2012

Valentine's Day spent driving in the bus, with Angel and the rest. They're all shooting stray zombies wandering along the roads. That it's hard to get a "killshot" is a sort of sport for them. Sometimes they'll shoot out a zombie's legs and pull over to take off the head with a shovel, sometimes they'll just not slow down and hit the zombie with the bus, knocking it off onto the side of the road. The fact that I'm keeping a journal has come front and center. "Hey college, you want to read me one of your poems?"

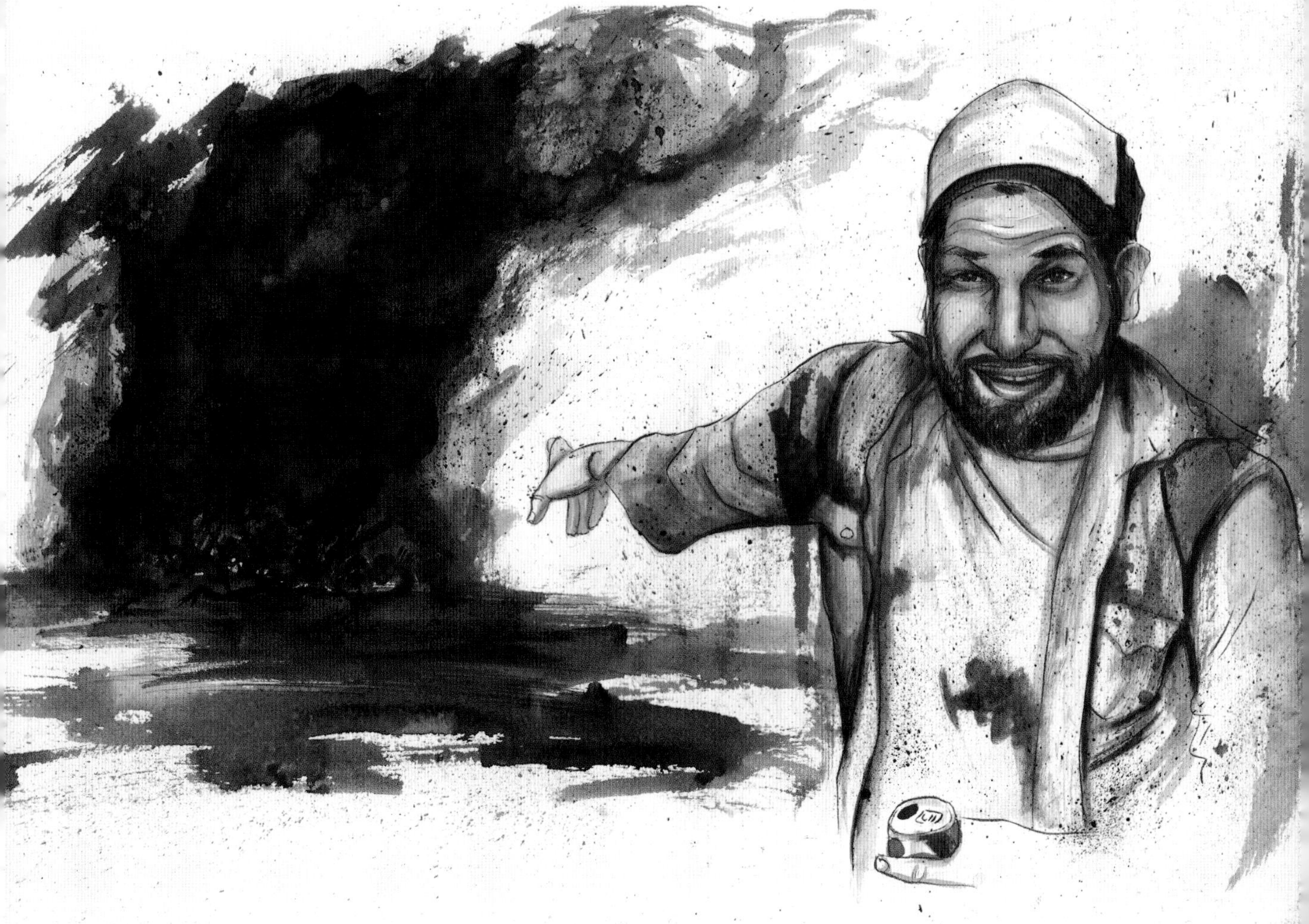

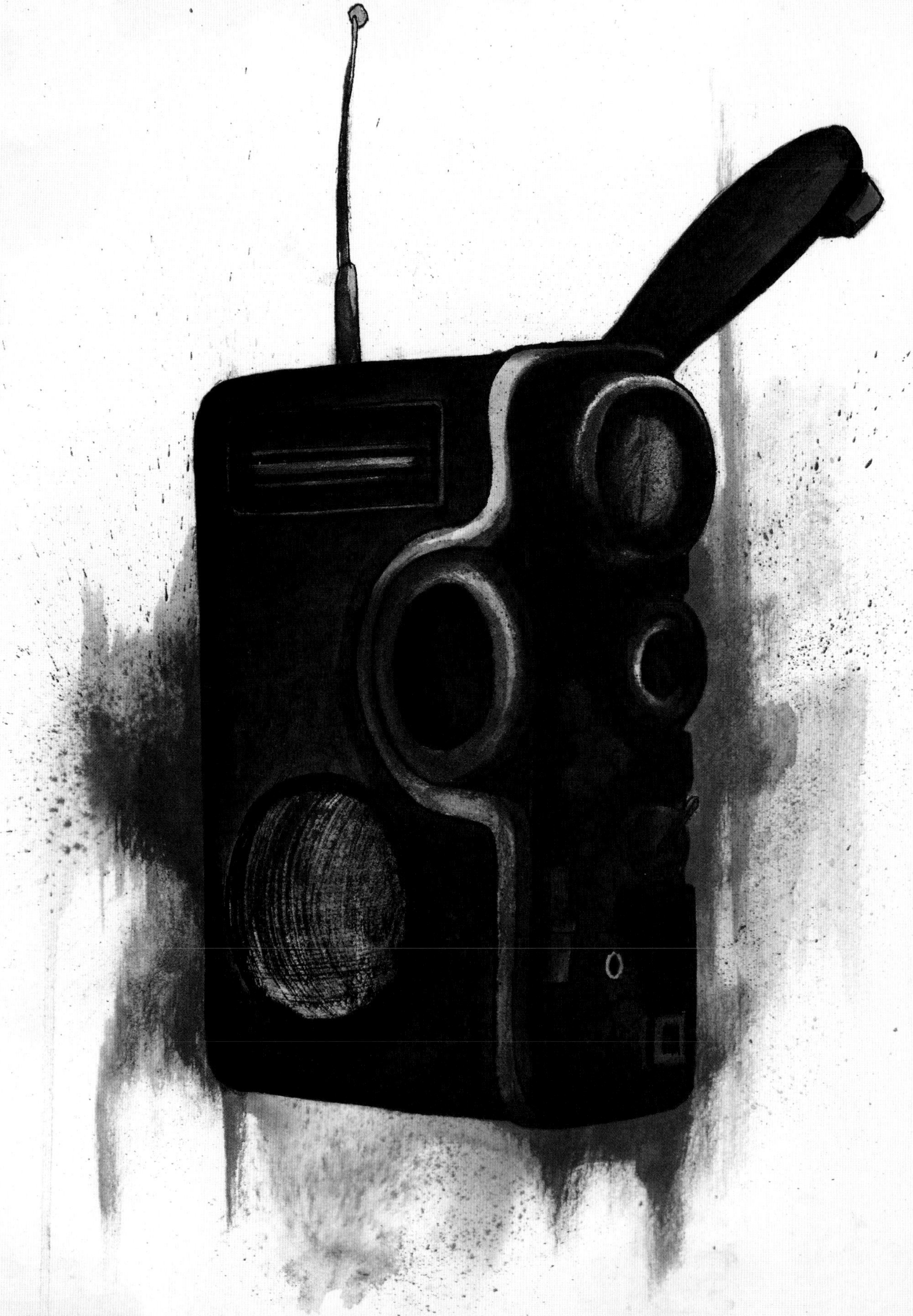

February 15, 2012

I left the camp last night to go "use the bathroom" at the
edge of the trees, after stuffing the bus's hand-crank radio
in my jacket. What were they going to do with it? After a
few minutes they noticed that I'd also taken my pack with
me and there was yelling and some shooting into the woods
in my direction, but no real pursuit. I kept moving. I need
the radio to find this camp up north. Intermittent
transmission, or at least I've only been able to get it
intermittently, on 1031 AM, from "The Farm" located
outside of Strawberry Ridge, Saskatchewan. They give
GPS coordinates and other directions. They're promising
food and safety. I'm not ready to give up, more convinced
of that than ever.

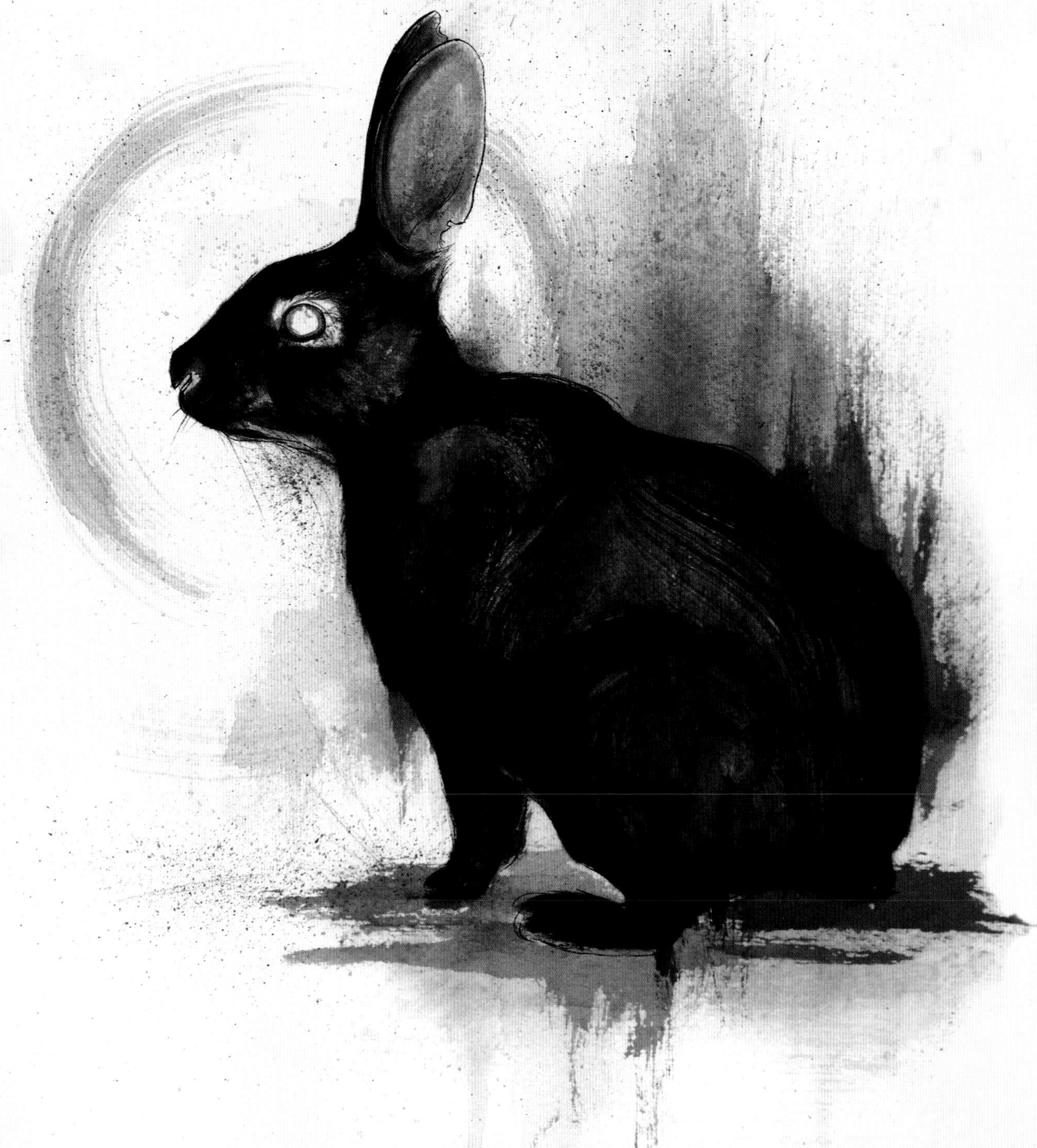

February 18, 2012

Been travelling. Using the GPS and a map. I am now in Canada and moving northwest. The Farm transmits a radio message every day. It says basically the same thing: Coordinates, band of survivors searching for the like, food and shelter from the plague of dead. There is optimism in the woman's voice—it's inviting. I eat what natural food I can find, berries, fish. I mostly go hungry.

The miles heading north have been taxing. I think I've burned through all my body fat. I'm shivering and I need food.

Tried to snare a rabbit using a shoelace. I saw the technique used on a TV show once.

After I made the snare, a simple slipknot, I put it in the path of some rabbit tracks I found. I was baiting it with some corn chip crumbs. Nothing so far.

I was checking my trap and a zombie came up on me, couldn't have been very fast, and it was wearing range orange so I don't know how I missed it—my senses are dulled. I bolted without thinking onto the edge of the frozen lake and the zombie followed, but went down on its back on the ice and like a turtle it struggled to right itself for quite a while. No signs of any other zombies following so I took time to sketch it. Perhaps this is a good omen for me heading north.

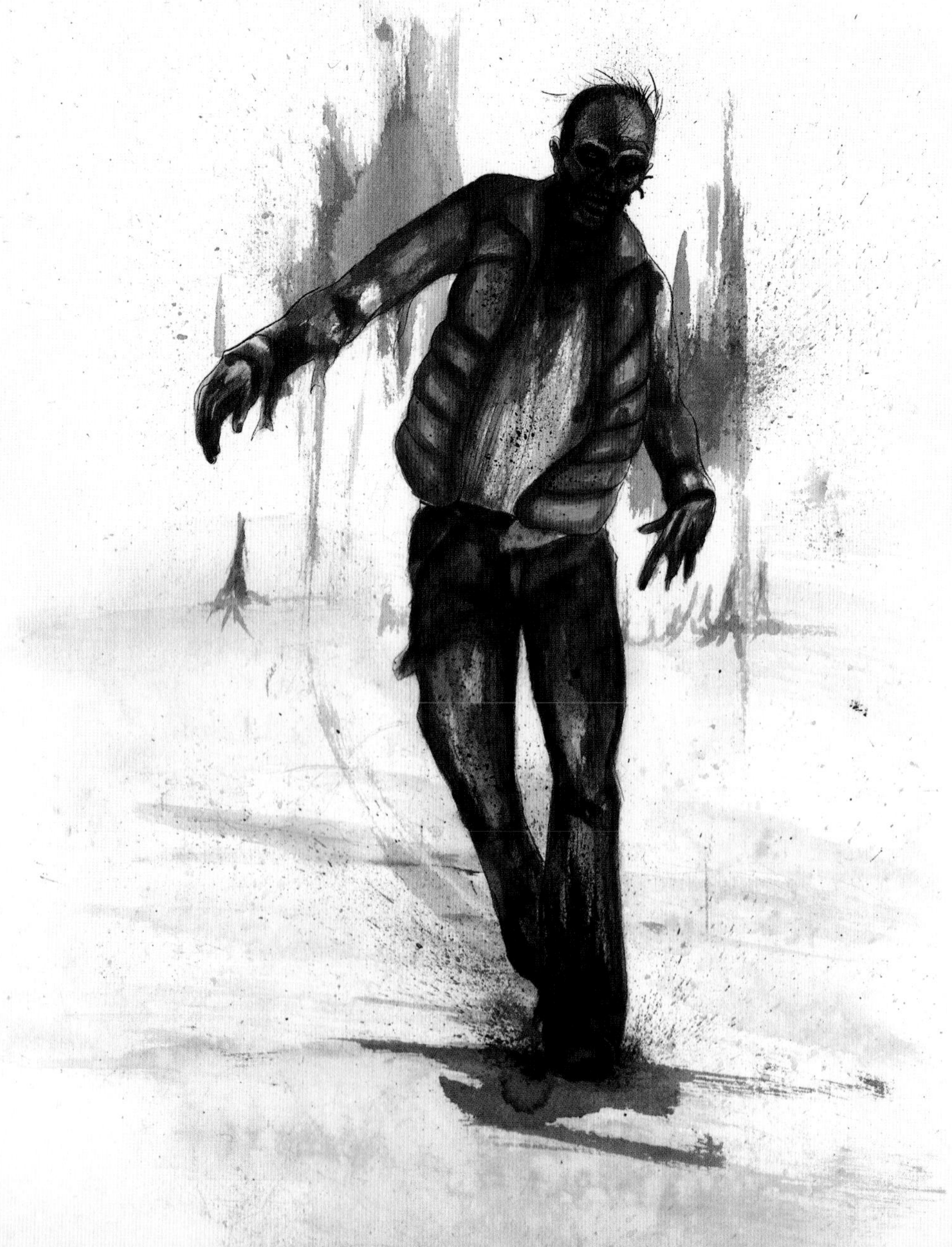

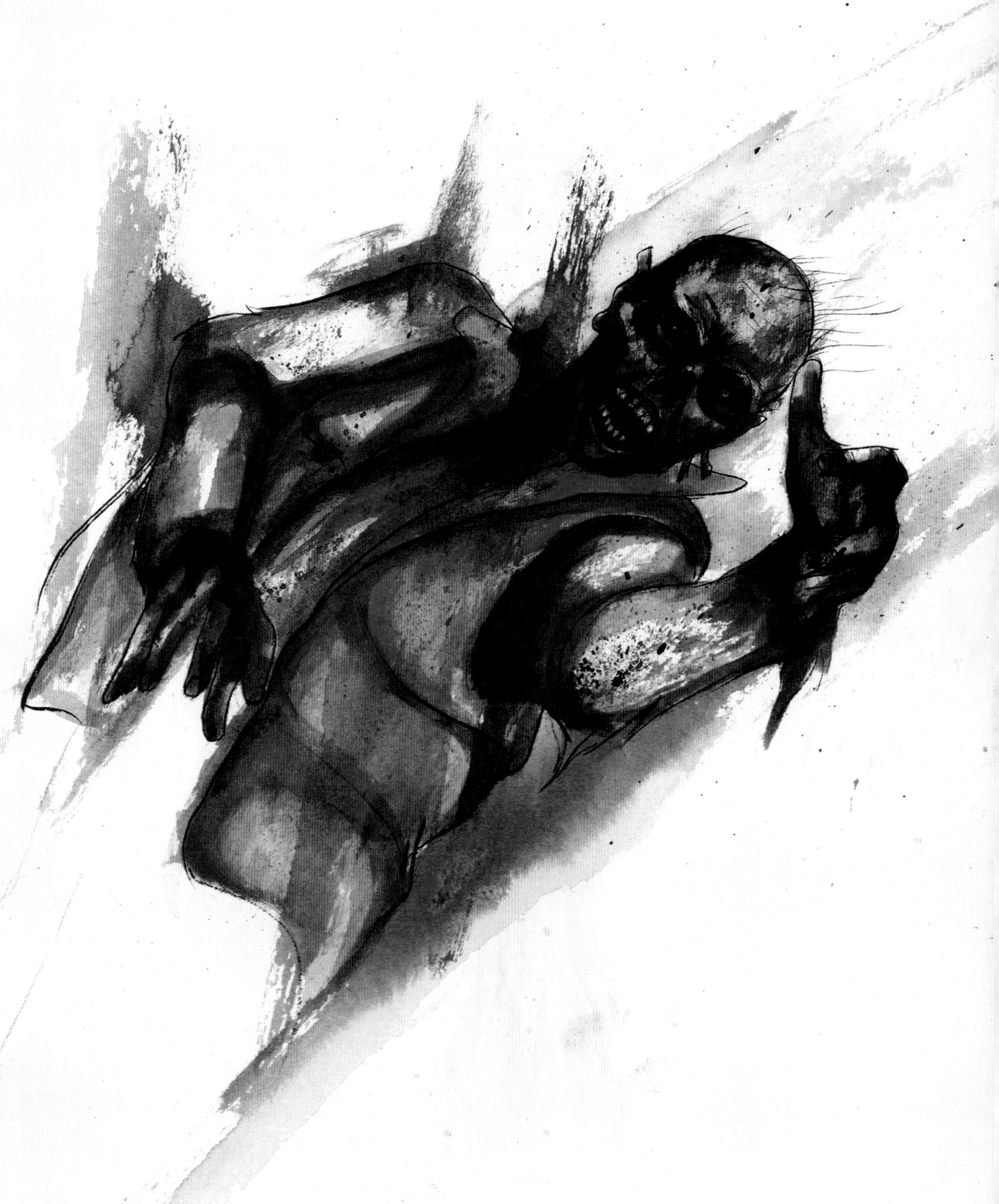

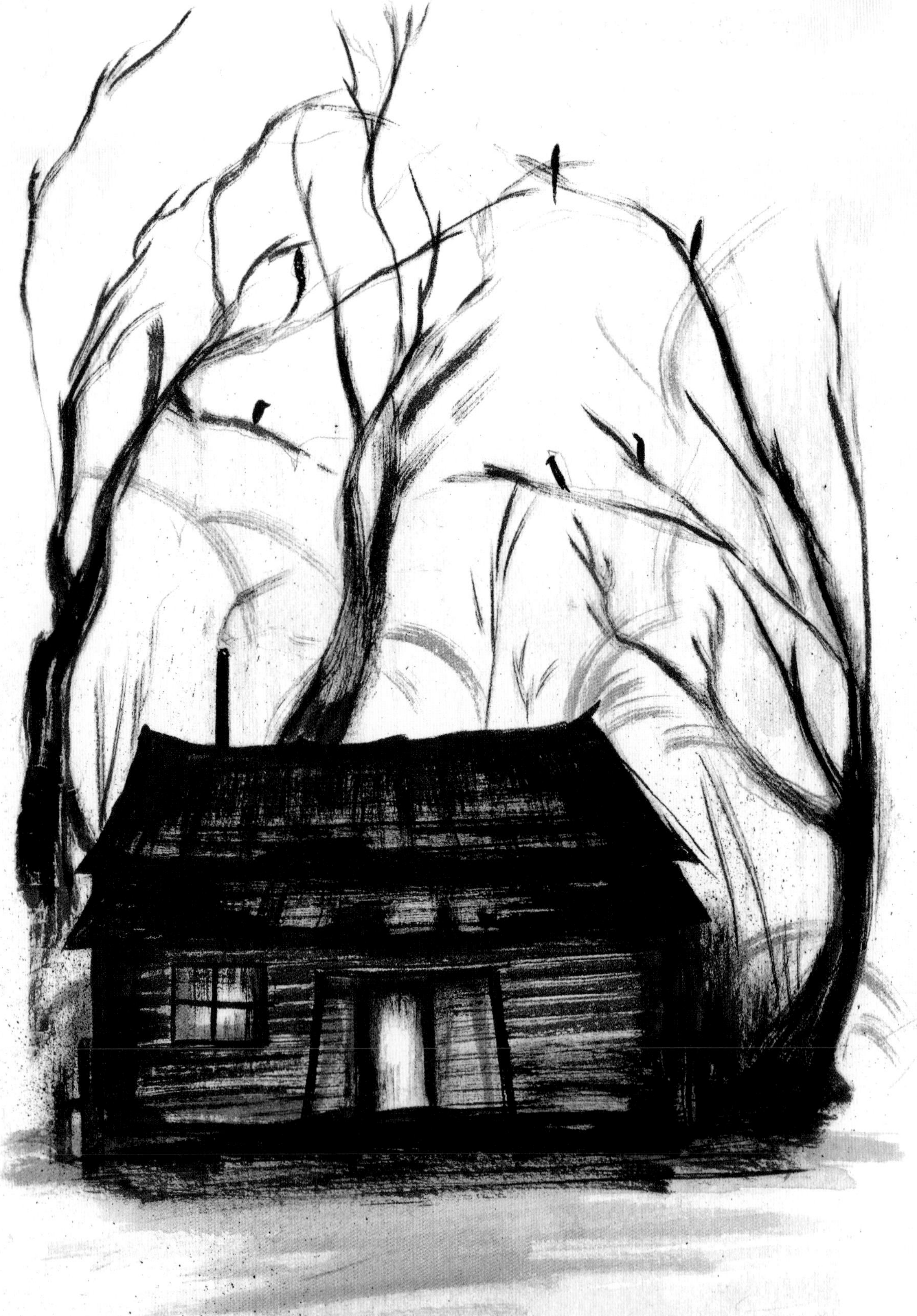

February 19, 2012

A night indoors. I found a small cabin in the woods that seemed unoccupied, until I opened the door. Zombie inside rose and came at me, an old man, moving relatively quickly. It got out past the doorway and even weak as I was, I managed to drop it with a piece of cordwood and bash its skull in with another. No one else inside. The cabin seems like an overnight, shack? I guess would be the way to describe it. The woodstove inside was still slightly warm, the old man must have been human not very long ago. Checking the corpse again outside, it had a wicked bite mark on its forearm that had been bandaged in a torn bit of shirt, pathetically, as if that would help. The old man didn't have anything with him. Where had he come from? And what had bitten him? It occurred to me that I probably should have killed the zombie from yesterday, but I'm just so tired. Tonight, shelter from the wind, a warm fire, and a securely locked door.

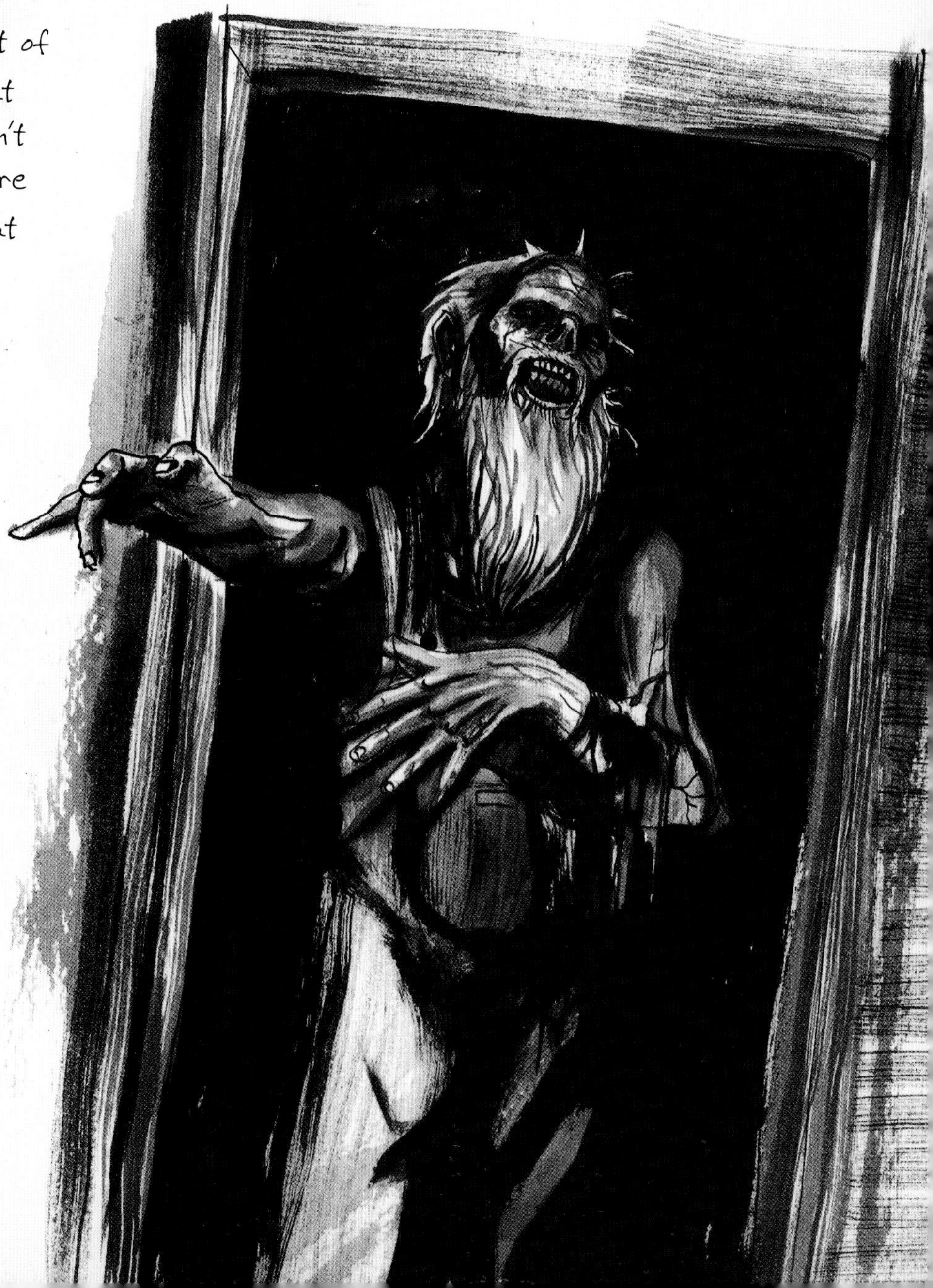

February 22, 2012

Slept and slept and slept. No sense of how long or what day it was until consulting the watch. Spent two days in the cabin and feel rested but also weaker, less willing to go outside. Sure, I could stay at the cabin forever, just go to sleep forever. Hunger finally drove me out and onward to a small town near the border.

Came across a truck stop convenience store/gas station. Inside, the smell of rotten food and decomposing corpses. The place had been looted, but in haste, so I've managed to find some cans of food here and there amid the debris, including a CAN OF BAKED BEANS, which I started eating immediately while still inside the store before noticing my surroundings, nearly threw it all back up. Some scattered, crushed bags of snacks clearly advertising "Flavor Burst" and other C88-derived benefits. Can't [redacted] I can't. It'll all be here if I can't find anything else. No one else left to eat it.

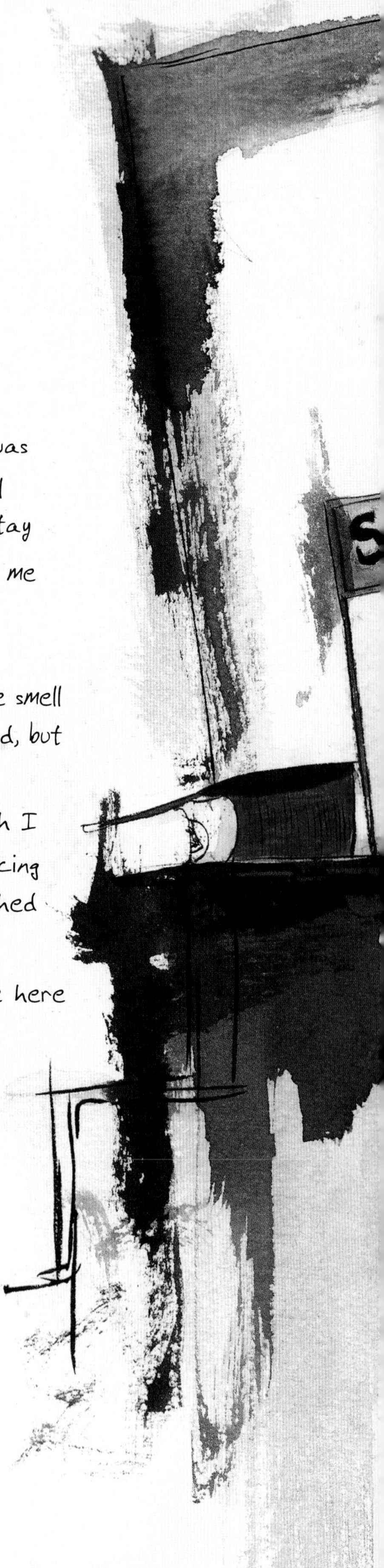

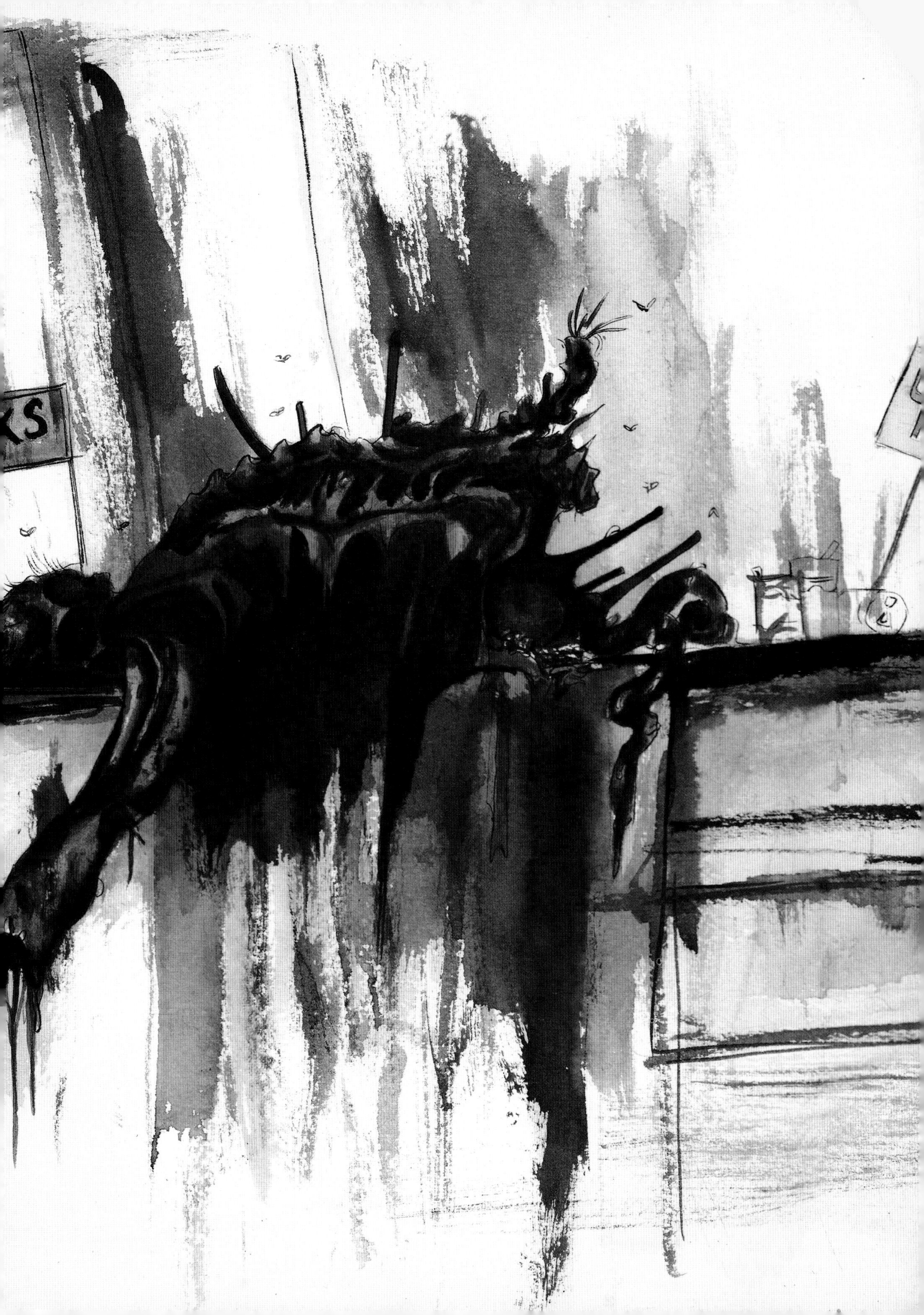

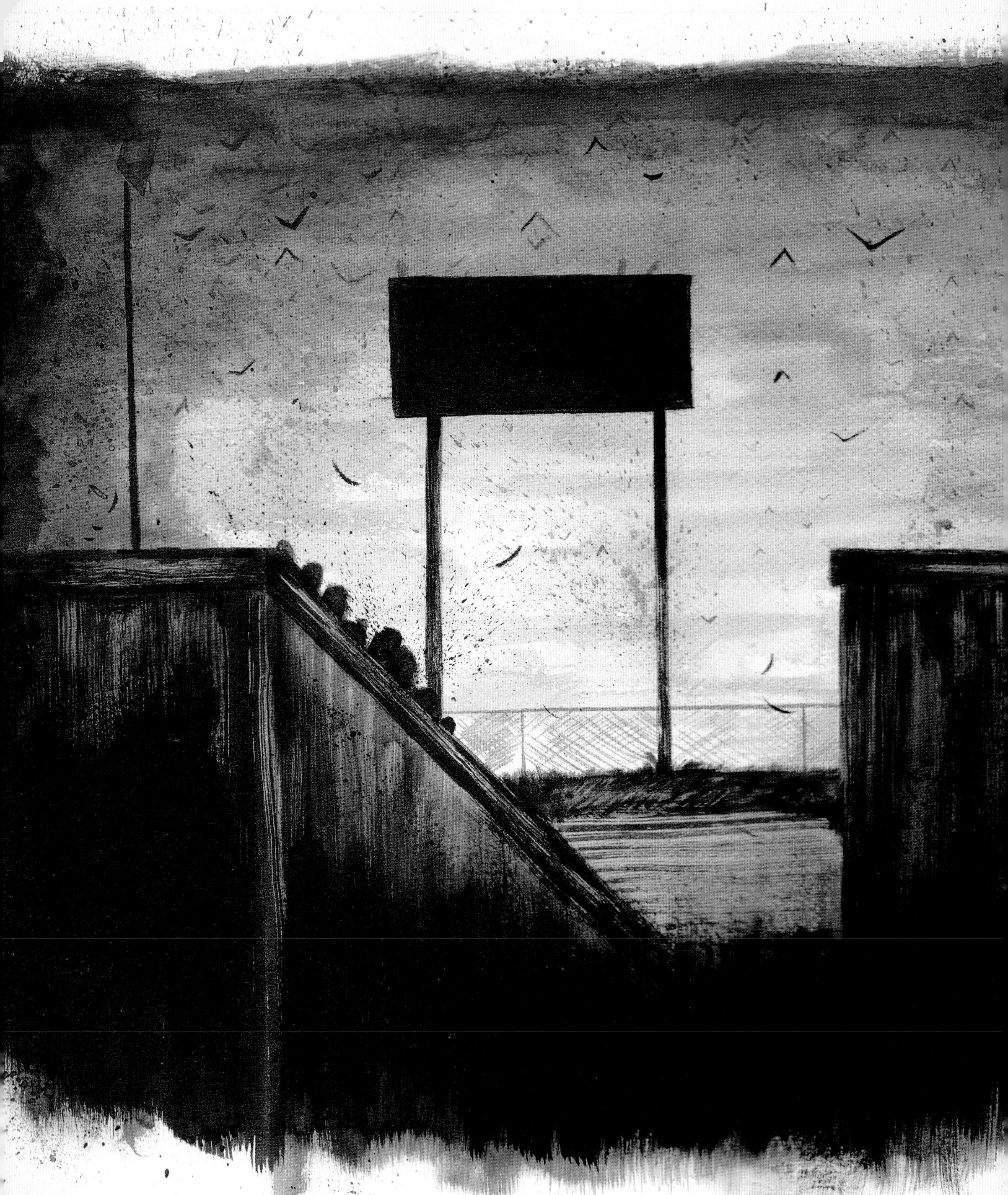

I was feeling better with some food in my stomach and cautiously roaming around—the town seems empty—when I noticed vultures circling above what turned out to be the high school's outdoor stadium. The parking lot was full of cars. As I got closer I could see ~~people~~ bodies in the stands, slumped over one another at one end of the stadium. Row after row of corpses with empty cups at their feet. A mass suicide? Why would these people ~~~~ were they uninfected, or fearing infection to come? What had they heard or seen to lead them to do this?

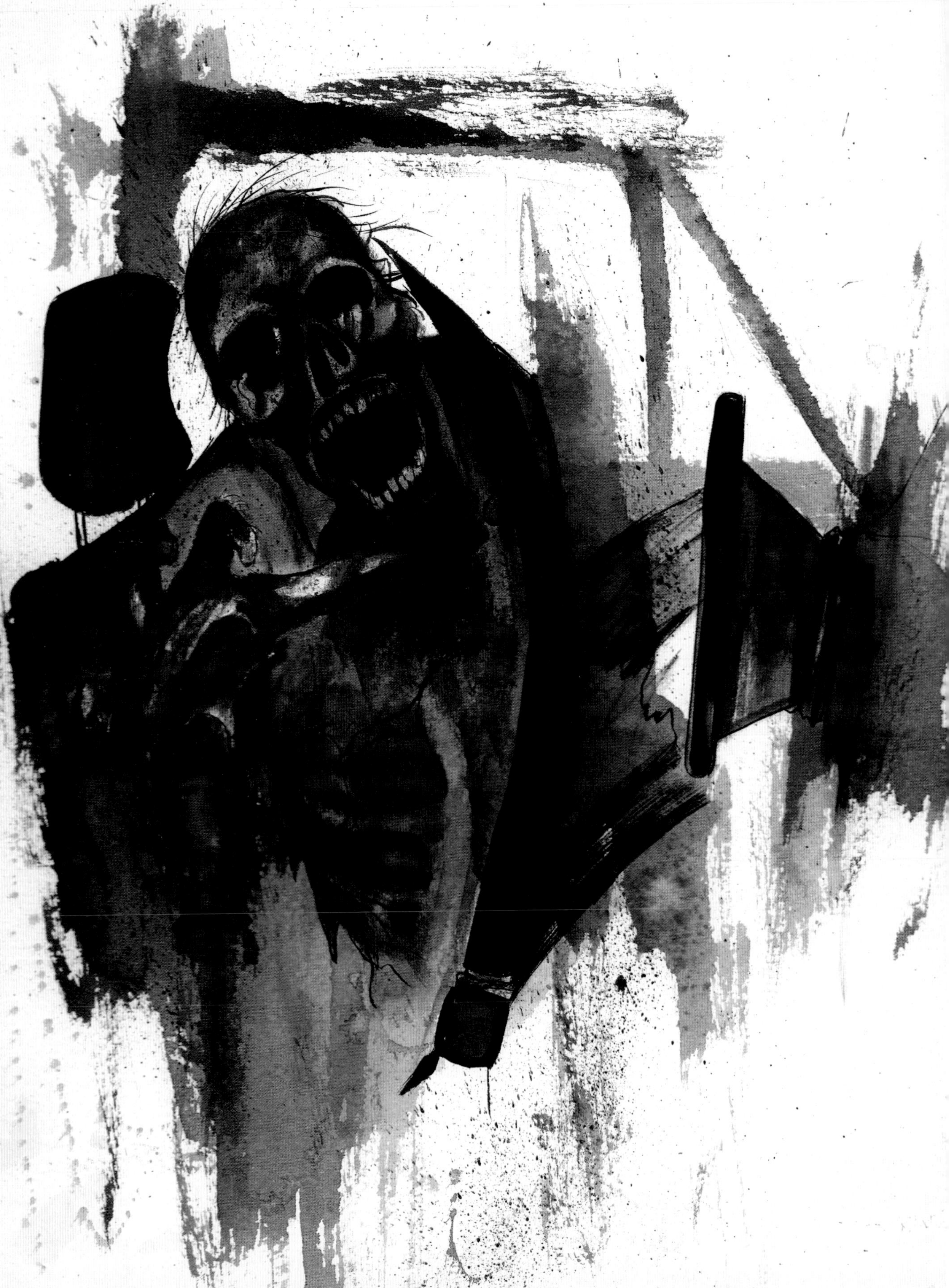

February 23, 2012

Signs of infection as I wandered through the town today.
Some human corpses, some zombie corpses? Dead anyway.
Not moving. Hard to tell the difference.

I came across a small car with its windows down. Cars. I could drive north.
I walked up and looked inside—nothing in the back seat. In the driver's seat, a
body still seat-belted in. The keys were in the ignition. I decided it was worth
the risk. I opened the car door and jabbed the corpse in the ribs with the
tip of my axe. No movement. I went around to the passenger side door, opened
it, and slid in so that I could unbuckle the belt. Its eyes opened as soon as
I reached for the buckle. For a second I thought it might be a human dying
rather than dead, but it wasn't. It grabbed my jacket but I was able to wedge
the blade to take off the hand and I jumped out of the car, the severed
hand still clutching. I tore off my jacket and threw it on the ground, shut the
creature back up in the car and ran. I should have killed it but I couldn't make
myself get close to it again even with it still belted in the seat. Nothing and no
one took any notice of what had just happened. No signs of life. After about 30
seconds I stopped running.

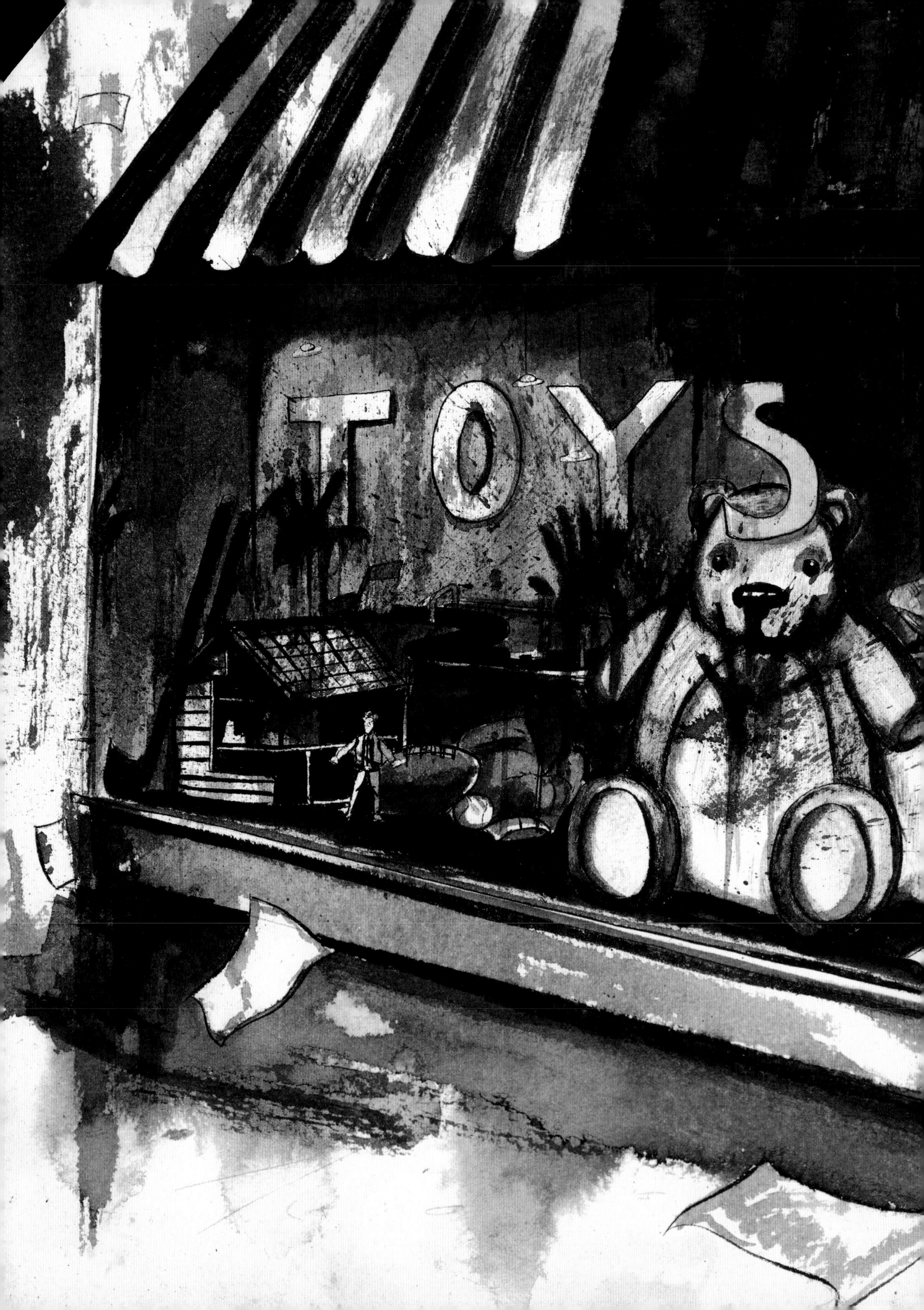
TOYS

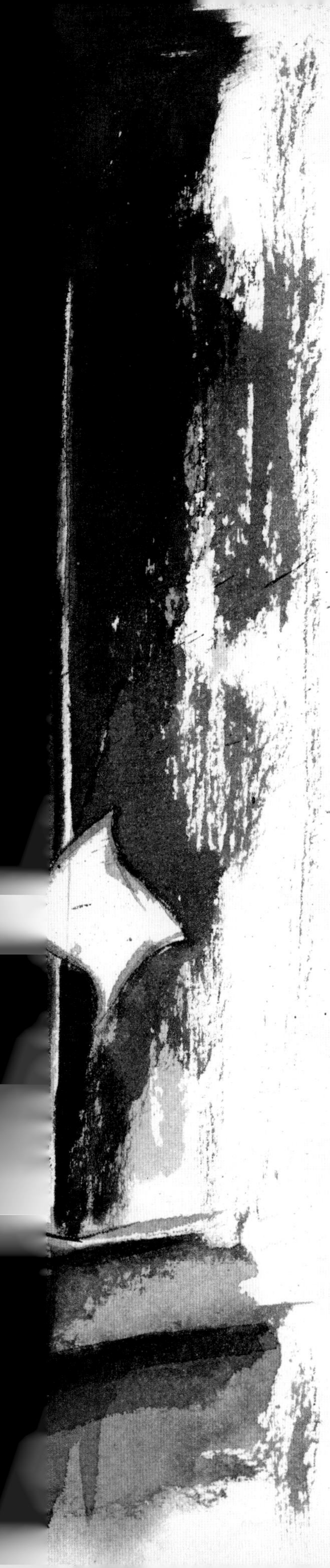

Downtown, such as it is. The town's dead, literally. I passed by a toy store window and found myself looking in. There was a slot-car track display set up, a new model updated from the kind I used to play with as a kid. Other toys, a princess costume, some stuffed bears, some toy guns—boy toys and girl toys.

There were children in the bleachers at the stadium.

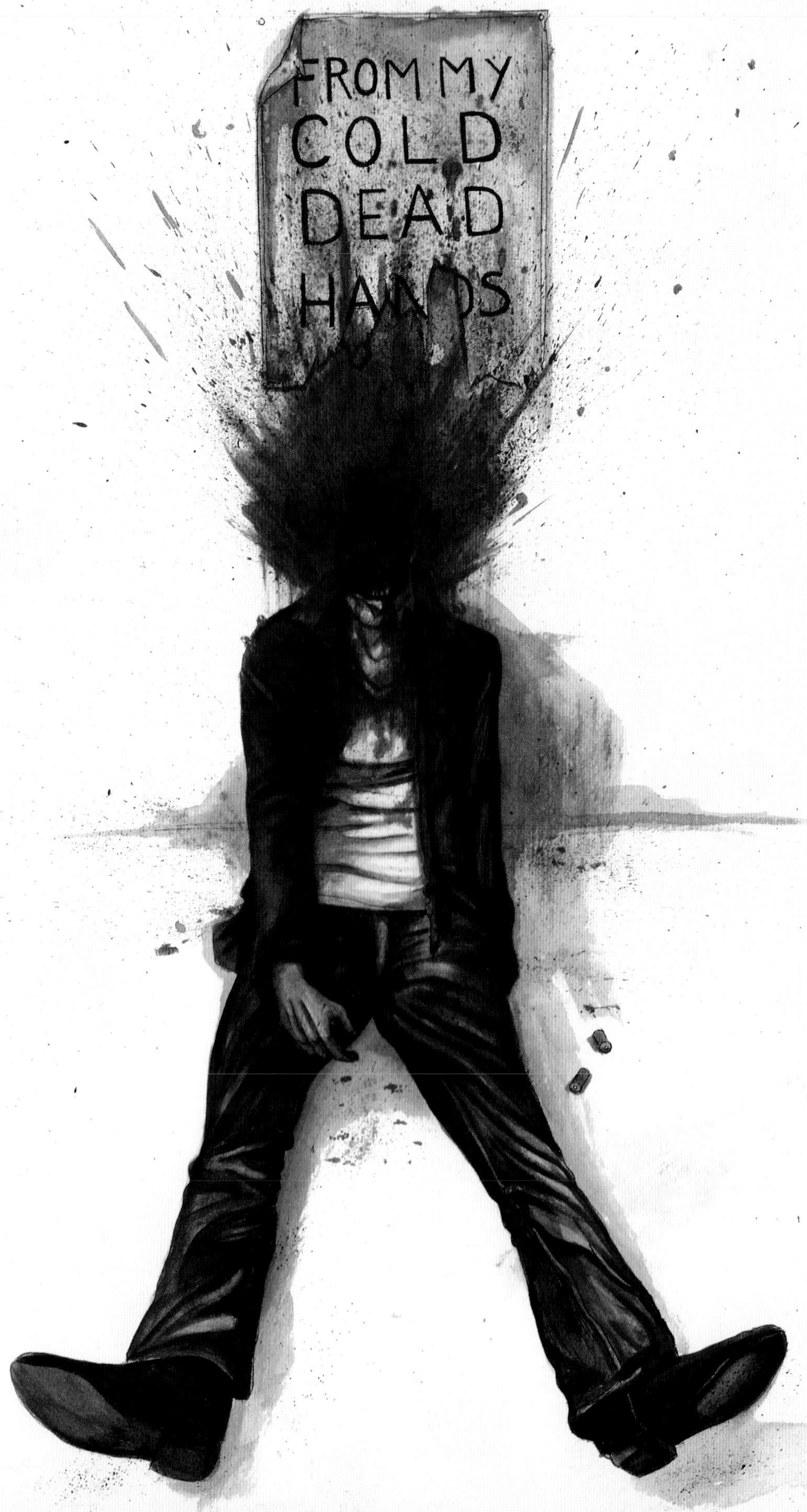
FROM MY
COLD
DEAD
HANDS

Spending the night inside Gus's Guns & Ammo. I've got new clothes, a few more layers of shirts and a down jacket from a back room inside the store. I've also got a pistol I found loaded in the office, where I also found what I assume was Gus. He looks like another suicide, a shot to the head, ~~not~~ nothing much left of his head. His hand is in rigor mortis in a trigger position, but no sign of the gun. The store has been pretty thoroughly looted, so not everybody in town gave up? I shut the office door and am sleeping behind the counter. Barricaded the doors and windows as best I could. Tomorrow I'll try the cars in the stadium lot. I have to get the hell out of here.

February 24, 2012

Almost killed the first human I've seen in more than a week. I was sound asleep when I could hear scraping metal and the front door barricade pushing in. I saw a head shape against the moonlight outside and fired, a bad shot into the wall, thank god. "Hey! Human! we don't mean any harm! Hello?!"

That turned out to be Joe, part of a band that's been living out of their van for the past few months. Logically, they thought Gus's might have weapons. There's four of them: Joe (guitar), Phillip (guitar), Ian (bass), and Stu (drums), all in their 20s from Olympia. And they have food! Finally getting out of town, heading north with them in the van.

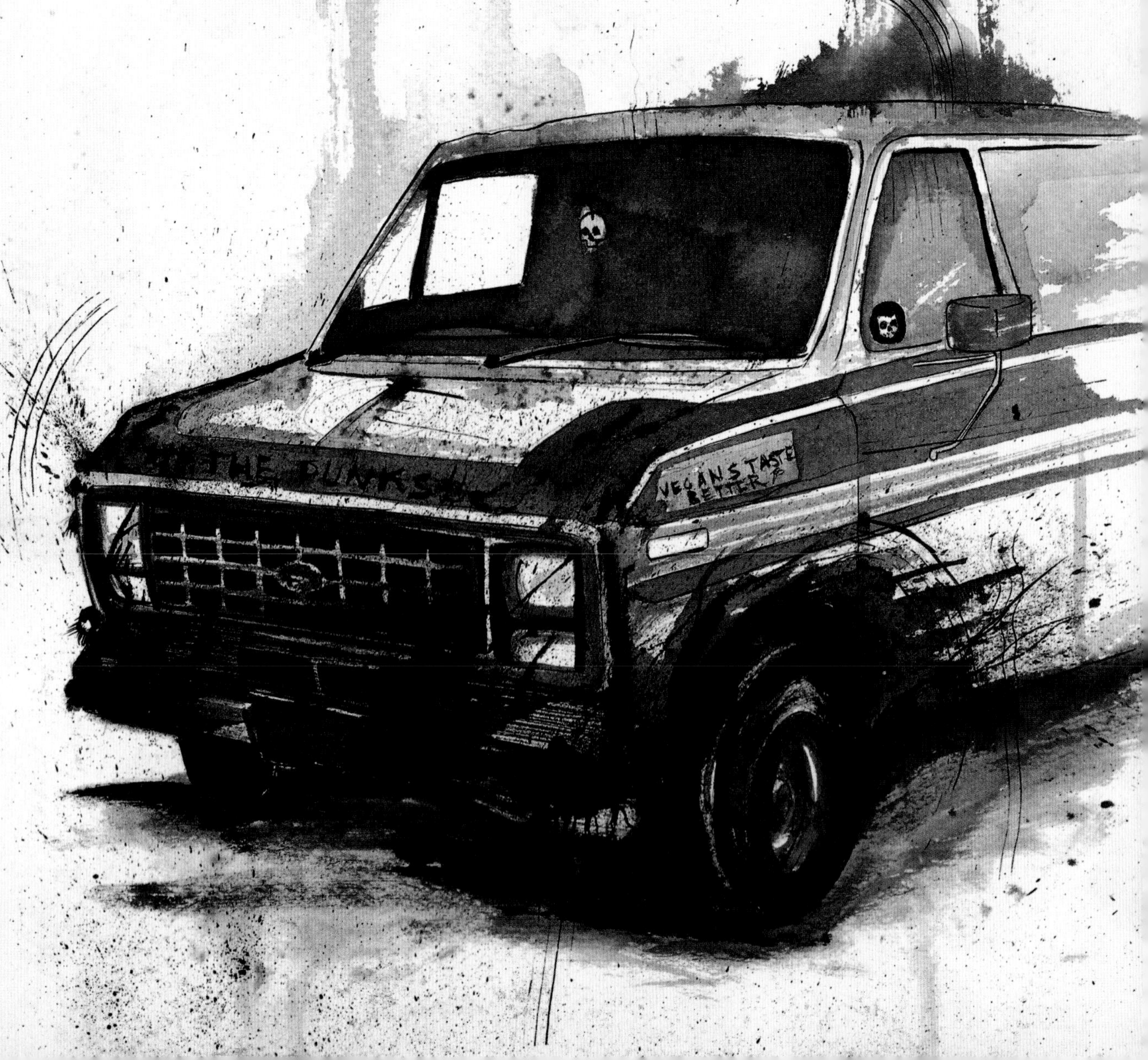
VEGANS TASTE BETTER

February 25, 2012

The guys take turns driving, one at the wheel, one "shotgun" to make sure the driver stays awake, two (now three) of us in the back. A different but I have to say better bad smell of a bunch of guys living in a van. A human smell. Also in the back are some cans of gas, sacks of food, various containers of water, sleeping bags. They ditched their amps and the drum kit but kept the guitars and bass, and noodle around on them sometimes. We're headed for the Farm now and spirits are pretty high.

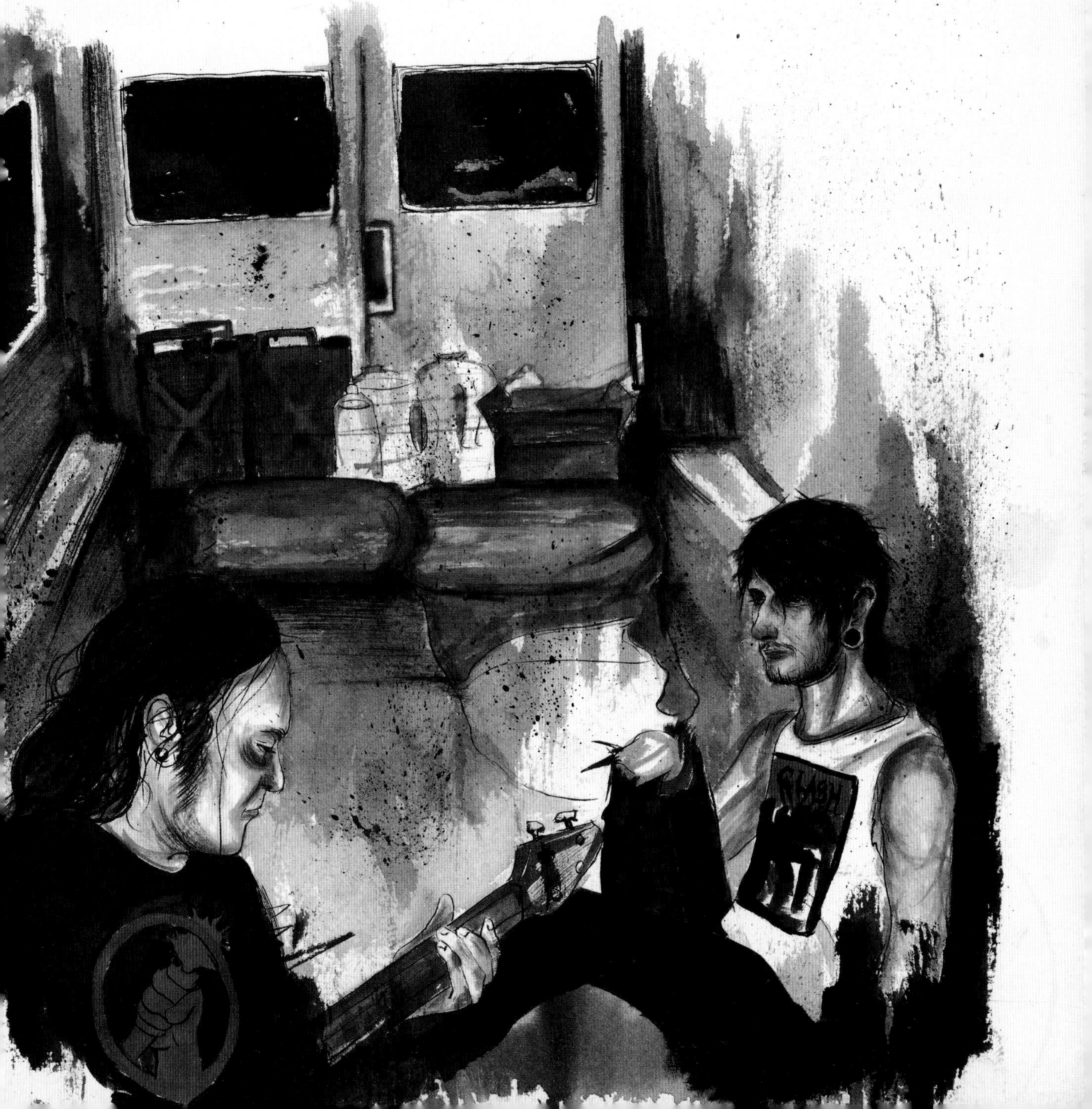

February 26, 2012

I'm recording Joe's account of what happened to them here.

"We were playing up and around Vancouver when people started getting sick. We're pretty used to cruising around and crashing with friends or having someone put us up for the night, the local punk house or like student co-ops. We usually cook for them and we always leave the house cleaner than when we got there, so we have this network. Things got bad in Vancouver, people just attacking each other, everyone with the weird fever, and so we started calling around when the phones still worked and made it to some friends who were kind of isolated, they inherited this house. When we got there . . . they were dead. We just kept moving after that. We've got plenty of food—when everybody looted everything they went for the packaged food, like in the supermarkets and stuff. Nobody's thinking sacks of beans and rice, like bulk, soup kitchen style, but we're vegans on a budget, and that's food. Been siphoning gas, been doing that for years when funds run low on tour."

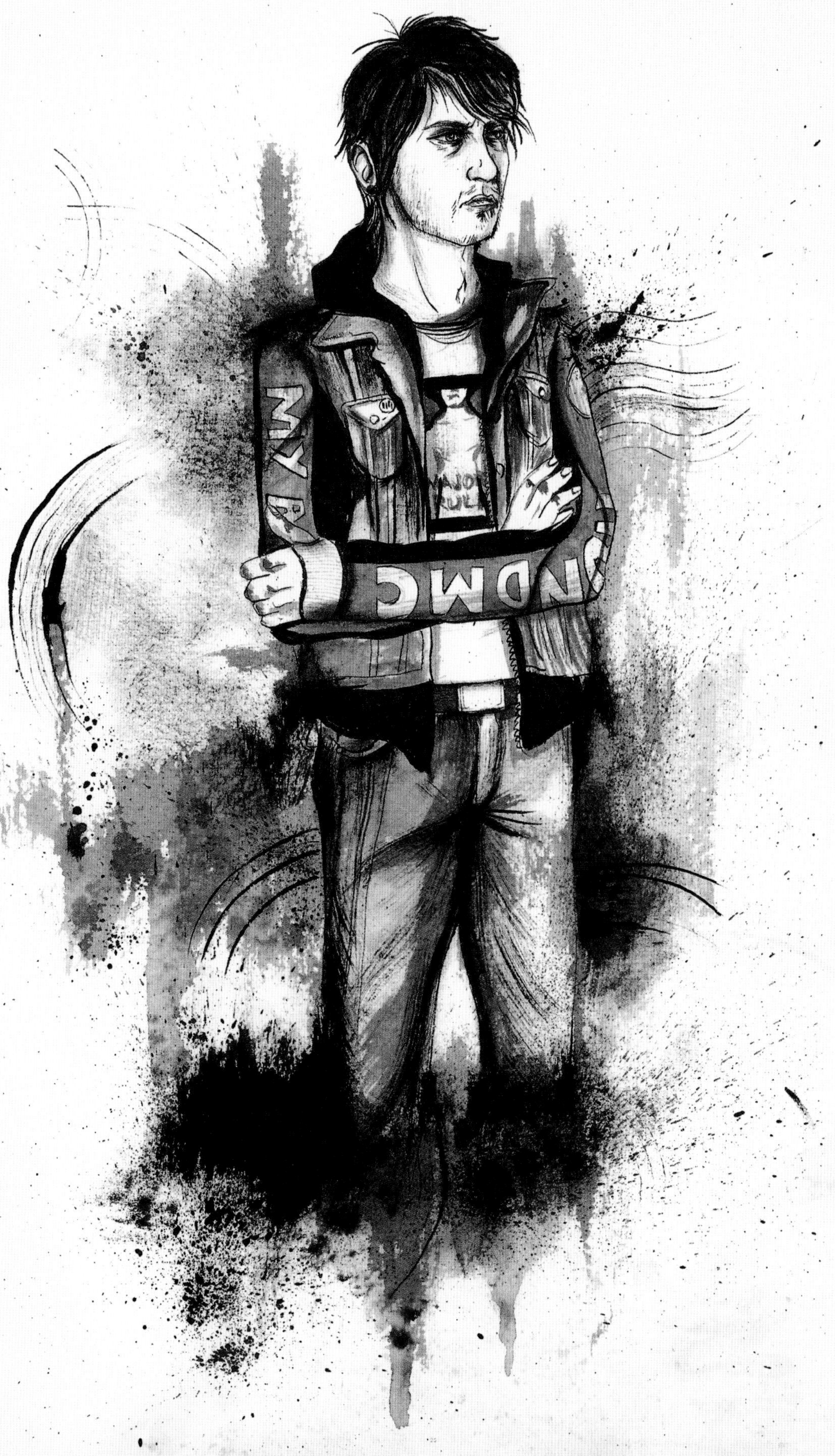

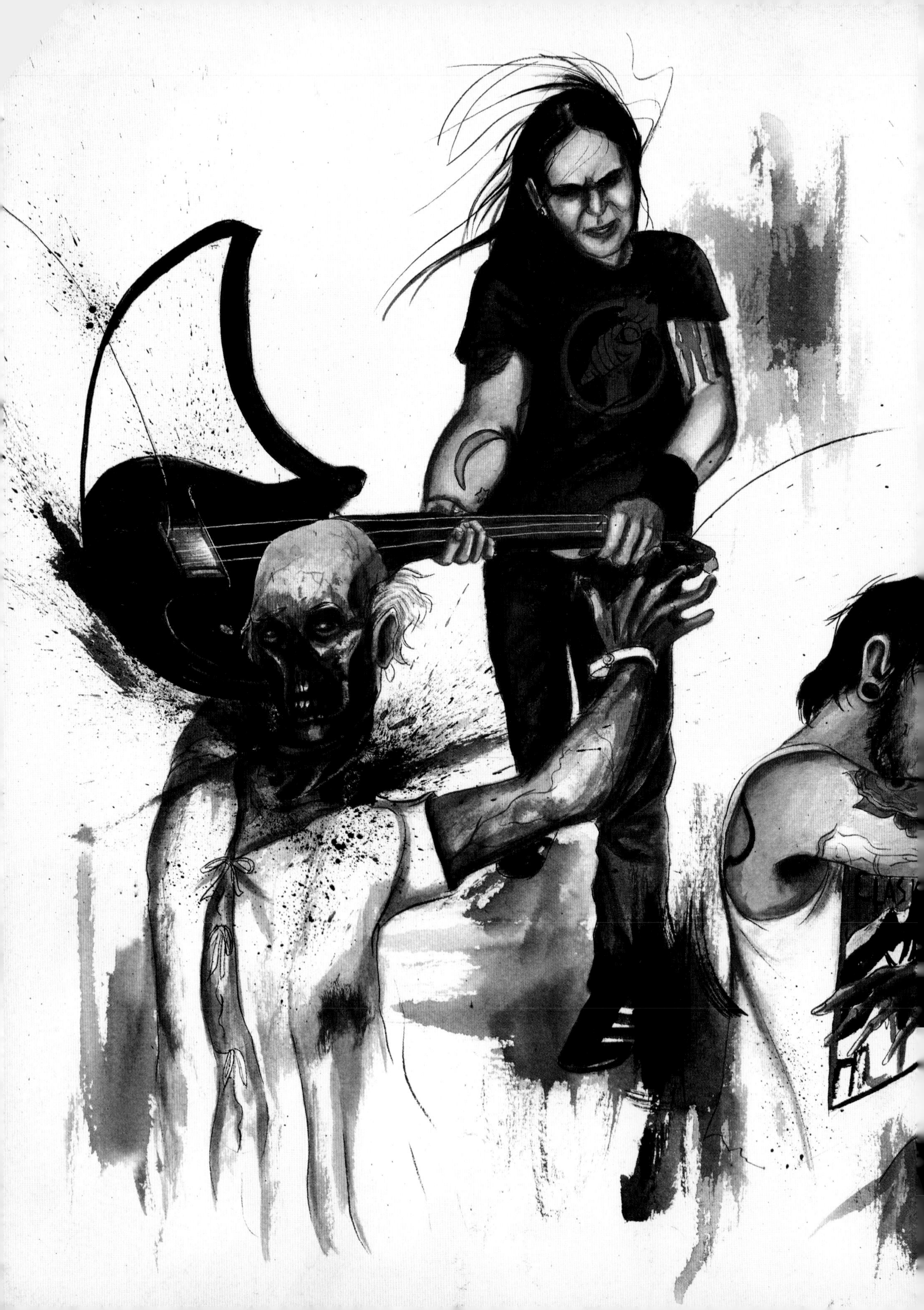

February 28, 2012

Finally making some real time. As we move north, seeing fewer bodies or broken down cars. Whenever we see stopped cars we'll usually check them out to see if they have any gas in the tank. It's almost more upsetting when the cars are completely, inexplicably empty, but more often there are bodies. We'll also occasionally pull off to do some cooking or just stand around a fire.

Loopy tired, we had a couple zombies come up on us while we were stopped. The band had been sitting around playing and Ian managed to crack the closest one in the head with his bass. We set them afire with the gasoline and kept them away with branches until they fell and burned out like cinders.

We always sleep in the van.

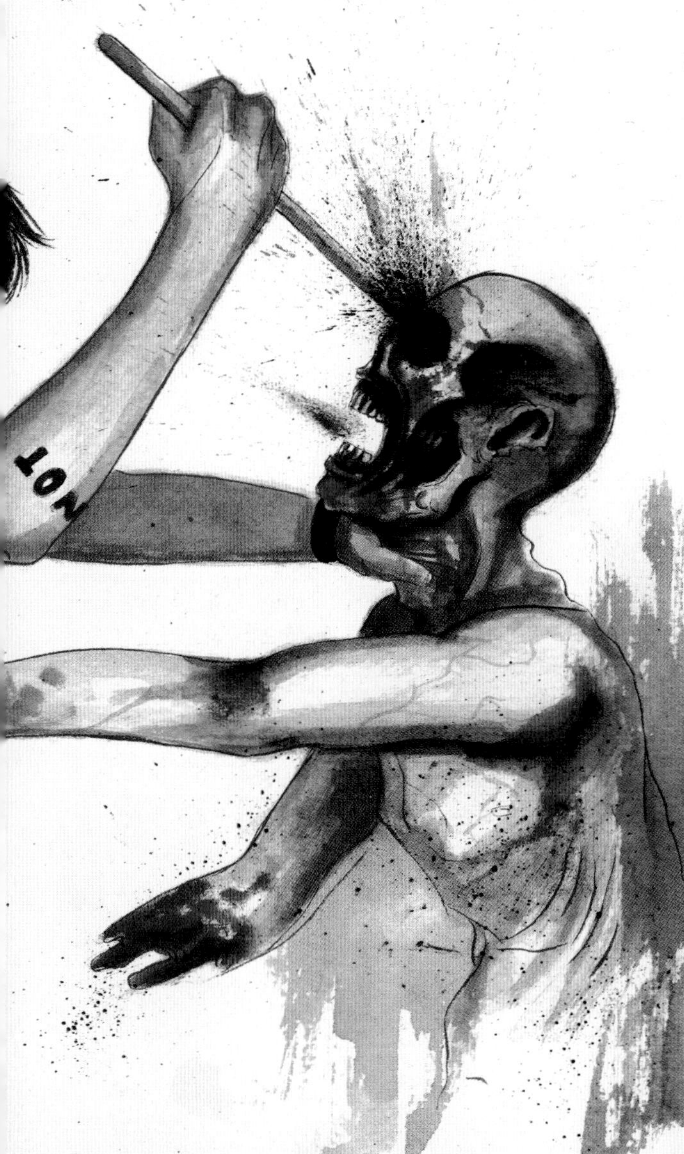
NOT

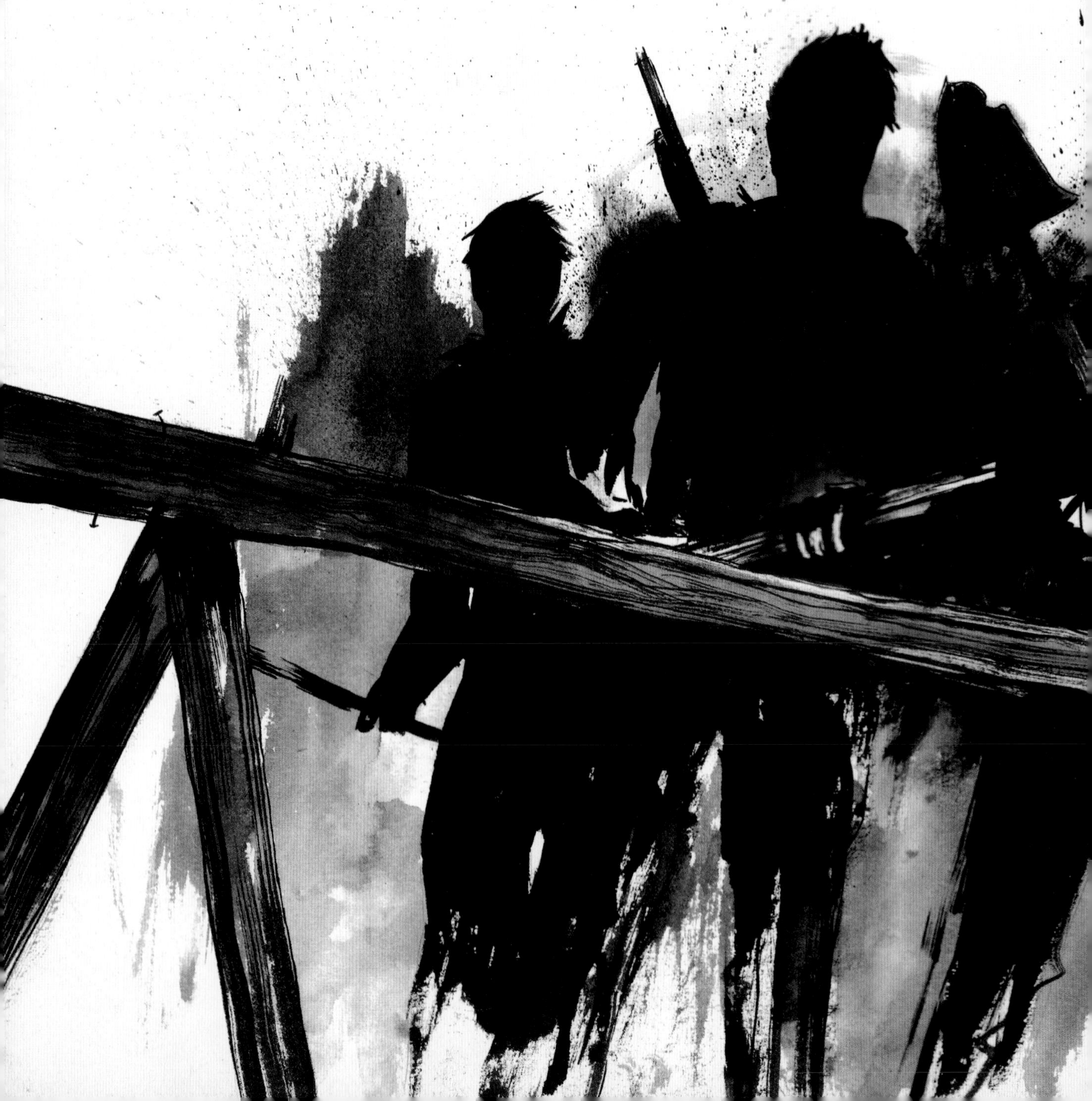

March 1, 2012

We've made it to the Farm. 500 miles it took us to get here. It's a small, semi-fortified, bucolic inn, located off a series of wooded country roads about 15 miles from the nearest town. We've been allowed through a checkpoint but instructed to sleep in a smaller cottage building for the night, I guess to check and see if they want to let us in. I was expecting an actual farm, though this is close enough, one of the people at the checkpoint was wielding a pitchfork. Nice long handle on that, good for keeping the dead at a distance. Some rifles slung over shoulders, but also gasoline or kerosene and rags at the ready. A few charred heaps dot the yard and there's a long low pit full of burnt human or zombie remains.

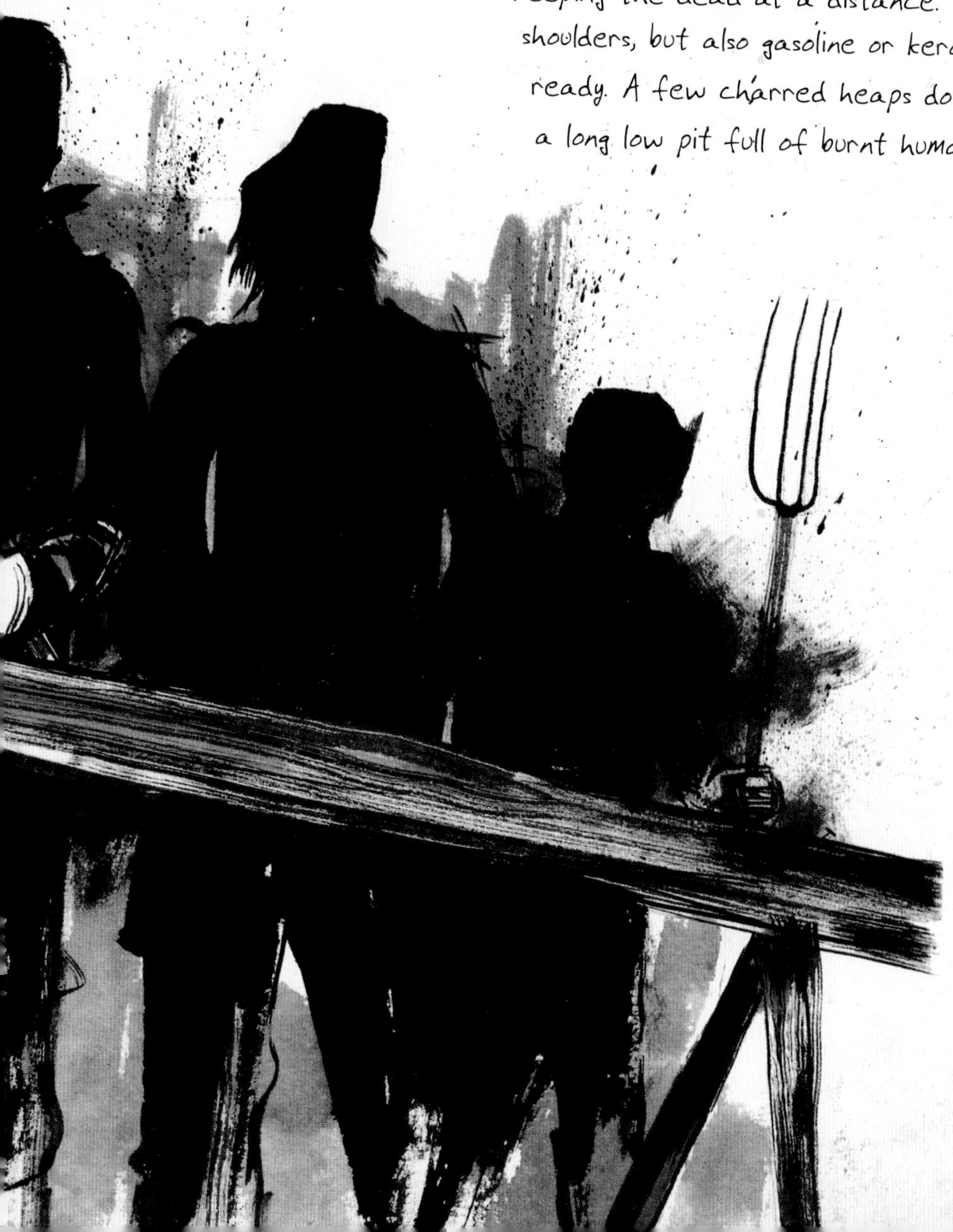

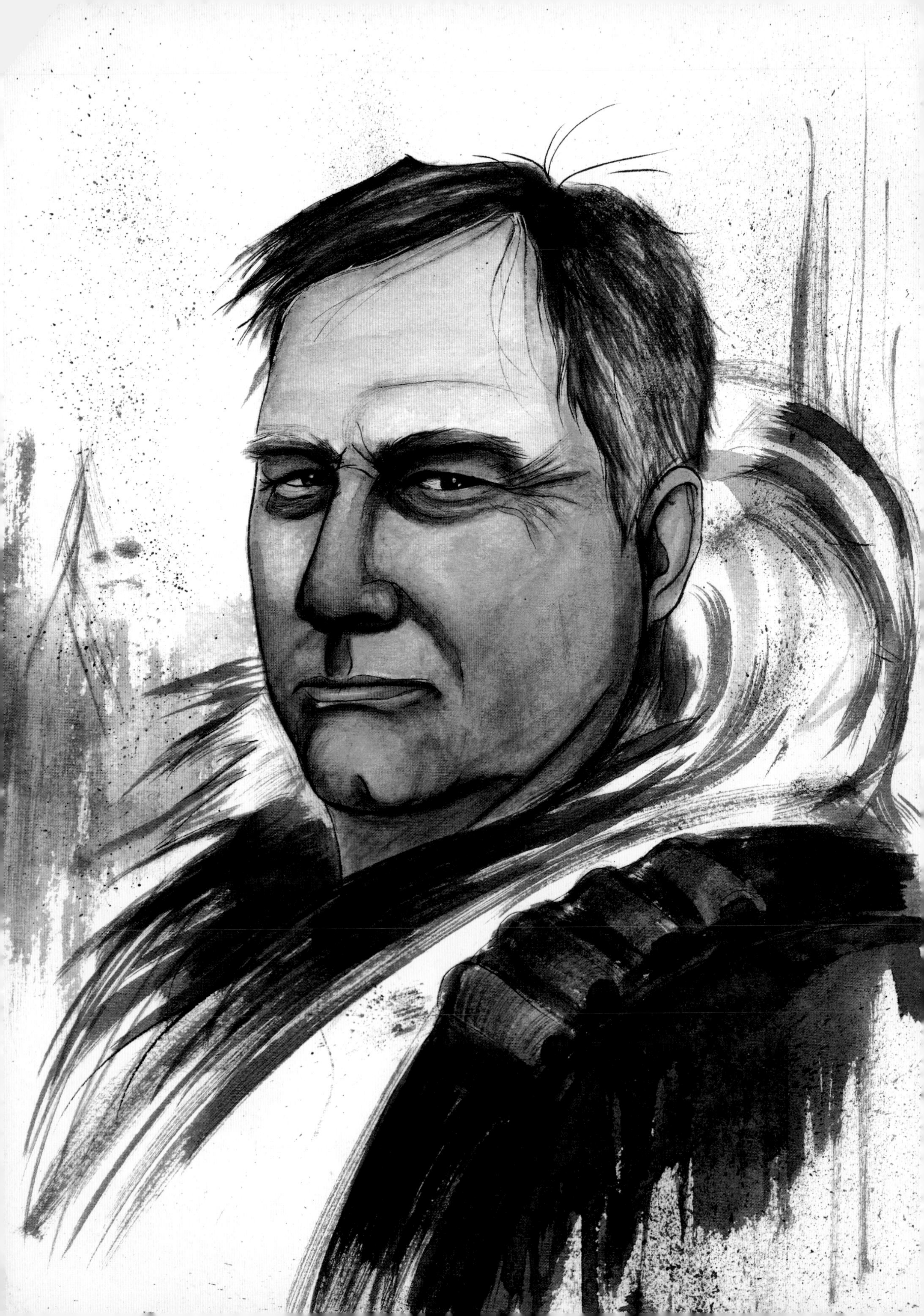

March 2, 2012

This morning a woman came in and took our temperature, shined a light in our eyes, asked a lot of questions about where we'd been and what we'd seen. Left and told us to wait. We passed whatever quarantine they wanted us to pass and we've been admitted to the big house.

The guy in charge is named Dale Fowler. I'm recording his story here.

"My wife and I came up here for our honeymoon one year. She's dead now. When the plague hit, and we knew how bad it was in the cities, I remembered this place. Off-season when I got here, so there weren't many people around. The few that were, I had to destroy—they had turned. Pretty soon, some other like-minded folks showed up. We just decided to hole up here a while until things got better. Obviously, that didn't happen. We fortified all the doors and windows, hunt the area for game, and for people who've turned, keep watch in shifts. Run the radio, hoping other people like you will show up. We need numbers, more eyes, more hands, for protection and to turn the place into a real farm by spring."

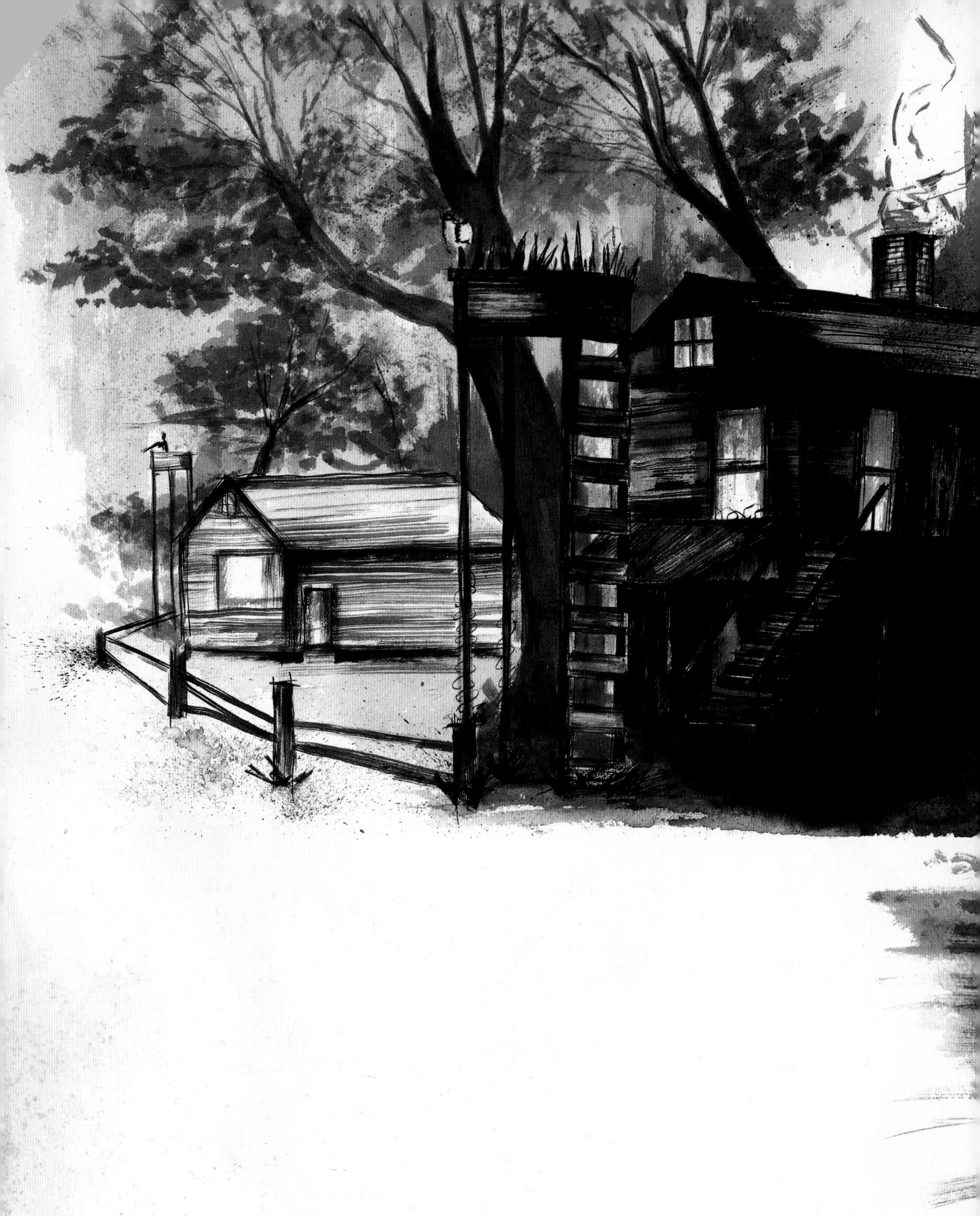

March 3, 2012

I've drawn the setup here as best I can. There's no perimeter fence to speak of, which worries me, though I'm not sure what they would make one out of, or how much good it would do. There are what amount to observation points that are a bit raised up and built out of odds and ends, which are staffed during the day, and always people watching from the top windows of the main building, day and night. They cleared the area around the Farm as best they can, but there are a lot of big old trees in the woods, so there's a limit to what can be done. The pit is where they drag bodies of zombies that have gotten this close. It's hard to tell, maybe 30 to 40 charred corpses in the pit?

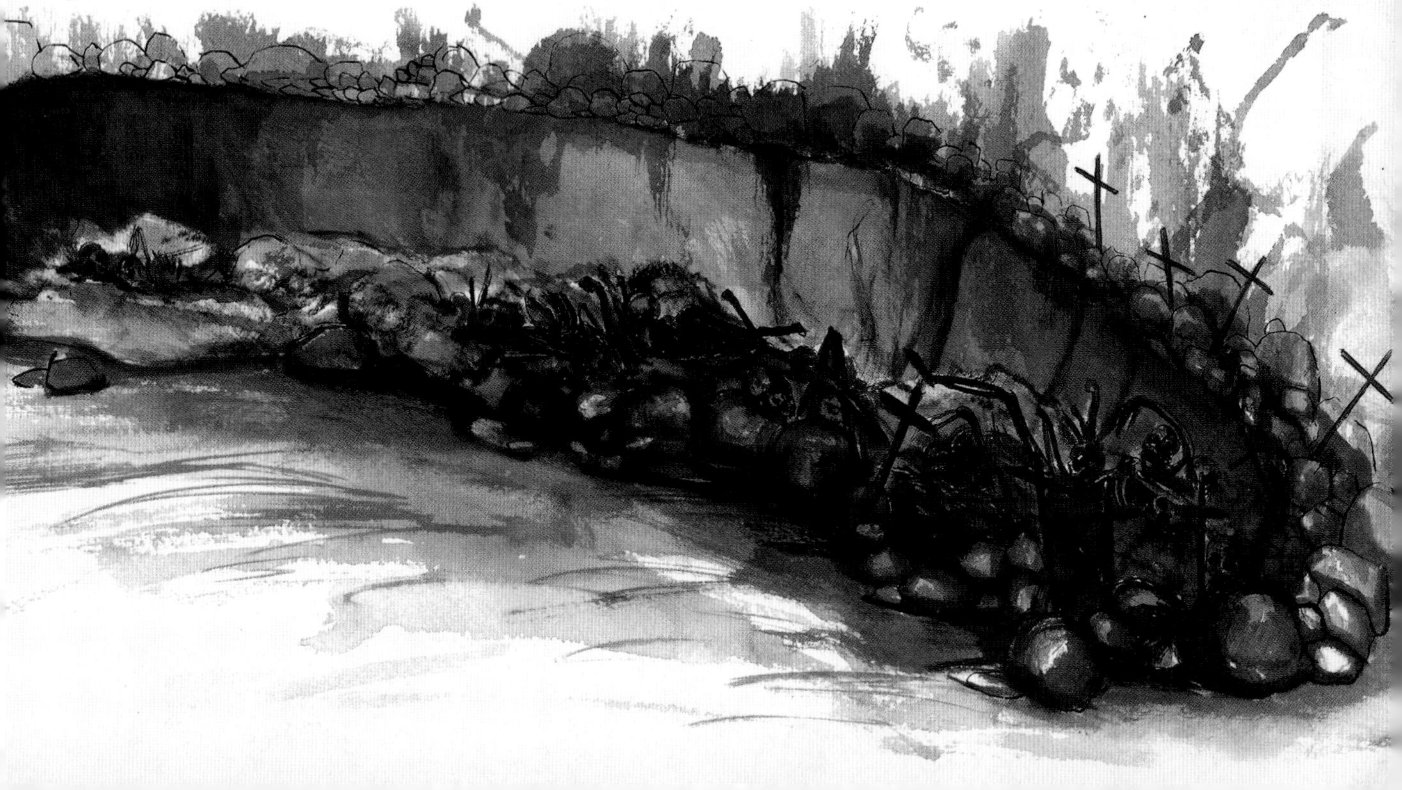

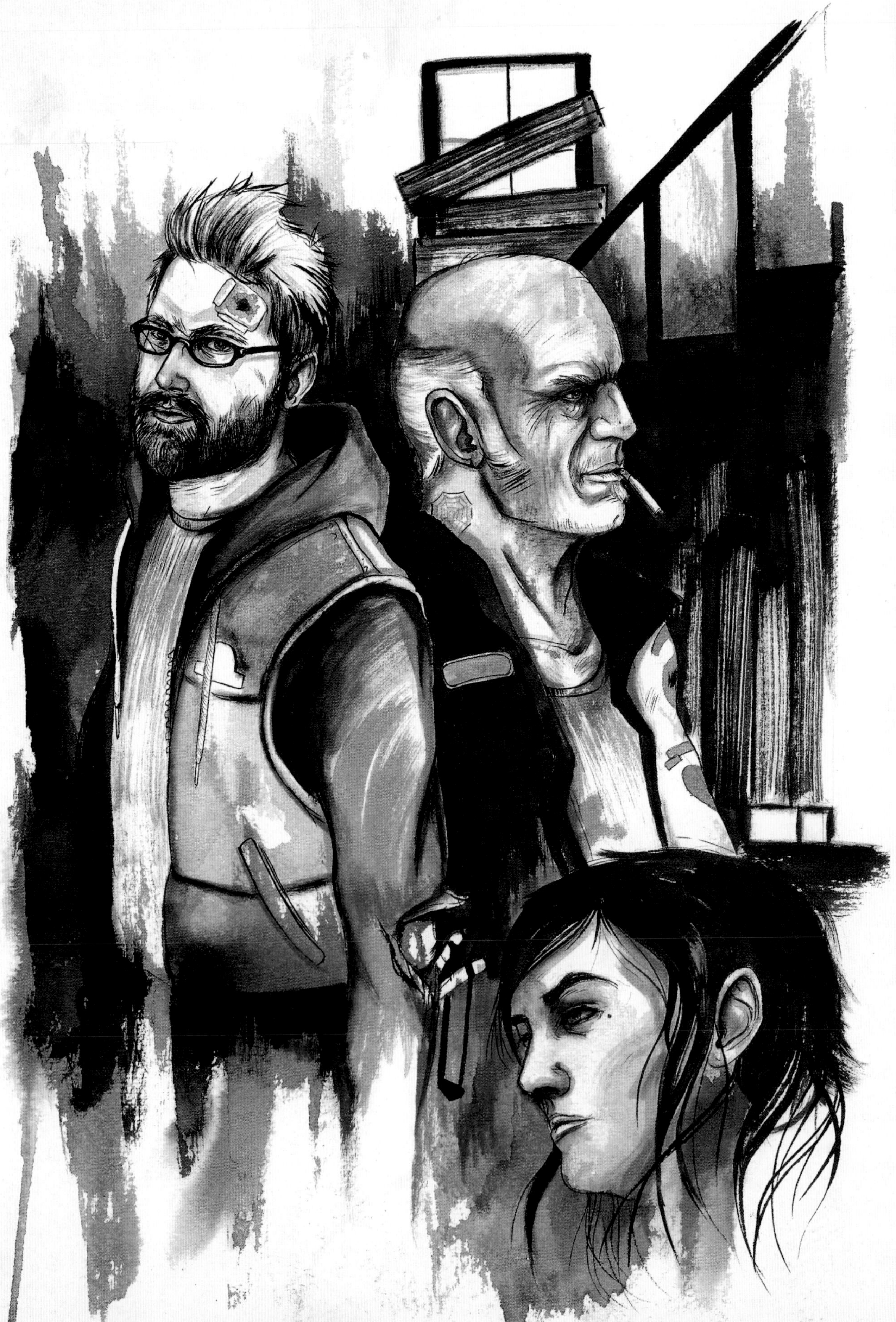

March 4, 2012

There are 15 other survivors here, so the band and I make 20. Some of them are from far, a few hundred miles—there are three cars and a motorcycle outside—but most came from one of the nearby towns, which are a dozen or more miles away from here. Apparently earlier on folks would venture to the towns to see what could be salvaged. There are great stores here of water, gasoline, clothes, tools, some lumber, bedding, etc. Nobody really bothers searching towns any more. "There's nothing there."

It feels good to be around people again.

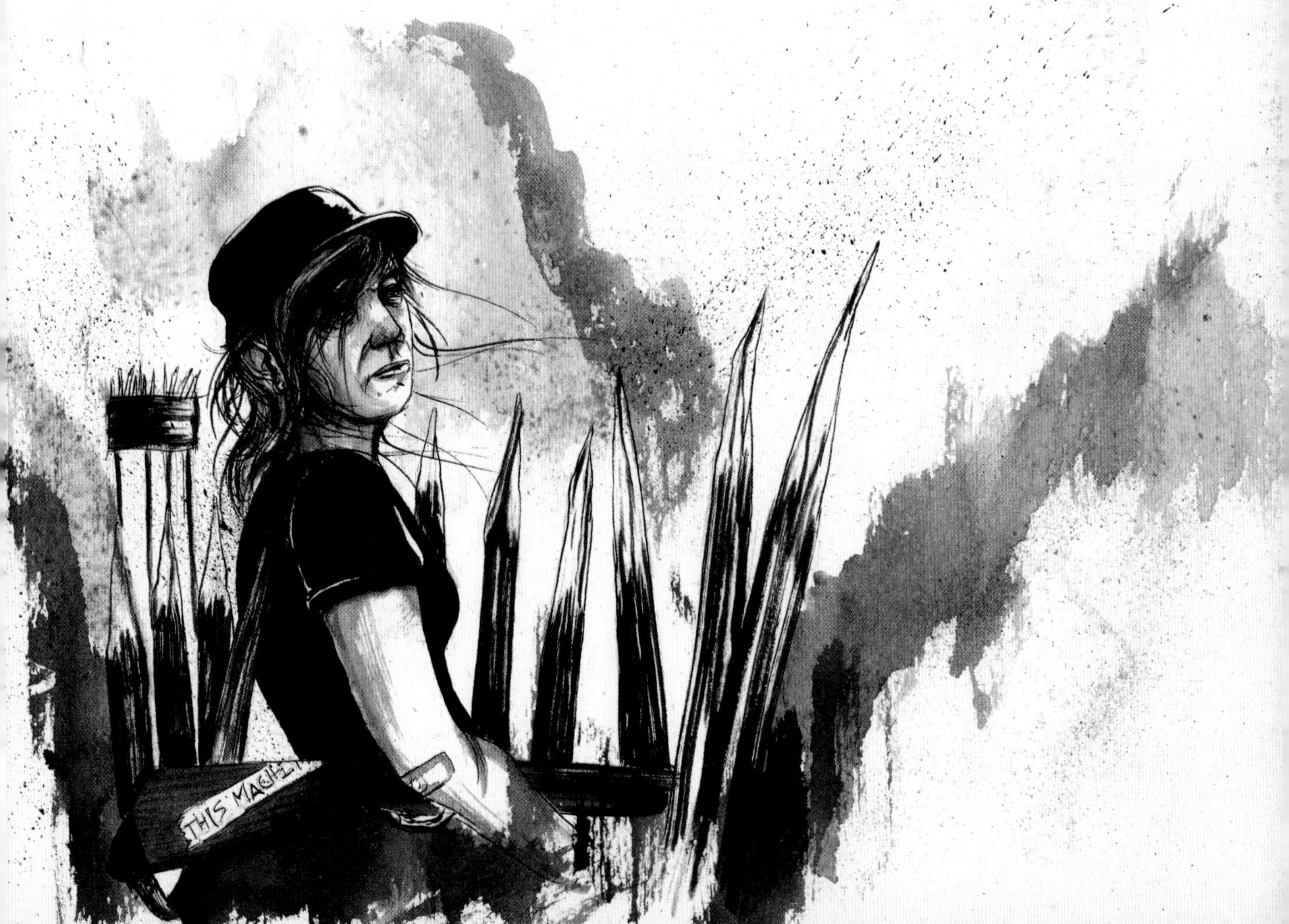

March 5, 2012

Doing my part around "The Farm." Cooking and cleaning. Laundry! Clothes hung on lines out of the windows during the day.

Went on a patrol today around the near woods. On the way back we saw two zombies trying to break open a woodshed door. One of them just clawing at it, but one of them had a log and was hitting the door. This is the first sign I've seen of adaptation and problem solving, and it's a bad sign. They were after a stray cat that had crawled under the door. Do they eat animals? Are they starving? We beheaded and burned them.

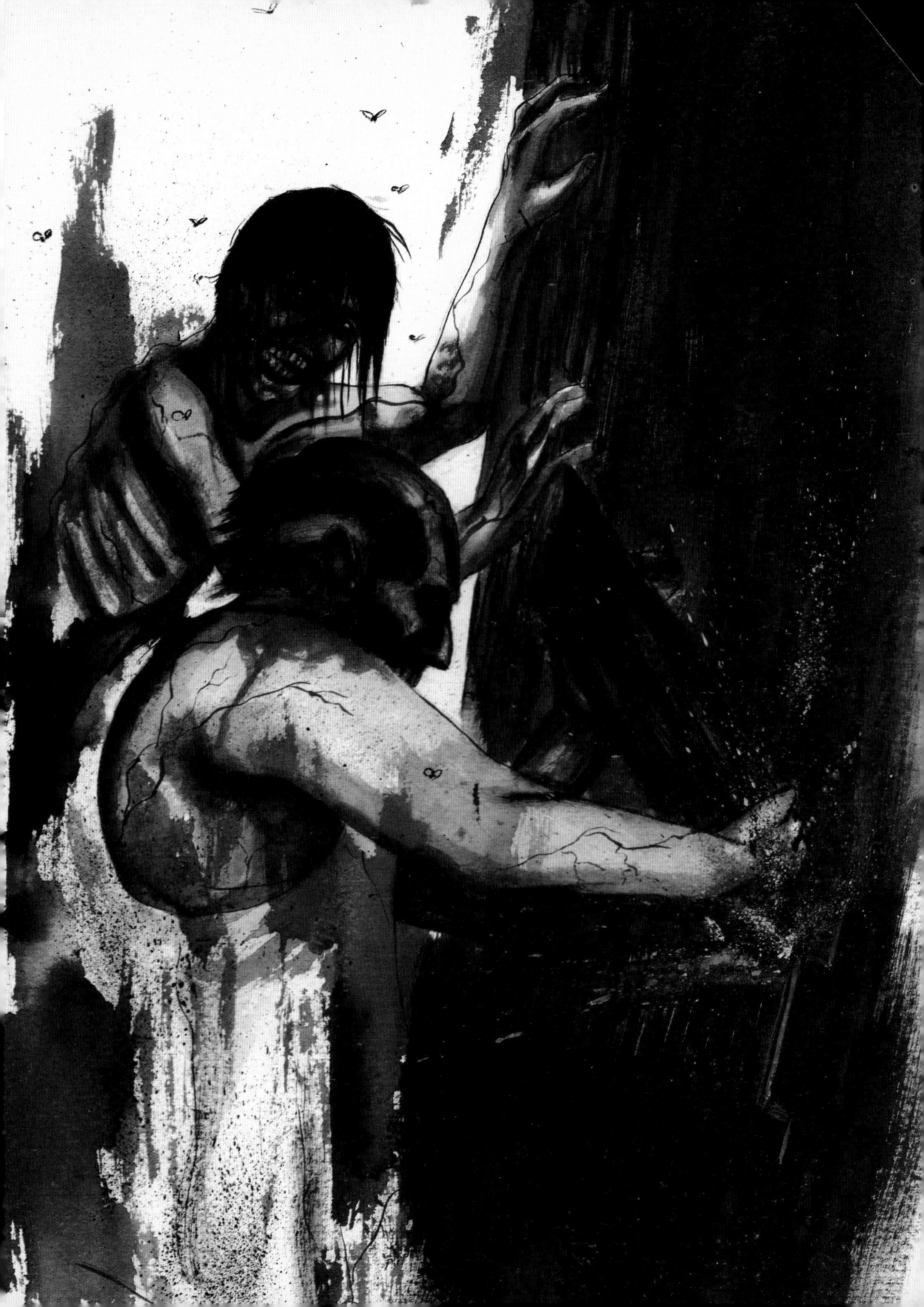

March 6, 2012

Killed two zombies who had come up to the house this afternoon. Deeper back in the woods we saw about two dozen zombies who just seemed to be watching? At any rate they only came toward us when we drew close. It took a big group of us but we managed to behead and burn the whole group of them before they could encroach the property.

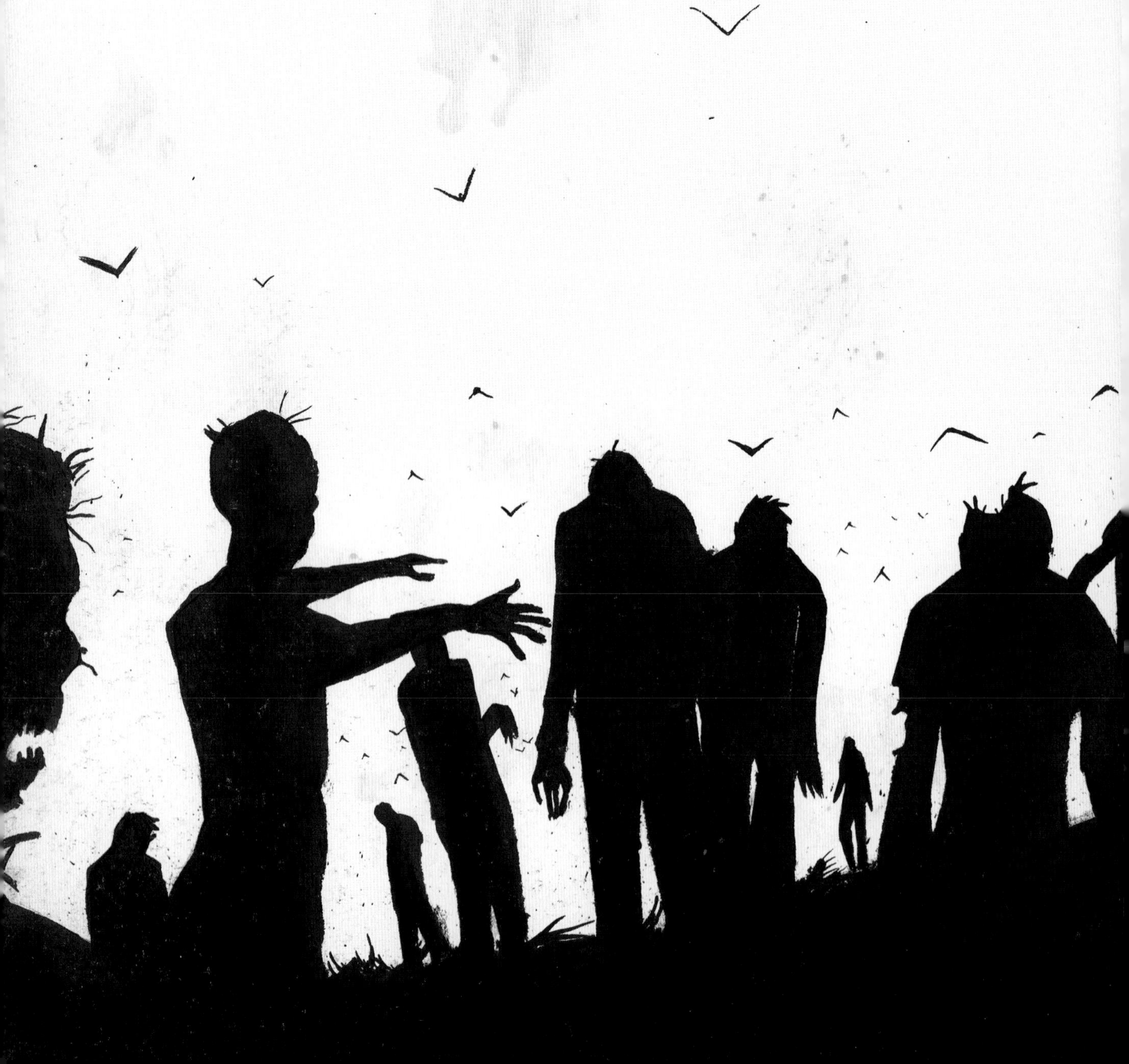

Tried the radio today to see what else we can pick up here. There are several other stations broadcasting, one from Regina, one from Churchill, Manitoba. Pockets of humanity are reestablishing themselves.

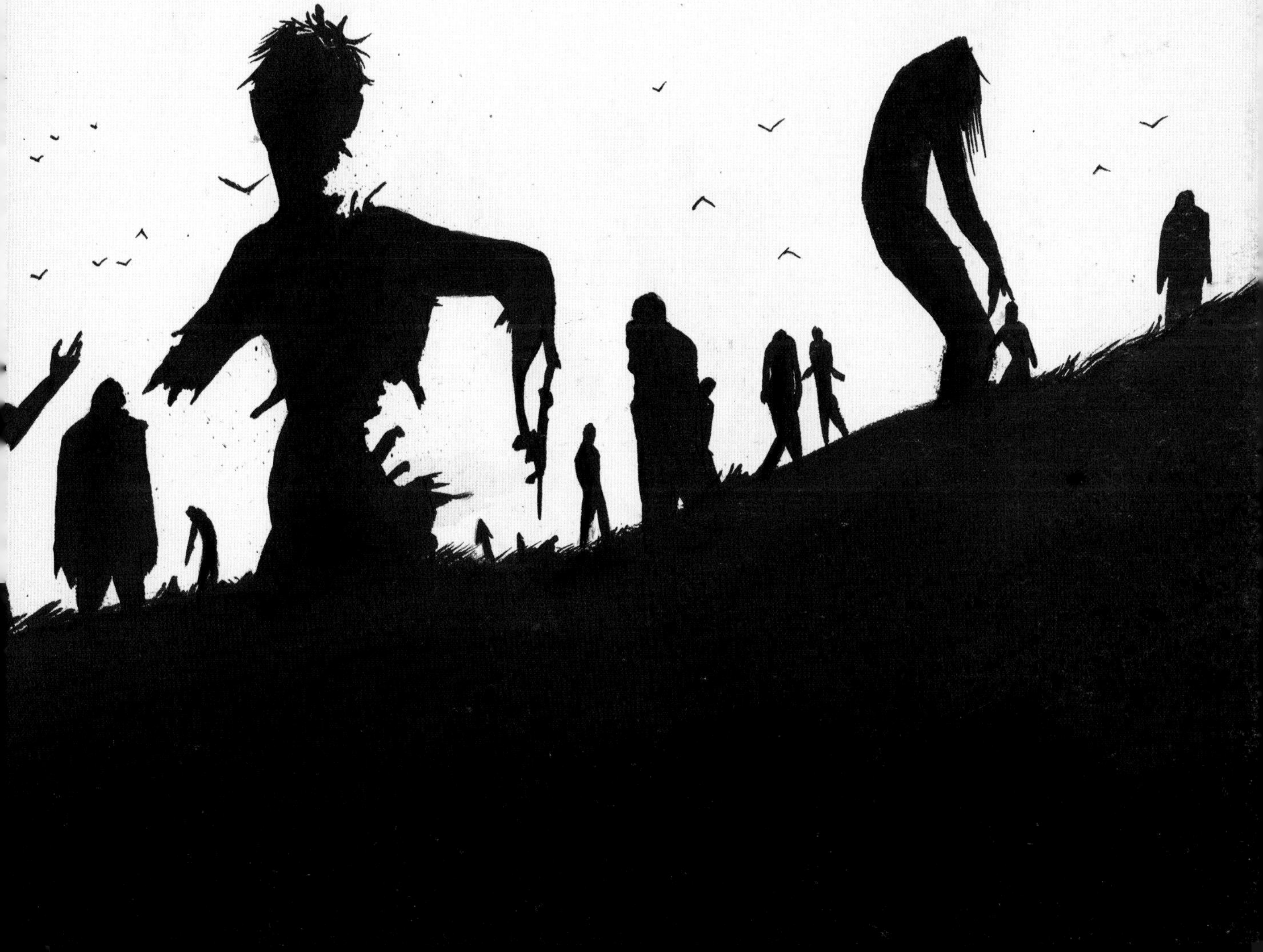

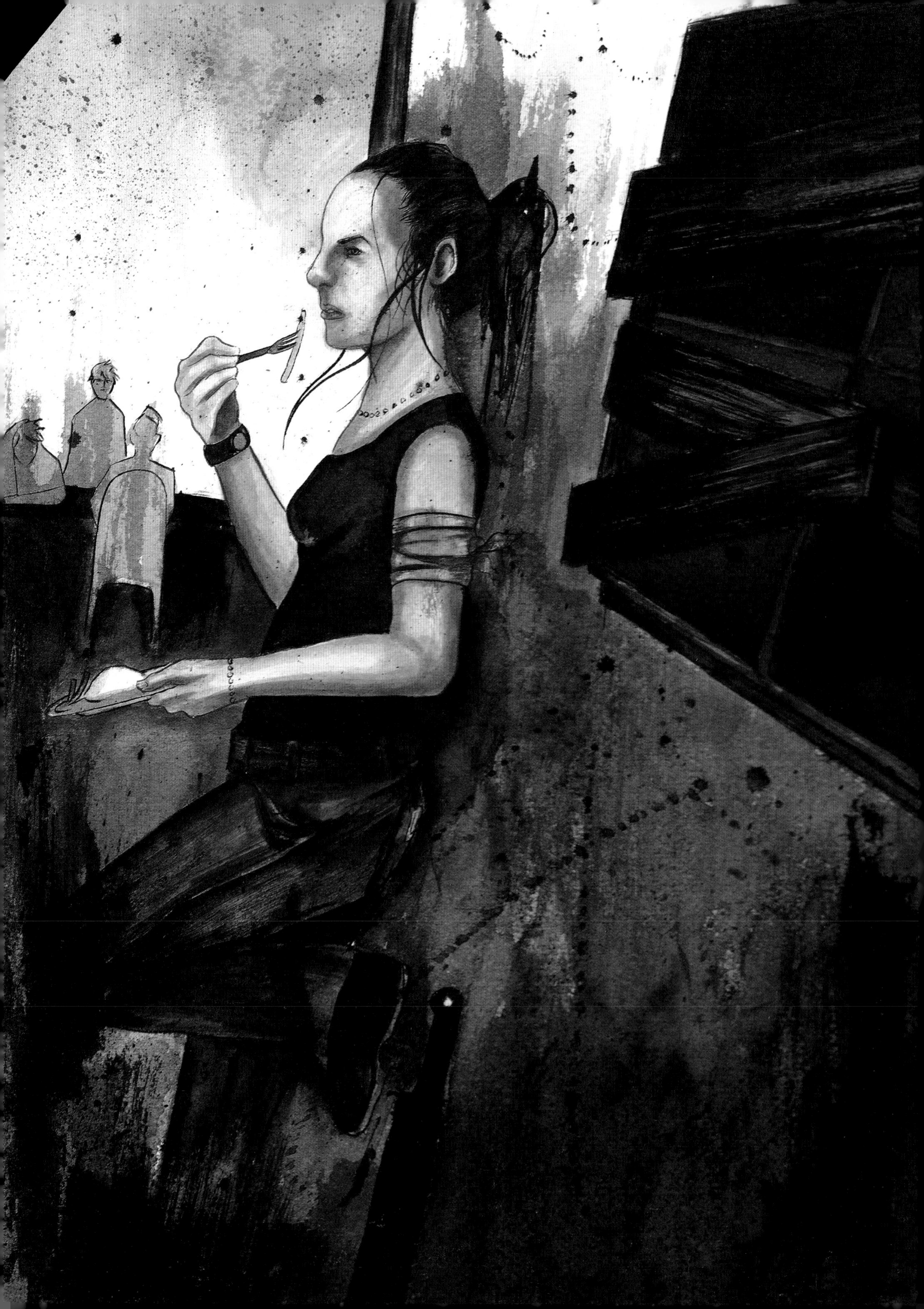

March 7, 2012

Katherine showed up at the farm today. You don't really expect to see people again, but she'd been the one who had told me about this place. She's driving a white delivery van with horrible smears and crumples all along the sides, front and back. She says that the towns she's seen are either empty or "full," meaning full of the undead. She stayed for dinner (potatoes, canned green beans). She's been here before, and they seem to accept that she'll be leaving again without discussion. When I ask her why she doesn't stay, she says, "there are too many of you here."

March 8, 2012

Todd Smith fell suddenly ill, symptoms identical to the early days of the infection. He hasn't been bitten, and no more exposure to zombies than any of us on patrols, no direct contact. We moved him to the cottage and have posted watch.

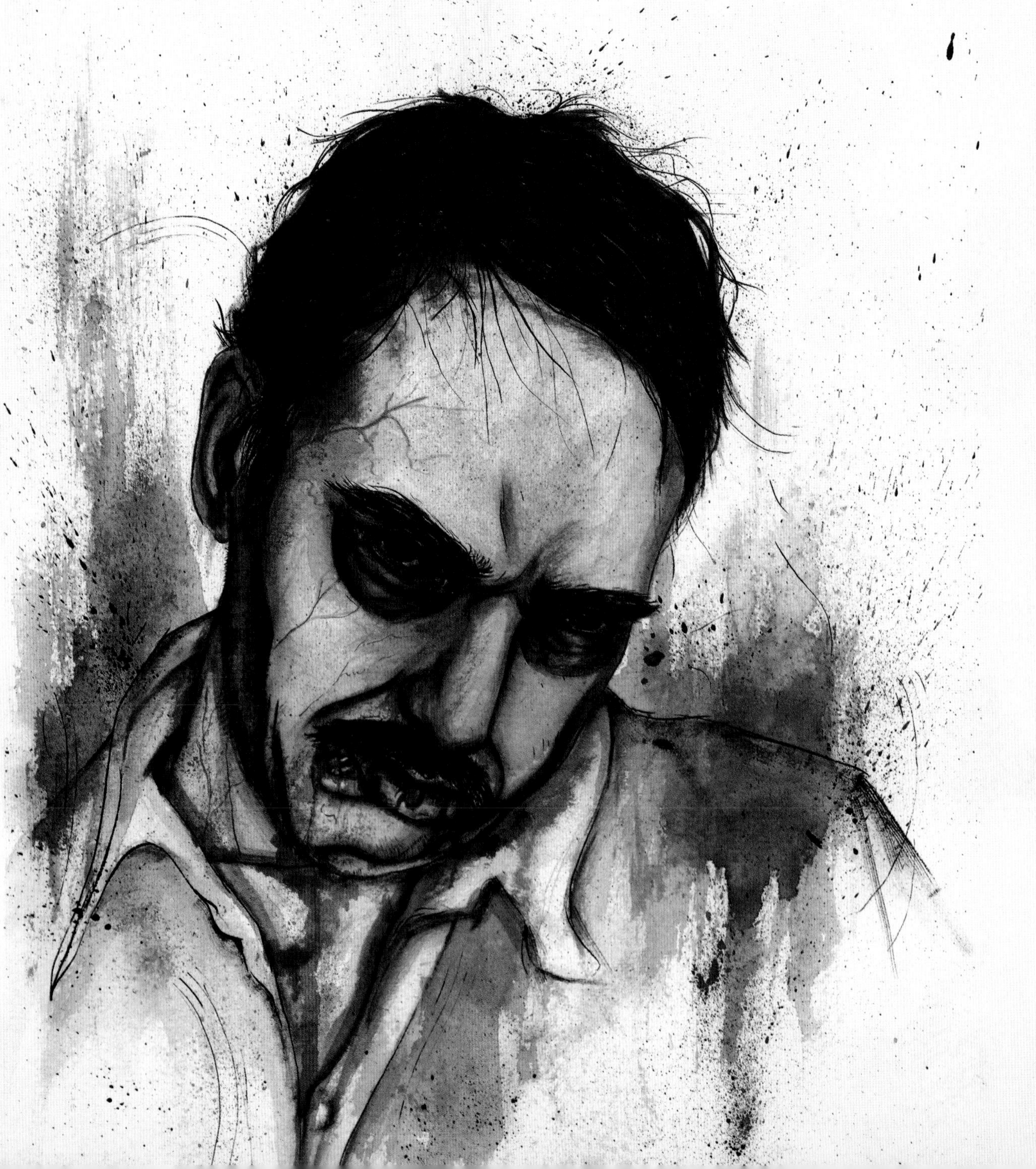

March 9, 2012

Todd's dead. Beheaded, burned. It happened fairly quickly. At first he seemed to know what was happening, then he seemed less aware, almost feral, simply reacting to whatever was happening in his system—the seizing up, the intense pain. People are still succumbing to the compound buildup in their systems. I asked Dale if this had happened here before and he said, simply, "Yeah." We threw what was left of Todd in the pit.

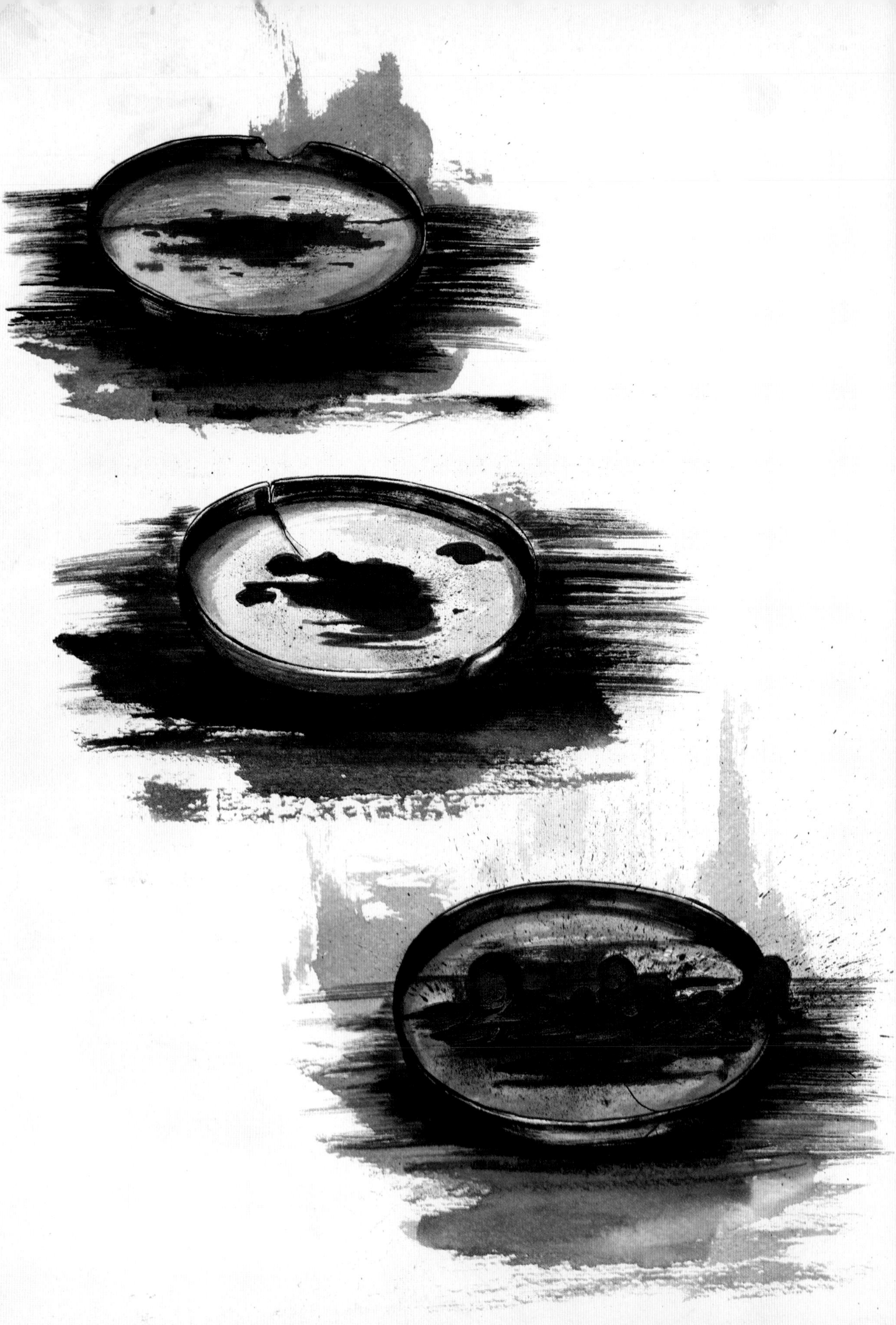

March 10, 2012

No zombies sighted today on patrols or watch.

I took a sample of Todd Smith's blood before we incinerated the body.
Not much I'm able to do with it in these conditions. I did manage
to get a reaction. I pricked the end of my finger and collected a
sample of my own blood. I bandaged, wrapped, and regloved my hand.
Then combined the sample of my blood with Todd's, ~~which attacked~~
The combination fizzed like peroxide on a wound, then clumped into a
curdled knot. Tried it again, same reaction. So at the state of Todd's
transformation the necrotic tissues have an intense and seemingly caustic
reaction to other human tissue. Additional human blood (mine again) added
to the combination infected and uninfected sample didn't cause the same
reaction, no fizzing, but it did curdle the new blood so that it resembles the
other dark gore on the glass in front of me. So what do we know? That
zombie tissue contact can have a corrupting influence on living human tissue,
and that the reaction is active ~~to the point of~~ I want to say "aggressive,"
even at the level I'm dealing with here, just a bit of blood. And when did
we know that? we knew that about two months ago during the first wave of
corruption of the living by the dead.

March 12, 2012

No sign of zombies on patrols or watch. That's 3 days now.
Disposed of the rest of Todd Smith's sample, no real point to
tinkering without proper equipment. Someone out there must be
working on figuring out what's happening. It's nice here when not
under siege. Been playing some backgammon. Tossing a tennis ball to
Marty, the farm's German shepherd.

My nerves are still raw. If you get hit with a stick every day, you come to
expect the stick. Everyone, apparently, has nightmares (I do), and because
of the watches we sleep in shifts, which means while asleep there's always
something to mishear and trigger the fight-or-flight reflex, or you can
just be scared to death by the sounds of someone else waking up from a
nightmare. My recurring dream has me being chased by my ex-girlfriend.
Undead. I trip over something, fall, and find myself pinned to the ground.
She's kneeling beside me with my hand raised to her mouth. Before I can
tear it away, she's chomped down, chewing . . .

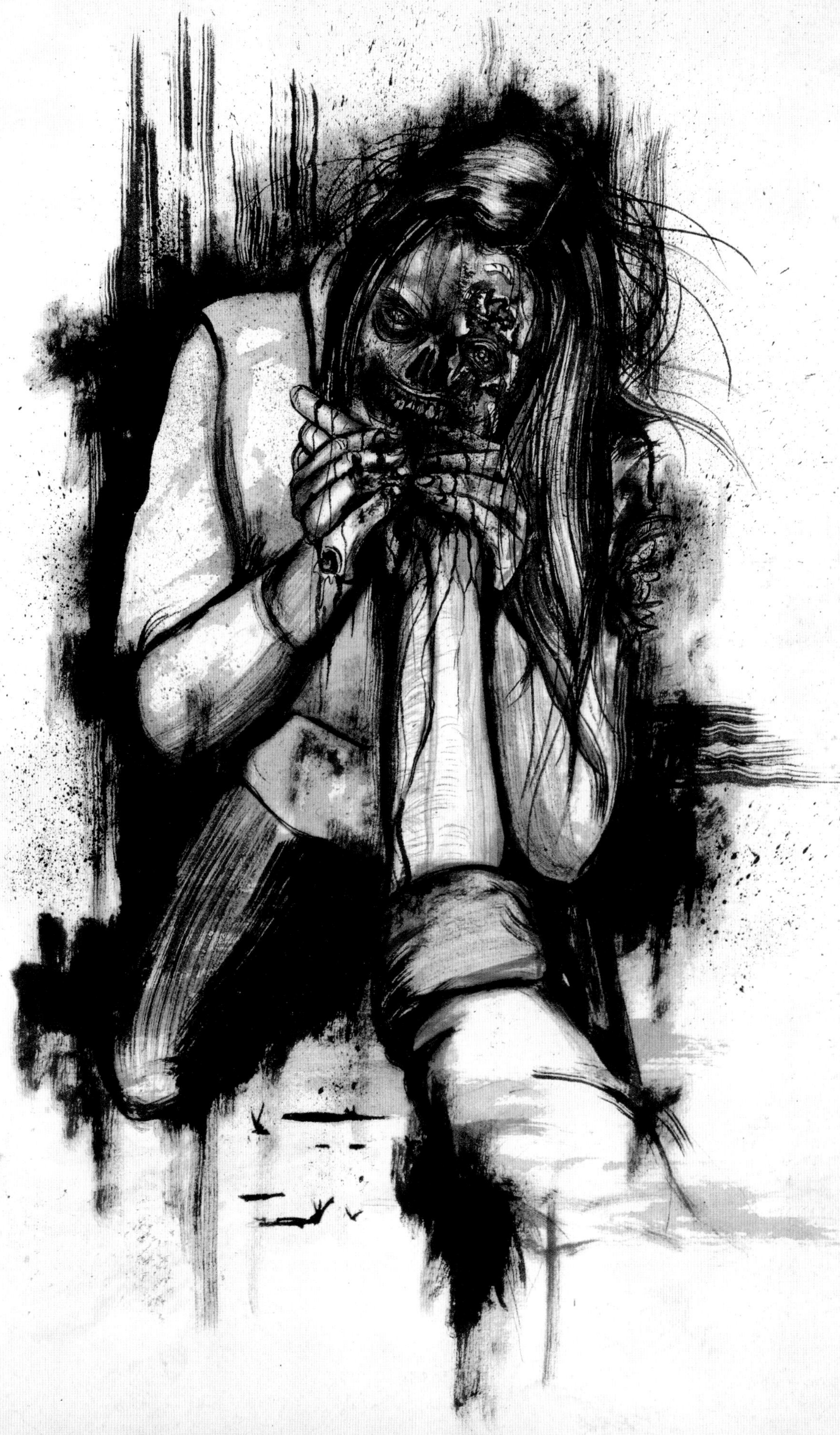

March 13, 2012

Fourth day with no sighting of zombies on patrols or watch, a record.

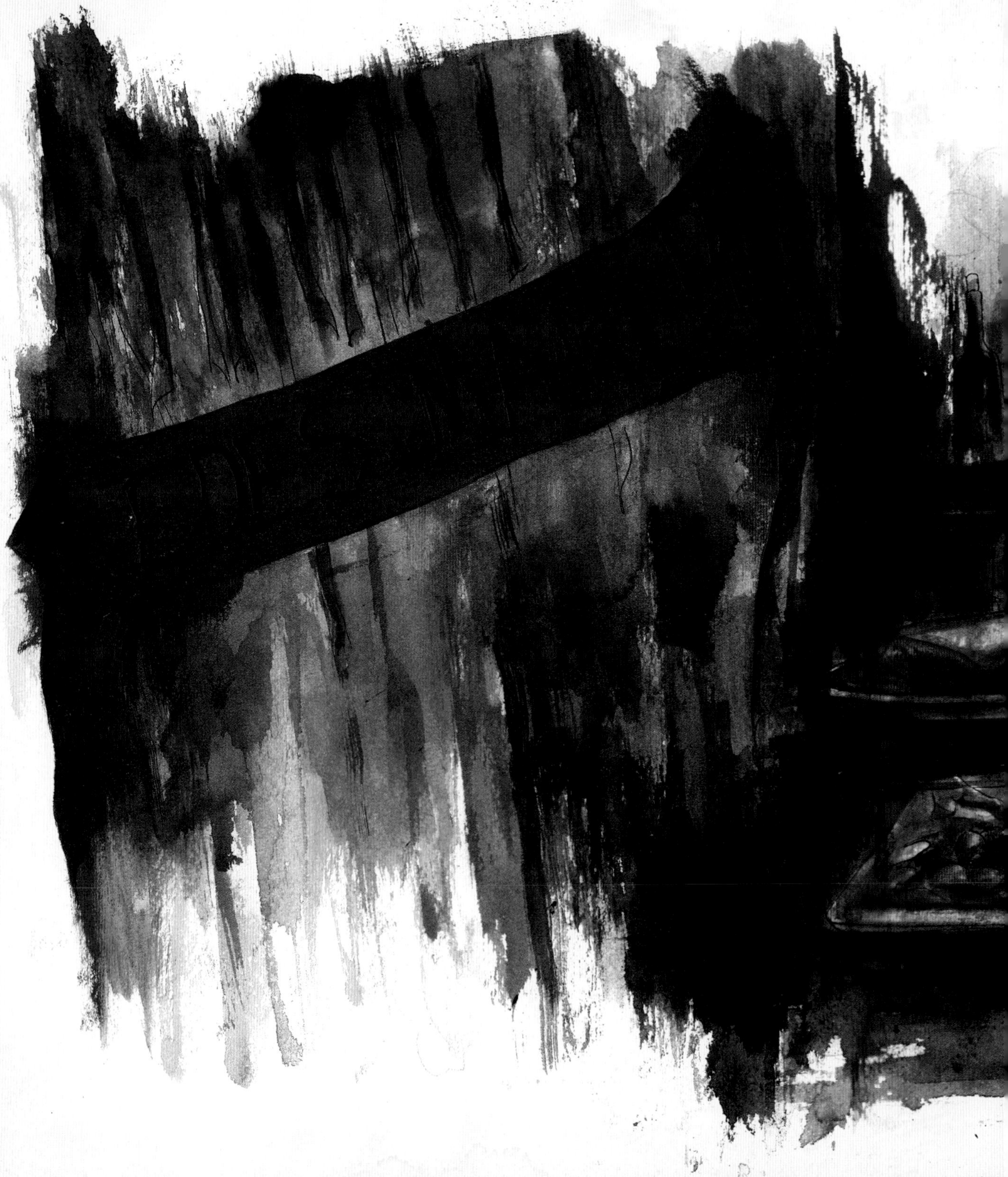

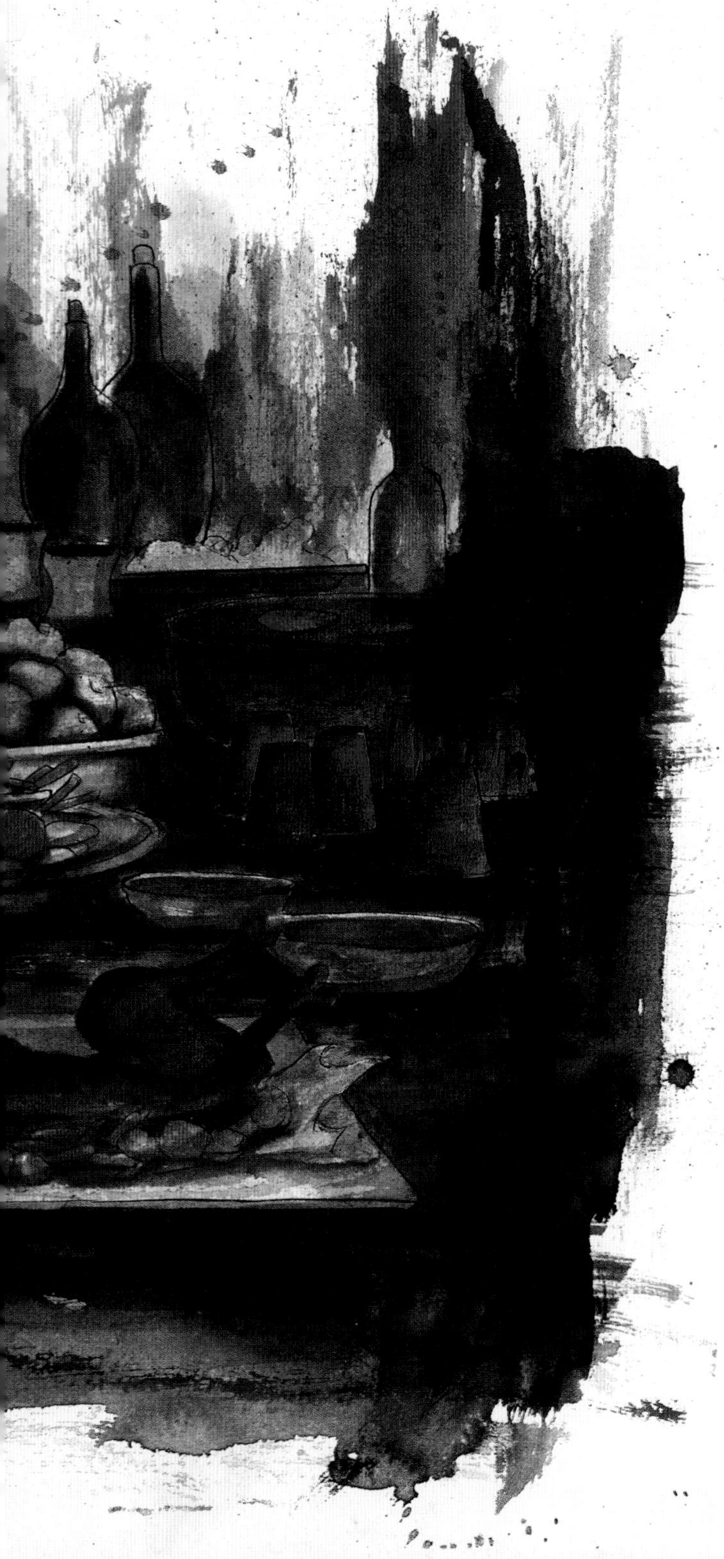

March 15, 2012

6 days, no zombies. Talk of a party tonight. Why not? I guess. I think we're stir crazy. Not really realizing how the constant threat of the zombies shapes everything, and no zombies for days! Some rum-fueled speculation as to what it might mean. Conservative view is it means nothing, we have to assume it's the same as ever. Others feel certain we've turned some kind of corner. We didn't really understand what happened before so why would we understand what's happened now? At any rate, a celebration, at least blow off a little steam. The guys are going to play tonight. Singing, dancing. Guards posted per usual, of course.

March 16, 2012

The farm's gone. ~~Kill everyone after~~ Hundreds of them. We were completely overrun. Somebody dropped a gasoline cocktail—we'd been throwing them from the windows—caught the main house on fire and sent us out among them. Dale was bitten and went down, torn apart. Joe locked himself in one of the guard posts but they swarmed it and it collapsed. Amy, Ian, Carl. As far as I know, Marty and I are the only survivors. We're sleeping in the band's van about 2 hours north of the farm, as far as I could drive before a massive adrenaline crash and I shook myself to sleep, or something like sleep. I killed— I just kept killing them but there were so many. <u>How</u> had they massed together out here in such numbers? I shot them, I set them on fire, I took off their heads. Still they kept coming.

Another safe house burned to the ground. ~~scribbled out~~ This time I managed to save the dog.

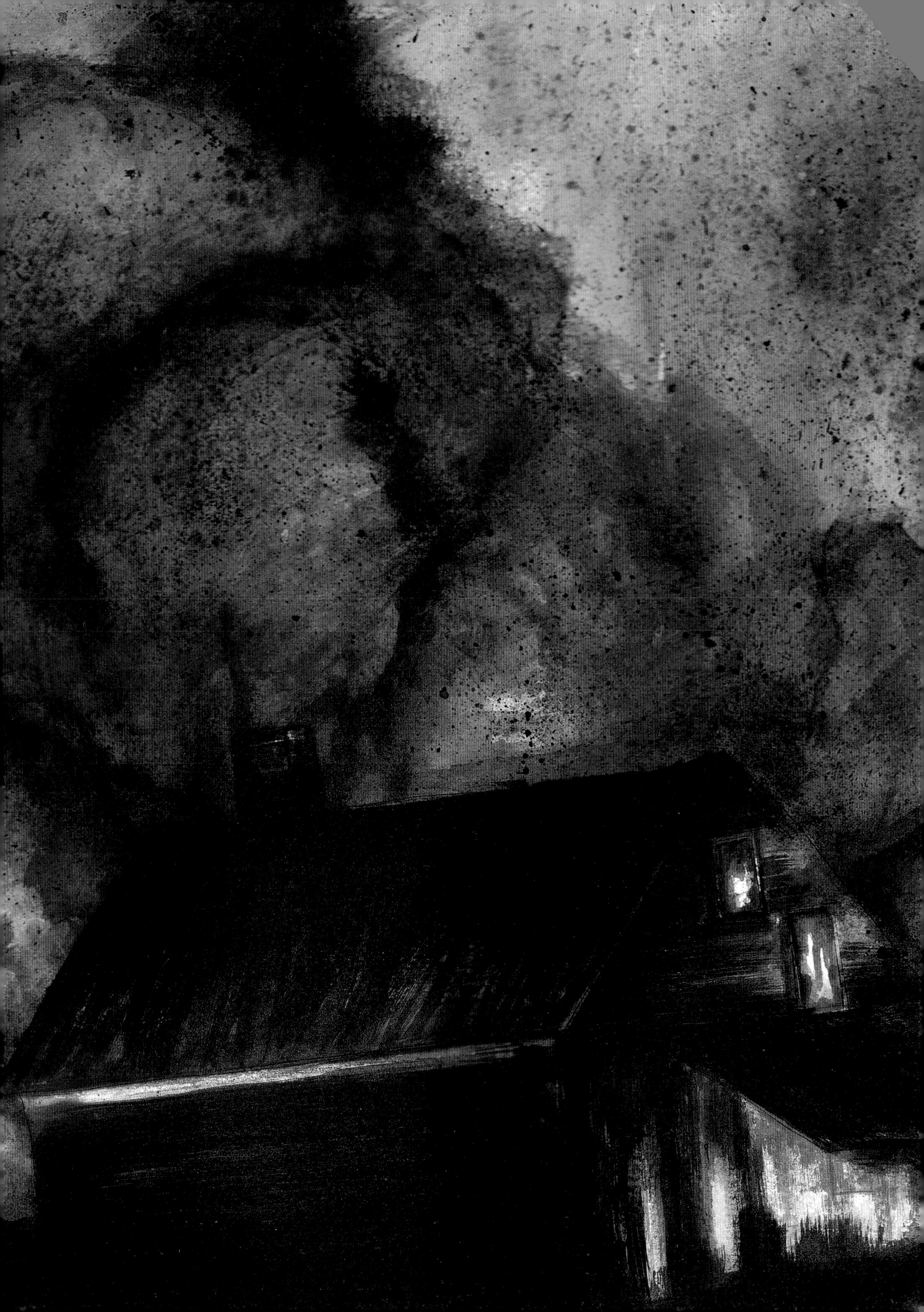

March 19, 2012

Drove for days before I remembered the van's radio and found
the AM signal for Churchill. I don't know what the point is anymore
~~except~~ except that, this is going to sound stupid, but I feel a
responsibility for Marty. To Marty. There's this deep, human-canine
connection that's developed since we started domesticating them. I'm
still human, and Marty's affirming that for me.

I'm also waaaay out here with my own thoughts, and ready to risk making for
human civilization again. I'm not sure what else is left to do.

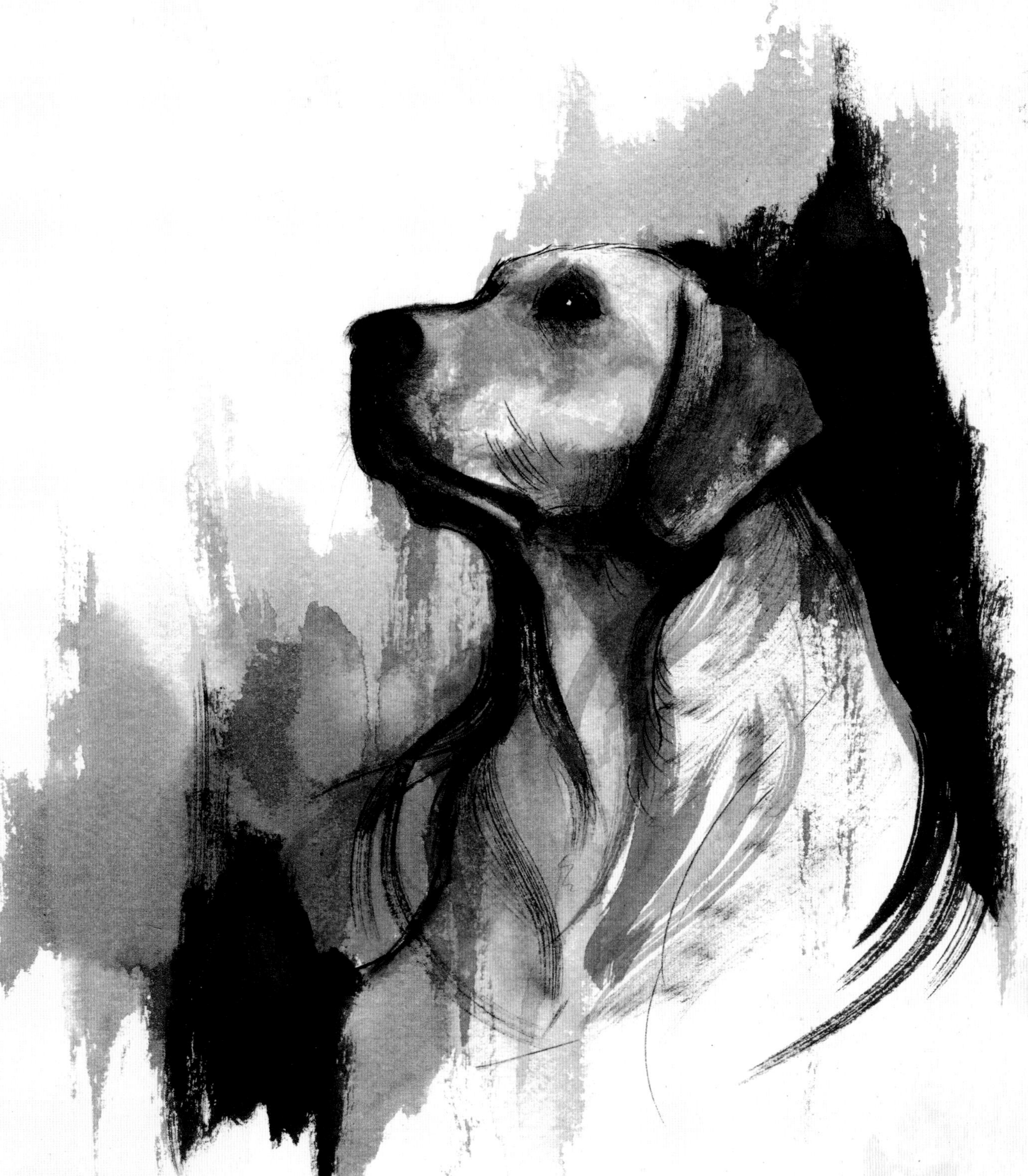

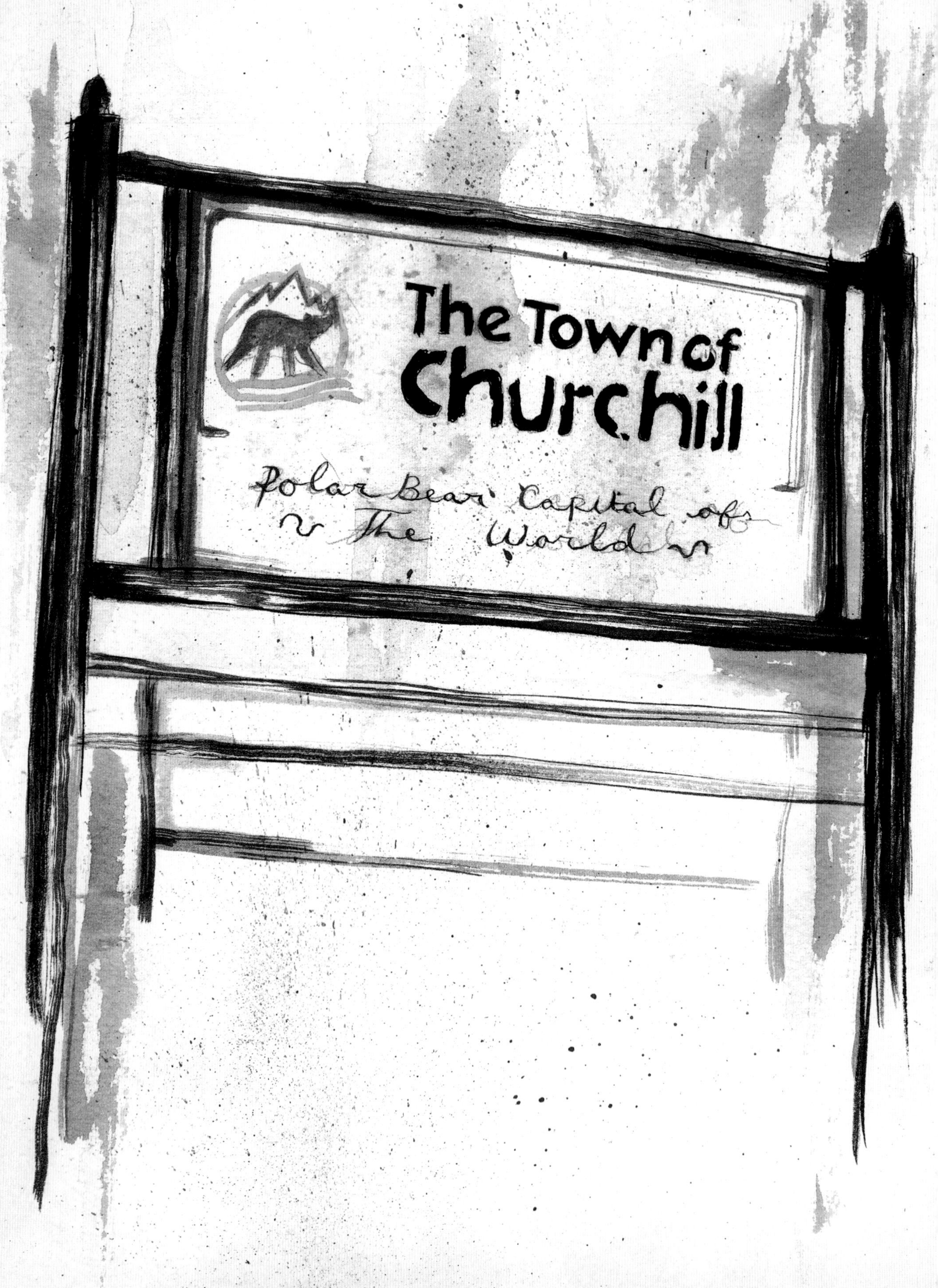
The Town of
Churchill
Polar Bear Capital of
The World

March 25, 2012

Churchill is a small town that's been re-imagined for a siege. There's something almost medieval about it. They've consolidated the townsfolk to a grouping of buildings facing Hudson Bay and surrounded these with an 8-foot-tall wall made from dismantled portions of the structures outside the perimeter. The rule is shoot or torch anything that moves, though I can't imagine much does. Everything is, literally, frozen up here. Since it's understood that zombies can't drive vans, Marty and I were admitted, after a thorough inspection, and some interest in the dried foodstuffs and our gasoline. Despite the radio signal, I'm the first vehicle to have made it up here.

Larry Wilder, who grew up in the town:

"We haven't had any of the trouble everyone else has had down there yet, but we're not taking any chances whatsoever. Nothing gets in here. We're self-sufficient people and always have been."

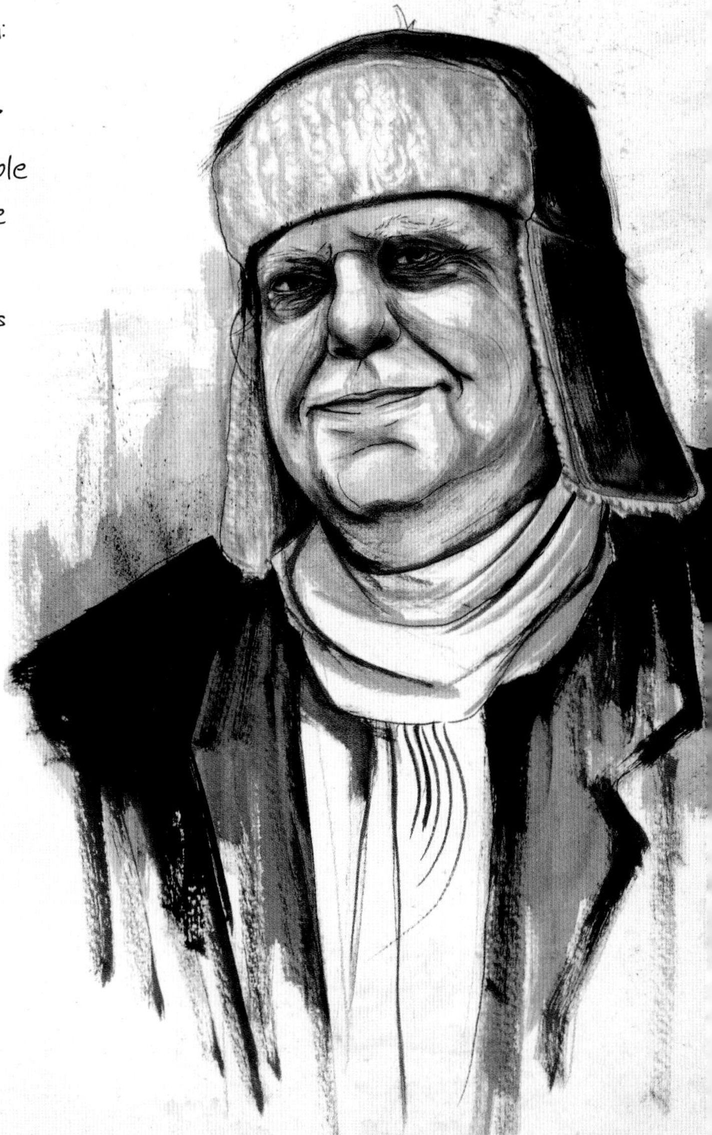

Nobody here has seen an actual zombie. It seems impossible—have I made it far enough north to have outrun, or to outlive this thing?

March 26, 2012

Marty and I have a room at a cottage on the bay that we're sharing with 87-year-old Nora Riley, another local who has lived here her entire life. Basically, they moved us into her space, and she's not thrilled about it. I have not really been forthcoming with any details of the life and death down south, and she's been preemptive. "You're from where there are all those 'dead people.' You seen any of em? Nothing happening up here. I just don't believe it. Government lies to us all the time." The fence around the town? "Larry Wilder's a kook. Gets people to do things they don't want to do. You're here, aren't you?" It's a little edgy around Nora, Marty picks up on it, hasn't really relaxed in fact since we got here. He does <u>not</u> like Larry. Anyway, we'll need to get along here.